HAPPINESS

Happiness

Julian C. Haines

Matador
Unit E2 Airfield Business Park,
Harrison Road, Market Harborough,
Leicestershire. LE16 7UL
Tel: 0116 279 2299
Email: books@troubador.co.uk
Web: www.troubador.co.uk/matador
Twitter: @matadorbooks

ISBN 978 180313 283 9

British Library Cataloguing in Publication Data.
A catalogue record for this book is available from the British Library.

Printed and bound in the UK by TJ Books Limited, Padstow, Cornwall
Typeset in 11pt Minion Pro by Troubador Publishing Ltd, Leicester, UK

Matador is an imprint of Troubador Publishing Ltd

To Everybody whose ideas have been shared with me and whose support has been given to me. Thank you.

CONTENTS

One

HAPPINESS AS THE END

WHY BE INTERESTED IN HAPPINESS?

We can often take the meaning of happiness to be obvious; it is that positive feeling we get that makes us glow inside. Yet, for all that it is positive, we can spend much of our life finding it very elusive and not that easy to come across. We should be interested in happiness because its presence can make life so worth living and yet its absence can be hard to bear. If, somehow, we can understand why it arises within us and what it is telling us, we could perhaps experience more of it, and feel life is better. Indeed, the purpose of our life seems to be a search for happiness. This chimes with some ancient thinking on the subject. The question as to the purpose of life is a very old one that has probably been around for as long as there have been human beings with time enough to think. It is the question of what the ancients called ends or simply what as a human being am I here for? The end can be considered to be our overall purpose that sits on top of our motivation structure. It is surely an attractive idea; I am here to be happy. The Dalai Lama has stated *I believe that the very purpose of our life is to seek happiness. That is clear. Whether one believes in religion or not, whether one believes in this religion or that religion, we all are seeking something better in life. So, I think, the very motion of our life is towards happiness* (Dalai Lama, 1998, p3).

Some of the ancient Greek philosophers were a group that saw the purpose of human life as happiness, although they tended to qualify different sorts of happiness (Devettere, 2002). Their word for happiness was '*eudaimonia*', literally 'care of the soul'. Devettere (2002) describes the end or '*telos*' as the Ancient Greeks knew the term as *the natural or designed goal of an organism or of a fabricated thing. The goal of a living organism is to function well and thereby live well; the goal or purpose of a thing is what it is designed to do. The complete and overriding end for humans is called happiness – living well and doing well* (Devettere 2002, p141). If we track back our reasons for doing anything, the ultimate motivation will be happiness, our own well-being. So, for example, I got up this morning to go to a job I hate. My aim here does not appear to be happiness as I hate my job, but in the schema of my motivations my going to the job may get me a good reference so I can get a job I want; it may give me money that enables me to do other things I want. It may allow me to provide for my family, which brings me joy, or it may give me some social status that impresses my so-called friends so they no longer think I am a loser. Behind our hierarchy of motivations, we will always find happiness lurking. This sets up the idea that we exist to have happiness as our end.

Within any culture there will be expected scripts to follow as to what to do in order to be happy. In our age, the quest for happiness is often dominated by achieving a particular role or status. This often starts when we are very young, say by wanting to be an astronaut, a sports star or a famous entertainer. As the realities of life hit home these aspirations will usually have to be toned down into getting a good job, nice house, good family and friends, having children and perhaps seeing a bit of the world, if we are lucky. For some, even these dreams will seem a long way off due to the blights of poverty or the stigmas of discrimination. For much of human history, dreams and aspirations were the things that had to be kicked out of you in order that the rest of the population could survive. Yet, some have always appeared to achieve their dreams and become an example that a privileged few can make it. With greater prosperity the ability of people to achieve dreams has been greater. Yet, for most, there will be inevitable disappointments as things rarely turn out the way we expect them to be. Things such as health problems, death of loved ones, financial problems, career problems, and relationship problems can all derail our aspirations. Even if we do manage to get broadly what we want in life, we will then be left with the aching question, now what? Do we continue within the rat race to look for an even better job, which usually means getting more pay and getting to order more people around but having increased responsibility and greater levels of stress? Do we look for even bigger houses, more luxury cars or better friends? We may well be left with the realisation that the dreams we once had were not all they were cracked up to be. Yet, few of us are asked why we entertain such dreams and how such achievements would enable us to lead fulfilled and happy lives. We could be left questioning whether any of this really brings us satisfaction.

This can lead us to attempt to find our own paths to happiness and fulfilment off the beaten track. Yet, being without a carefully considered reason for being in life can lead us to be without direction or an anchor. It may mean having no compass for making decisions and being left adrift on the sea of life, left at the mercy of the moment. If you have no thought-out schema for yourself, then you will either be without aims altogether or derive them from others, from family, friends, peer group, media or tradition. This can lead us to looking at what we want in life and seeking our own path to happiness. What happiness means for us and what makes us happy become central questions. When, however, we try to turn this observation into a way of living, we immediately run into some obvious problems.

THE PROBLEMS OF HEDONISM

The ancient Greek philosophy of hedonism places the achievement of personal happiness and pleasure at its centre. It was usually dismissed as ridiculous, even in Greek times. Some examples should make clear why a simple pursuing of one's own pleasure is problematic. People find all sorts of things make them happy, including some things which others will find bizarre or unpalatable. For example, some people find happiness in running others down or making other people miserable. It could also mean one person trying to grab as much for themselves as possible: the biggest house or the most opulent lifestyle. One person's happiness often results in another's unhappiness, whether directly in causing harm or because a small group of people are grabbing everything for themselves. If we can afford to spend all our time in pursuit of idle pleasures, no necessary work will get done either. It is also possible to conceive of situations where happiness is far from being a great good. If a pill were invented that meant you could have continuous happiness without any effort, would that be a good thing? If you were demented but left in a blissfully happy state, would you lead a good life? Would it be better to be a tortured genius or a happy simpleton? From all this it could be possible to conclude that the pursuit of feeling happy does not always lead to a life well lived. This may appear a fatal flaw in the argument that the purpose of our life should be seeking our happiness. It could be argued that what we need to do is rein in our happiness so that we can consider the well-being of others and to benefit our future self. Therefore, for all that happiness may appear a good candidate to be the end, there are also concerns about its suitability. We can summarise the issues with happiness under three broad areas. If we pursue happiness as our end this can lead us away from reality, if we pursue happiness as our end this can lead us away from what is morally good and if we pursue happiness as our end this can lead us to undermine our own future. We will now examine each of these problem areas in turn.

The real world can be a harsh one. We can see life characterised as relatively short in which we make a relatively tiny contribution and then leave to be rapidly forgotten. In seeking to be happy we may end up deluding ourselves about reality. We may think we are kings of the whole world and have large amounts of money to spend these thoughts may make us happy but if they are not based in reality the consequences are we could spend money we don't have. We may be happy because we regard ourselves as stunningly beautiful or talented, yet everybody else sees us as vain and stupid. We may have lost our memory or intelligence, but we may be happy with seeing the same object repeatedly as if new all the time as if it is the most exciting thing that has ever happened to us. We may believe we have been abducted by aliens and they have imparted a secret knowledge in us that only we know about. This makes us especially happy that we were lucky enough to be chosen for this task. In our current state, would we really want any of these things for us? We would be cut off from the world around us.

It can also be argued that there are good reasons to feel the whole range of emotions. Emotions can be invaluable in pointing out to us when something is wrong. There are good reasons why we need to feel unhappy, angry or fearful. If a loved one has just passed away and we feel happy, it would be odd. It could mean we deny negative emotions and force ourselves into a happy charade. To concentrate on promoting happiness could lead to a world of fakery, where the real thoughts and feelings of people would have to be censored by self or others. Society could become full of false smiles and pleasantries and create a public and private split in our emotional life where we project outwardly only those emotions that are found to be acceptable. Only in private would we reveal a self that is very different. Instead of happiness as the end, it is possible to consider that honesty should be. That honesty rests upon an appreciation of reality and truth. This suggestion sets up the possibility that truth could be considered a better end than happiness.

A second issue concerns happiness and its relation to the moral good. There are many millions of people in the world, not including other species who also share our planet, and in order to get along and work together in order to provide all the basics of life have to play by a certain number of rules, whether made explicit or accepted tacitly. Yet people are different and find all sorts of things make them happy. Serial killers may find murder makes them happy. Imperialists may find conquest of other countries makes them happy. Racists may find attacking and ridiculing a person of another race makes them happy. Misogynists may find attacking and ridiculing women makes them happy. Power-crazed individuals may find that the bullying and belittling of others makes them happy. Fundamentalists may demonise those who do not share their beliefs about the world and are only happy when in the company of those who share their world view. Just because something makes you happy does not make it right and can do a great deal of harm. Just pursuing what makes you happy can lead to an erosion of the rules of greater society and make it progressively more difficult for the vast number of people to live in.

In addition, a person may find going to parties all the time makes them happy, perhaps staying in bed all day, eating lots of food indulgently may make us happy. Perhaps it will be gossiping behind others' backs from which we derive pleasure. Maybe it will be the pursuit of lots of lovers or collecting lots of trinkets or visiting lots of places. If we never get out of bed, constantly eat, have one lover after another, always go on holiday, many would accuse us of wasting our lives and being selfish. This leads to the accusation that happiness is fundamentally selfish. Only we can experience our happiness. It is the result of our stimulation of our senses. Dividing what we come across into the pleasant and the unpleasant and discarding the latter can mean we do not play our part in promoting the communal good. Our own happiness can be at the expense of others.

Yet, we are far more efficient as a human race if we manage to work together and share our wealth of learning and experience around. Our communal ties may thus be poorer as a result. Self-sacrifice begins to look unjustified in a life dominated by the pursuit of such a sensuous happiness. The ultimate virtue was to lay down your life for your friends but such actions could never be justified by an ethic dominated by the pursuit of individual pleasure. Some people would argue that the pursuit of happiness has led us to a society of pointless consumption. A society where lots of goods nobody really needs are manufactured at great cost to the world and the environment. It is done so in an unsustainable fashion that will eventually lead to the ruin of the planet and ultimately of humanity itself. Humanity should do without so much pleasure if it wants to survive. Happiness also, it can be argued, seems to abnegate fairness and justice. The pursuit of happiness may cause me to favour certain people because they subconsciously make me happy. I may favour the beautiful over the ugly. The person who is like me rather than the person who is different, the person who praises rather than the person who criticises, the person who has a good story to tell rather than the blandly truthful. I may seek the company of the entertaining rather than the challenging. I may fight alongside my family, those of my faith, or my race, even though they may be in the wrong, simply because I owe them for past happiness.

Another way of characterising happiness is to see it as part of our biological adaptation that allows us as human beings to survive evolutionally. Just because something enabled us to survive does not mean it will lead to moral and civilised values today. What tends to make us happy are those things that tend to make it more likely that we will be able to pass on our genes. Oatley (2004) gives the example of the sort of thought experiment from science fiction where alien creatures take over human bodies in order to replicate themselves. It is almost as if our genes do this. As long as they continue to replicate themselves, they will be immortal. They need a human body to survive once their job is done, though the body can be disposed of. If we look at genetic replication in these terms, we could begin to see happiness as a natural impulse to trick us into gene replication. We can then see the impulse to freedom and culture as the resistance to this imperative. The quote from the film *African Queen*, with Katharine Hepburn saying to Humphrey Bogart 'nature... is what we were put in this world to rise above', encapsulates this well. We could see happiness as part of that nature, trapping us into patterns of a biologically determined existence. The issue of the moral good often splits human beings into part animal and part civilised layer. The pursuit of happiness is then seen as part of satisfying our animal instincts and urges, whereas only by controlling our urge to gratify ourselves do civilised values become possible. For those that accept this it is not happiness that should be pursued but the greater moral good. It would thus also seem plausible to regard the ethical good as a suitable candidate to be our end.

The third area where the pursuit of happiness can be an issue is towards our future self. Happiness brings our focus to the present. It leads us to merely look as to what makes us happy now and not look too far into the future and therefore reduce things to the immediate situation. There are perhaps powerful reasons why emotions such as happiness have evolved to focus on the present because if we fail to survive the present there won't be a future to have. Yet, this tends to favour us living in the here and now and against planning for longer-term futures. So, we may spend our schooldays playing truant because it is more fun than sitting through a dull physics class. We may favour doing drugs and partying rather than working hard at our job and career. We may enjoy driving fast without considering that this increases the likelihood we will have an accident and get seriously hurt or hurt somebody else.

Happiness is our psychological reward for getting what we want. It is perfectly possible to trick our brain into giving us pleasure when it isn't appropriate. We have a range of pleasure-giving substances such as alcohol, drugs and sugary foods. Sex is a major means of pleasure for many. Exercise is a major source of happiness. Most forms of addiction stem from these short circuits to happiness which can, when taken to excess, lead to lives that are less than full. It is also possible to conceive of situations where happiness is far from being a great good. Going back to the pill mentioned previously that meant we could have continuous happiness without any effort, would that be a good thing or would it mean we would make nothing of our lives? It is possible to argue that many drugs in effect behave a lot like this, although there are other consequences when we come down, don't have any money and are left craving. The nature of addiction is such that for every high, there is a low to follow. So, when the pleasure passes, as it surely must, there will only be emptiness and pain beyond. Yet, many have fallen into this trap and, if you do, it is then difficult to do this and to have a career or a family or to save money up. All that matters becomes when the next fix is.

In order to achieve great things, we need to be able to put in effort and hard work and this involves a certain amount of pain. Pain is unpleasant and therefore it might seem a good idea to get rid of it. Yet, those unfortunate souls who are unable to feel pain are unfortunate indeed. They are subject to horrendous injuries as they are unaware of when they are confronting a serious problem. Many emotions serve as pain receptors for our mind in a similar fashion to pain (Damasio, 1994). They are there to let us feel what is important. If we were to let our entire outlook be dominated by happiness, we would no longer be able to determine risk or know significance. Damasio (1994) has found that when the emotional centres of our brain our damaged we find it difficult to make decisions. We need to be able to push through a certain amount of pain in order to win a race or to reach the top at business. Let us think of the truly great characters throughout history, people such as Mahatma Gandhi, Mother Teresa and St Francis of Assisi, for example. The list is very far from exhaustive and many other heroes can be added to it. Is what marks out these people as truly great not the pursuit of happiness but their ability to take on suffering for a far greater cause? The pursuit of happiness can be seen as leading us to look to our own comfort at the expense of the pursuit of great and noble causes. Thus, the cause of anti-slavery may never have happened if people had been obsessing over interior design or which new cocktail to try. The fight for human rights, against poverty, for votes for women may not have happened if people were only searching for the next high. Great artistic and scientific endeavours may not have occurred if we could only see our next banquet or sexual conquest. Achievements can be seen as being built upon to delay our gratification and acquiring skills and abilities that can take a lifetime to master.

Imagine you have had the happiest day of your life. You have just achieved all that you ever wanted to achieve. Then, you wake up the next day and wonder what to do with the rest of your life. Just imagine what life would be like if we thought we had reached the pinnacle and everything would be downhill from now on. There is not only a problem of constantly working for a dream to come true but, if that dream comes true, what are you left with: a few days of euphoria and then the rest of your life without purpose? The only way out is to dream of some secret in which a point of happiness is reached and then sustained for the rest of our lives. We seem trapped between a self that wants to live in the present and a self that also needs a future in order to make that present bearable. The choice seems to be take our pleasures now and possibly mortgage our future or have pain now and then have no guarantee that what dreams we have will be fulfilled anyway. Such are the dilemmas of the human condition. It seems that if we prioritise happiness now this may be at the expense of our future self and instead focusing on being happy in the future, getting a particular role, maybe we should focus on becoming the best we can be and living a worthwhile life as an alternate end.

From this discussion it may seem that happiness should not be our guide through life. We have also found some potential alternatives to happiness as things we could use to guide our life. Over the next five chapters, the book will examine the possibility that truth, the moral good and becoming the best self we can be, could be the best end we could have as our supreme motivating factor. Yet, from the discussion above, it is possible to reach a different conclusion regarding ends. Happiness remains an attractive proposition to be our end. An alternative suggestion is that, rather than looking for alternate ends, happiness actually remains a good candidate but we need to understand it more. That happiness is a term that actually covers a vast array of positive emotional experiences and some of these can be helpful and others aren't. Some we should have as ends and others are questionable. Instead of regarding happiness as a simple feeling, maybe we need to acknowledge that happiness is a more complex entity that could still when properly understood be a good candidate to be our end. It is this possibility that will be considered in the second half of the book.

Two

TRUTH AS THE END

THE SELF-OTHER BOUNDARY AND THE
SEARCH FOR REALITY OUT THERE

If there are question marks about happiness as the end for humanity, we are left with the question as to what other things could be our end. One option is the pursuit of truth. Truth, however, can mean different things. One thing that truth can mean is honesty, the opposite of lying. It is not making things up or bending things to get a personal advantage. Honesty is the moral quality of truthfulness. If honesty, though, is to function as a moral quality it needs to have a reference point which excludes our own wants and wishes. That reference point could come from other people, defining truth through the opinion of others, for example. Yet adhering to the truth can mean opposing those we love and going against community will. Truth can slap down the great and undermine the powerful. It would be a great advantage to be able to get to a position of certainty about how things are. This leads on to a form of truth which is about the search for reality; that to which we can attach ourselves with the full weight of our conviction against the storms of fickle and changeable opinions. It makes it far easier to be honest if we can be so from having the conviction of reality. If we can find reality, all we have to do is use this as our reference point and we can be honest. If we cannot find such a reality that can be known, then there could be a danger of everything collapsing into everyone's opinion, not being able to locate a reference point in order to be honest and not being able to tell truth from lies. All then can be seen as a competition for personal advantage. History has been littered with those who have been dressed in conviction which has turned out to be misguided, false or a disguise for self-promotion. The conviction of reality can be held on supposition without proof or the subject of interminable and irresolvable debate. Would it be possible to have a reality that could be proved beyond doubt and held in conviction by all? If we define something as real, we automatically create its opposite, which is 'unreal' or delusional. So, in order to have truth based on an achievable reality as an end there must be some way of telling the difference between it and delusion. There must therefore be some discoverable and usable mechanism of getting from delusion to reality. If reality is too difficult to find, though, or regarded as impossible to get to, people may well give up searching for it. If reality is too easily found then it is difficult to see how this can act as a perpetual motivator. A reality possessed would mean truth could no longer be an end. We may wish to propagate the reality we have or use it for other things but getting to reality would no longer be our motivation.

Truth can be conceived as a project about placing boundaries upon the world as we find it. Let us start our search for reality by placing an important boundary on our map. That boundary is the self–other boundary. This is the starting boundary in the search for reality. It is that which divides the self from other. In order to have a reality at all there must be an observer to that reality and this boundary creates the viewer and the viewed. It is one of the first boundaries we construct, to realise we have an existence and are different from others. The presumed existence of the self then potentially creates an experience of inner and outer where either something is internal or it is external. It becomes far easier to control what is on the self side of this boundary but, as we learn to interact with what is on the other side of this boundary, we can begin to develop strategies which help give us more understanding and influence over the other. We can then locate reality in relation to this boundary. Reality is commonly conceived of as something independent of the self discoverable as being 'out there'. This conception firmly places reality on the other side of the self–other boundary. It is given and human beings have to discover it. Greater influence is achieved by accurately mapping the boundaries of this reality.

The goal in this conception is to draw boundaries on what we see as other with a view to getting them to correspond and match to what is already there as much as possible. This means there are boundaries in the space of other that are actually there; we don't just create them. We just need to align what we see with what is there already. A failure to grasp our reality is very dangerous and not a mere academic question. There is often a need to understand what can be controlled in a universe that often seems chaotic and dangerous. If we fail to appreciate it, we will probably suffer an untimely death. We must learn what reality is and fast. This sort of truth allows us to chunk up our universe into plants that are good to eat and plants that are poisonous. It will tell us what may kill us and what may let us prosper. Such a truth, however, is engaged in not for its own sake as some end in itself but to promote our survival. It allows our functioning in what can be a hostile and unpredictable environment. What we are aiming for is to gain as much understanding as possible so we can increase the influence we have over the self into other as much as possible. Taken to its logical conclusion, this view would mean to have total security we would have to seek total mastery of the other in order to dissipate the fear that lack of control often brings. An end is the ultimate driver beyond which there is no other motivator. So, if we want to know reality because it brings us survival, then truth is not our end. A person who bases their truth on the need to overcome their fear is a person looking to control all that they see. Truth becomes about gaining control over our environment, which makes our survival more likely. Control instead could be suggested as a better candidate as end. This suggests that reality has to be formed out of the ability to predict and control the environment. If control and survival, though, are our ends we are left with a question as to why. We are left in a potentially hostile environment to survive for as long as we can until our inevitable demise. If our demise is inevitable, why simply bother to survive at all? If, however, we still need or want to know more about our reality beyond our mere survival and the avoidance of negative emotions, this could lead us to investigate whether truth could be an end.

Let us suppose, though, we have gained enough influence over our environment not to be living in fear all the time. That we realise that trying to master all that we see is a project that will hit reality and will eventually be doomed; we can never become kings of the whole world. We can still be left with the dream of matching boundaries upon the reality we see. Such a prospect removes the urgency of immediate danger and allows us to reflect for longer on the scenarios we face. The starting point for these techniques is to try to make sure our viewpoint does not interfere with the boundaries we want to place. There has to be a viewer who uses their senses to detect reality, but, once reality has been established, we want that viewer to have as little significance as possible. One reason for this is the fear that having a self in the equation could distort the perception of reality and skew it. Truth must be obvious to all whatever the perspectives the self may hold. This could not be achieved if the self is too prominent. Besides, once we start placing boundaries 'out there' logically, we must place them on the self, which in turn is rendered an object of study. This reduces the self to 'out there' as well. Therefore, in this form of reality, the boundary of the self is minimised as much as possible whilst 'out there' or other is expanded. This conception of truth also goes by the name of empirical truth. It is about establishing truth in what we can see, touch and hear. Reality does not change, only our perceptions and understanding of it change. For example, the Earth has always gone round the Sun. Just because the bulk of the human population thought differently makes not one jot of difference; the earth went around the Sun then and goes around the Sun now. Thus, when the understanding of that reality changes, it is not that reality has changed but that we did not understand it properly. The boundaries placed on reality were not properly understood.

Yet the problem with finding truth 'out there' is it is impossible to escape from the self. It doesn't take too long to realise that this outer reality we can dream of is unreachable. This is because outer reality amounts to a representation we access through our senses and our brains. No amount of minimising of the self will ever remove this. There will always be an observer with senses and our senses are open to distortion. We only experience the world as we do because our brains have learnt to picture it that way. For example, the blind spot results from the nerve that connects from the back of the eye and sends the collected information to the brain. This means there is a point in the eye that cannot collect sight information. Yet, we are unaware of it because the brain performs a trick that ensures the gap that results is not in our general awareness. In other words, our brain helpfully fills in the gaps that exist within our sense information depending on what it expects to find there. This is also true of our memory. If an event is shown to any group of people, what is remembered is often very divergent. For example, if there is an altercation in the street that is witnessed by several people, what we are likely to find if those witnesses are interviewed afterwards is a lot of varying accounts of what happened. People confabulate, which means, in much the same way as the brain fills in for our blind spots in sight, it fills in with what it expects to find in our memories. We genuinely believe things happened because it fits with our underlying assumptions.

It is also experimentally possible to electronically stimulate areas of the brain which then replicate the experience of sensory excitation. This phenomenon raises even further questions about how sure we can be about the world we appear to experience through our senses and memories. In many science-fiction films this subject of not being able to know reality has been a popular topic. For example, in the film *The Matrix* (1999), humanity was being farmed by aliens for their energy. In order to keep humans within this role a computer-generated world called the Matrix was created so that humans would accept their plight and produce the energy required. This may seem far-fetched but it is perfectly conceivable that the world is experienced only as we are designed to view, hear and feel it. The thought experiment called 'the brain in a vat' puts the situation another way. It is possible to conceive that I am a brain in a vat and that electrical impulses received I interpret as the life I regularly live (Poundstone, 1988; Dennett, 1991). The limitations of our senses and memories mean our minds are apt to fill in what we expect to find in the world we inhabit. There are many assumptions we make about ourselves and the world around us. We could assume that the world is a projection of our minds and is some grand illusion. We could assume that the world is a manifestation of some greater being or intelligence, far greater than we would ever understand. We could assume that the world is mine because I am special; I have rights over the world that will only become revealed once my special task is completed. We could assume that the world around us is something determined by those who are most powerful around us. We could assume that the world is the result of our collective imaginations. In order to produce something wonderful we need to be as friendly and cooperative as possible. We must concentrate only on good things and keep hoping for a better planet.

Another set of issues stems from knowledge about reality not coming from direct personal experience but the accumulated wisdom handed down to us from others. I know the Moon is a lump of rock orbiting the planet Earth not because I have been there to find out but because I have been told this is so. Others, though, from different cultures and different times may have genuinely believed the Moon was the goddess of the night riding her chariot across the sky. I have never seen a unicorn and I have never been to Antarctica. This may cause me to disbelieve in the existence of both, but I am only inclined to disbelieve in unicorns. The accumulated wisdom tells me that Antarctica exists but unicorns do not. Unless I have good cause, that is what I will believe. Yet, the accumulated wisdom can be wrong. Even our direct experience has come to us interpreted through the equipment bequeathed by previous generations making truth inherently social, mediated through the opinions of others. This means that truth has behaviours analogous to a virus. We accept a new truth 'virus' if we are persuaded to share certain opinions. Truth can be caught like a cold. This will involve a combination of argument and evidence but a certain degree of emotional persuasion as well. Depending on my disposition at the time, I may decide to accept the virus of this truth into me or I may reject it. This acceptance or rejection will often depend on the sort of truth viruses I have caught before. Such ideas turn truth from a lens with which to see the world into property connected with who we are and how we situate ourselves in wider culture. Truth can become part of who we are. For this reason, we may become more preoccupied by who is telling us information than what is being told to us and whether this is a trustworthy source. Much of deciding truth becomes not about conducting experiments but about working out the validity of what somebody is saying. This means we must develop a methodology to weigh up evidence from particular sources. Often, we tend to categorise people into certain camps: those whose opinions I will trust and those who I will disregard. This creates in-groups and out-groups, often based on commonality and likeness. Within the in-group there are shared bonds of trust; others who are like me. Having identified such a group I also create a group that is not like me. Having in-groups and out-groups means that we can sometimes see only the point of view of those we perceive as like us and ignore evidence from other sources.

THE PROBLEMS OF SOLIPSISM AND DELUSION

These problems create difficulties in reaching certainty about truth. The situation where we can map boundaries onto some pre-existing reality will forever elude us. Potentially, if we conclude externality is impossible to reach, we could conclude reality is therefore impossible to map. This would lead us back to the place where we are all living in a form of delusion and that there is no way of reaching any truth. So far, a boundary between self and other has been drawn. A division between internal and external has then been placed upon this, with self roughly corresponding to internal and other to external. If we conclude we can never get beyond the self, this means that other collapses. Consequently, the boundary of self becomes expanded to all that we see, feel and touch. In this situation we potentially fail to even recognise the existence of other. This is the experience of solipsism, where self is all there is. If we accept this version of reality, everything is already part of me; it is just a case of realising this, putting on the right pair of glasses with which to see. This version of the truth, though, does not enable us to achieve reality as sought at the outset of this chapter. Instead, if we can find truth at all it would be entirely personal. If the existence of others is acknowledged at all their truths would be almost entirely inaccessible. Potentially there is a failure to recognise even the existence of other.

Thus, potentially, we are all living in a delusion and there is no way to prove otherwise. It is perhaps beneficial at this stage to change our perspective from one looking at what reality might mean to one where we are concerned with what unreality could look like and how practically we could live in such a situation. The world without the prospect of truth begins to look like a very strange and disorientating place. For a start, the statement 'the truth is that we cannot possibly get to the truth' is logically problematic. This is a claim to the truth and yet the same statement is a refutation of the possibility of truth. Any statement that claims to be true and yet to be a refutation of the truth is a logical tautology. So, for a start I begin to be unable to make any truth claims whatsoever, even to deny the possibility of truth claims. It can neither be true nor untrue and we enter a world where we cannot be sure of anything. It means we have nothing to anchor any truth claims to. Everything becomes a circular argument where the logic of one thing becomes dependent on something else that cannot be proved. It is a state of perpetual uncertainty.

Yet, delusion also has a specific meaning, which often means we are so drawn into the self that we fail to acknowledge realistically the point of view of others. If you are seen as having delusions you hold a fixed belief that is not widely held within wider culture but also it is not amenable to change with evidence. So, whereas in the philosophical understanding the state of solipsism is suggestive of a position of constant uncertainty and unknowing, in the medical condition delusion actually implies a certainty that is beyond evidence. Often, as long as your truth does not bother my truth, we can all live with that. At the point of delusion, however, truth has reached a point where our agreement of toleration has broken down. I could believe that all elephants are pink, for example. I could then be shown hundreds of elephants that are grey and not one that is pink. If after all of this I still insist that all elephants are pink and there is a giant conspiracy of people going round painting the elephants grey with paint that can't be removed, I am likely to be seen as suffering from a delusion. A delusion therefore is not just about cultural norms but an inability to weigh evidence and learn from experience. It is of interest to note that despite the theoretical possibility of a great many delusions they actually tend to fall into a narrow number of categories. Not many people genuinely believe that elephants are pink but many claim to be a great and important person despite evidence to the contrary.

Two of the most common kinds are persecutory delusions and grandiose delusions. Persecutory delusions have their route in the emotion of fear. They involve a person believing they are being threatened or mistreated by others. Rather than a having a sense of trust in the world around us which leads to confidence, we could see the world and those who populate it as essentially threatening. It means that the self is founded in suspicion. So common persecutory delusions include that others are talking about us behind our back, perhaps that others can read our thoughts, or have bugged our room they might be trying to kill us or do us down in some way. These are perhaps based on familiar experiences but in delusion they are taken to extremes. If, however, we have lost confidence in being able to get to reality, have constant uncertainty as to what is really going on and are unable to make reliable predictions, fear is not an unreasonable response. We have lost any ability to trust in other or our ability to react accordingly. In grandiose delusions, the person believes they are extremely significant, possessing important knowledge, power or ability, contrary to available evidence, and this is not amenable to argument. We may believe we have great wealth, have high status or be an important historical figure. Maybe, we consider ourselves to have great religious significance. Grandiose delusions boost our perceptions of the status we have in order to appear to ourselves and others as more important than we actually are. These delusions seem to allow a decoupling of happiness and truth. For grandiose delusions, unlike persecutory ideas, make us feel good. Grandiosity, though, is often compensatory for feelings of inadequacy or confusion. If we can make ourselves appear powerful we can overcome feelings of inadequacy. Like many such compensatory schemas it is flawed. In order to sustain delusions, we must reinforce barricades against contrary evidence. It also makes likely the existence of both grandiose and persecutory delusions coexisting in the same person at the same time. If we regard ourselves as being important, logically others will be jealous and will seek to undermine our status. If we are not amenable to seeing evidence of our position, we have effectively walled ourselves off from contradiction. Yet, if there is no reality, we are essentially free to believe whatever we like. There is great apparent freedom if we do not have to contend with any reality or interact with other. The truth can be whatever we want it to be and, if reality is a harsh and unpredictable place, being able to imagine it away can be highly attractive. It is just that most people do believe there is a reality to contend with and that although we can find times when we can escape it, we must return to face it at some point.

We thus have two versions of delusion, a philosophical one of solipsism and a medical condition, and they appear opposites. The former implies a total lack of certainty and the latter is a certainty beyond evidence often coalescing around particular themes of fear or grandiosity. Yet, these two positions have more in common than possibly first appear. Let us return to the construction of that all-important boundary between self and other and suppose many people are able to construct this boundary and an imperfect model of how the other functions. This need not be perfect but as long as it enables us to survive and follow some social rules that allow us to interact, for many it will do. Many, though, may well find for a variety of reasons they are unable to do this. Some may find their sense data is interfered with and that the information they are receiving is confused and overwhelming, which makes mapping other problematic. In order to live with a model of other there must be some means of making it explicable and predictable, otherwise it can turn into a very scary and dangerous place. Alternatively, we may as an intellectual exercise try to map other perfectly but realise this is impossible to do. In either case, the self–other boundary will become problematic because we cannot really tell where it is. In the former case we are probably likely therefore to find the situation frightening and come up with various techniques for managing this. In the latter case it is probable we will learn to ignore the imperfections and revert to our learnt map of how things are. If we were to try to live with an ill-defined boundary between self and other this would leave us in a very frightening and vulnerable situation. This can cause us to barricade ourselves off from other and build hefty defence mechanisms from an otherwise unpredictable and inexplicable place. If we cannot understand or predict what is happening because our ability to construct a model of reality has broken down, then it is possible to understand how fears can grow and the responses needed to gain confidence also grow. What we can find is that the self becomes so large that certain emotional responses become magnified and in particular it becomes possible that fear and grandiosity take over.

THE CREATION OF PARAMOUNT REALITY

There is, therefore, an imperative to escape, at least for a lot of the time, from the clutches of solipsism and delusion. We cannot, though, escape ourselves and get to a place without a viewpoint.

Instead of suggesting that everything is self, though, let us suppose everything instead is part of mind. This is seemingly a statement of the obvious. Everything we experience must be an aspect of mind. Let us suppose, though, mind is made up of both a conception of self and of other. Both self and other are facets of mind. One way of achieving self within mind would be to see self as the executive and mind as representing the more unconscious, animal side of our behaviour. This is not what was meant by this suggestion. Instead, mind is seen as all-encompassing and self an aspect of mind along with other. In this case mind is conscious of being a self and is able to examine itself critically. This suggestion is somewhat counterintuitive to normal English usage. Self and I are often used as the main actor and everything then becomes a possession of the self. This includes both mind and body. It is possible to have 'my mind' and 'my body' as possessed by a self. This suggests the self becomes before both mind and body. In other words, self exists prior to either mind or body which are possessed of a self. The proposed schema suggests the reverse. That self comes after mind and body and is created out of both. Logically, though, this idea has some appeal. It seems to represent experience better, for, when we are born, we are a mind and a body but a self is something that has to be nurtured. This alternative schema suggests that all experience is mind but not everything is self.

This potentially means the experience of solipsism is the expansion of the self such that it takes over the entirety of mind and other is excluded. It also means that other is as much of a construction of the mind as the self. This would make terminology such as my mind meaningless. Mind would not be something that could be owned; instead, it would be a platform out of which a self, the experience of being I, could be constructed. Mind becomes the basis of existence and from this ground we then construct both a self and other and the boundary that exists between them. It means we have to mentally construct a model of a world that appears to be outside us within the mind. In order to function within it our sense must be built up that it appears real to us, far more real than anything else. We have to create a model of this paramount reality in order to survive.

The search for reality begins with questions. A question is an expression of dissatisfaction with current understanding and is the starting point to reshape knowledge. In searching for truth there seems to be a need to discover reality to give life meaning and purpose. Wilkinson (2007) outlines some of the areas where we human beings seem to need answers. These include answers to where our universe comes from and where it is going: how our world works. We also seem to need to know where human life fits into that cosmos, where we come from and where we will go. In addition, we seem to need to have an account of how our pain and suffering fits into that overall scheme and some means of guidance as to how we should behave in order to get through our life in the best way possible. These sorts of questions shift us away from questions of immediate survival, pressing as these often are to the great existential questions of the self.

As adults we may think that reality is obvious or common sense. Reality, though, is something we have had to learn over many years from our parents, peers and teachers. That is why children are often asking questions, if the pursuit of truth starts in questions and results in the creation of boundaries, categories and trajectories. To answer a question such as what something is we need to create a category. For example, a question such as 'What is a chair?' is about a category called chairs and the boundaries that demarcate it. If we make an attempt to answer this question, we will have to come up with a definition of what is included within the category, for example a piece of furniture used primarily for sitting on. A category is a way of chunking up the world around us by use of boundaries. A boundary is how we divide one thing from another. We tend to see the world as chunked up into bits rather than as a seamless whole, and that is what boundaries do for us. They make a chair different from a typewriter or an orange different from an apple. They also make self different from other. We can form categories either positively because included objects possess certain characteristics or negatively because they don't. Categories often exist in hierarchical relation to each other with larger categories on top of smaller ones and boundaries separating each. We shall term these boundaries core and firmament. The firmament exists at the top of a category and is where the category begins to merge into other larger categories for example, chair exists within the bigger category of furniture. The core of a category exists at the bottom of category and is what goes to make it up. Thus, a chair would be made up of legs, a seat, a back all made of wood. The creation of categories enables answers to 'what' questions.

To answer a question such as how something is made or why something happened, we need to string categories together, elongating them over time to create a trajectory. A trajectory joins things up across time, giving categories both a past and a future. It is a process or chain of causality that gives an explanation for something. If the question is how we make a chair, the explanation given may involve breaking down the chair into its core components and telling the story of how they are put together again. Thus, it may begin with a category called a tree from which shapes can be fashioned. These shapes of wood can then be assembled to form a chair. The use of boundaries in trajectories is different to those in categories. In a trajectory a boundary demarcates an important change or transformation. Rather than unifying objects in a certain class, they are change markers. Thus, what is important in the story of making a chair is the change from being a tree into a piece of wood, which is then fashioned into shapes which then change again into a chair when assembled. When a tree becomes wood, when wood becomes shapes and when the shapes are assembled into a chair. There is an overall narrative or story. The most important change markers are those that mark the beginning and end of the trajectory, which will be termed the foundation and the end. The foundation will be what caused the category to start; this may be why we human beings decided to make a chair in the first place, the end we have already introduced as an idea in relation to the self, but is about what something will become, its purpose. As a self we experience the end as what ultimately motivates us but it is possible to see all trajectories as having ends. In terms of making a chair it will be when the assembled chair has been put together as the finished item, its 'chairness', or we could extend the trajectory beyond this to when the chair ceases to exist. An important way of understanding any trajectory then is to either go backwards to its beginning or foundation or to project forwards to predict its future or end.

Symbolism and language are the most powerful tools we have for creating boundaries, categories and trajectories. A symbol is anything, whether it is a sound, a picture or a diagram, that is a way of representing something else. The most obvious example of this is language. In spoken language we use different vocal sounds to stand for practically everything around us. If we find something new, we invent a new sound or at least a way of joining sounds together. This allows us to communicate with others about the world around us and learn from them and hand down information. It also allows us to communicate within ourselves. This is called reflexivity and most of us have a constantly chattering inner voice speaking to us in words as well as pictures. Written language represents these different sounds pictorially, again an amazing tool for communication and manipulation of concepts. We chunk up our universe and give each of these chunks a name and a picture, maybe even several words and several pictures. For a word unites in the form of a concept, disparate objects that all have something in common. This creates a category and can be further extended into a linked chain to form a trajectory. The ability to chunk up the world according to certain patterns or regularities in the way that language allows means we can do a lot more than we otherwise could. We can expand and contract boundaries depending upon the characteristics we are using and form trajectories by elongating or stringing together categories. The ways categories are defined or joined up are made by the particular language we are using. Languages and the way they make sense of what goes on can be very different from each other and draw very different pictures of our world. As such, any language we use will give us the sort of boundaries, categories and trajectories we can use. This in turn is a reflection of the culture from which the language is derived. A culture is the adapted patterns of behaviour evolved to cope and manage in a particular environment. This does not mean such categories and trajectories, like any culture, are set in stone; any language can change over time with changing experiences and new technologies. New words and forms of language can be created to accommodate changes. It does, however, mean that the categories and trajectories we use are limited to those we have been brought up with, have common acceptance or can imagine using. Although such symbolic or representational systems have brought great advantages, they do not get us to outer reality. By definition they seek to represent it using the equipment at our disposal. Any system may attempt to represent the world but it also can create that very world which it attempts to represent. For example, if I am born into a culture where there is a concept of happiness, do I learn to label certain experiences as happiness because of the experience or because I have a word I can use?

Specification and generalisation are two movements we can use in constructing a provisional reality in relation to category and trajectory. Specification is the movement of breaking something apart and seeing what it is made up from; it is very often the search that is essential in any category or trajectory. Generalisation means building something up to expand it from where it is. That might mean expanding a category or linking categories together in some way; generalisation expands validity. One way of understanding generalisation and specification is through classification. Classification is the means by which categories can be ordered and subdivided. Some categories exist as opposing classifications (this will be discussed below) but here we are concerned with the classification of categories in a hierarchical relationship to each other. All categories will have boundaries at the top which will be termed the firmament and at the bottom will be the core. If we generalise a category, we are exploring what the category we are looking at has in common with other categories and potentially merging with them. We are exploring the firmament boundary. So, for example, let us take an example of a cat. We place the cat in the category cat, but we can then go on to place it in the category mammal or the category animal. We could go further and place it in a category living being, or earthling. If we take generalisation to its furthest point we get to a place where categories cease to exist and the universe becomes a seamless whole. So, a telephone, a plant, a human being and a chair are in fact all the same thing really. Such a position is usually confined to the realms of the spiritual. Specification in a category represents the movement towards the core boundary and the contraction to what is essential. Here, we chunk up our world into ever smaller and smaller discrete entities to try to get to what is the essence of any category. If we go as far as we can, though, we get to a point where all is in minute, discrete categories in which everything is unique. This ironically is also a position held by more spiritual philosophies. For, rather than seeing what is in front of us as like other things we have also seen, we see it afresh as something unique and different to what we have seen before.

Let us look in more detail at what constitutes specification in a category. If we have named something as a table, what is it that makes it a table rather than a chair, a mat or a shoe? The application of scientific study has achieved a high level of specification, for example the number of atoms that make up a chemical or the genetic code that makes up a living being. Water, for example, can be described as made of two hydrogen molecules and one oxygen molecule. Such specification, though, is always a game of

Russian dolls. When we get to one level there is always a smaller component to be studied. Thus, when we reach the atomic level, we must then study the subatomic. By breaking an object down into ever smaller components we could hope to reach reality: the place where we get that links us to outside. This will never happen. It does, though, allow ever greater understanding in definition of a particular category based upon a small, specified core that all examples within the category share. Therefore, all human beings can be defined as human due to sharing a particular genetic make-up, for example. This potentially allows us to manipulate that code such that we then can create particular trajectories. It then allows us to understand the bigger category human being and reformulate that generality differently. Yet it can be argued that breaking down a table or a human being into its smallest core does little to capture its essence. For example, breaking down a table into given chemical components does little to explain what a table is to a Martian friend. A table is potentially made up of a variety of materials, such as wood or glass, for example. Materials in this example are not always the essence of the meaning of the word. Rather, we often have to look for the meaning of the word table elsewhere. It could be argued that a human being and a table are far more defined by common social understanding than by what they are made up of, as useful as that may be.

When we say a 'table' we probably come up with an idea of what we consider a table to be. We will probably imagine a piece of furniture possibly made of wood, of a certain shape or size, probably a table we ourselves are very familiar with. The example I start off with as an archetype of a table might be quite different from yours. Our starting points can be quite arbitrary. We can then change a lot of the constituents of what we have described to see if what we end up with is still a table. If we make our furniture very small for example, is it still a table, a doll's house table, for example? The answer is probably yes. If we use our table for eating off or for putting lots of junk on does it remain a table? Yes, it remains a table. What if we change the shape of the table, say we imagined a square table and instead make it round? Does this remain a table? Yes, it remains a table. What if we change what the table is made out of, say from wood to metal and glass? Yes, it probably remains a table but what happens if we make it out of paper or cotton wool? We could possibly make it table-shaped but would it remain a table? We may be reaching the limits of what we would call a table. This is not so much because of what a table is constructed out of but that the materials should allow the performance of particular functions such as the ability to put objects upon it. What would happen if we went back to our original idea of a table but sawed the legs off; would it remain a table or would we just be left with a table top? By mentally fiddling about with the facets of what a table is we can work out the boundaries of what we would consider a table.

Eventually, though, we can end up with a definition; for example, a table is a piece of furniture, which has a flat top and is supported by legs which can be used to eat meals off. This suggests that we are defining the core of an object not by finding the smallest part of it but by anchoring its meaning through using multiple other categories. We define the category here not by breaking it down into smaller and smaller components but by seeing what the category relates to and how it interacts with other related categories around it. It means that there are a variety of things that go to make up a core of a category. Meaning comes through the use of other categories together. The important thing is to begin to look at all the different facets of any object that we can fiddle about with to determine what is core. So, for example, to arrive at what is core for a table, we could look at the colour, how it was made, what smell it had, how it looked, how it was being used and vary each of these to see if this would still render the object as a table. In this particular example, one key area is that the size, shape and materials must allow it to fulfil a particular social function. It is not necessarily a positive approach. It is often about determining what cannot be a table as much as what could be a table. Just because this is the current word boundary in the English language doesn't mean this will be the same in any other language and the word for table may be used differently elsewhere. It may vary over time or from individual to individual. If there are great differences, however, this is going to lead to large misunderstandings. So, if we have a word for table and I think of a wooden oblong piece of furniture and you think of a round one, we can probably accommodate this but if you think of any space used for eating, considerable confusion could entail. It also means that, if a core is defined through other categories, each of these are apt to be defined and the means of doing this is through the use of other categories in an endless circle.

Thus, we have started off attempting to specify what is in a particular category, but, in order to carry on this process, we have used other categories to provide linkages. Understanding has become the use of both specification and generalisation together. Generalisation is the force that brings categories together. The merging of categories together to form a larger 'super-category' in a hierarchy is one means of achieving this. Thus, a table is an item of furniture or a cat is an example of a mammal. Yet, forming larger and larger categories on their own is often not that useful any more than making something smaller and smaller. If I want to know how to interact with a piece of furniture, I really need to know whether I have a table or a chair in front of me. Generalisation is also the linking of categories together. We can generalise by joining up categories in a number of other ways. We could, though, join up categories in manifold other ways as well such as through rhyming; table rhymes with cable, fable or able, for example. Alternatively, table could be the opposite of something or have other meanings we can link it with such as times table. It is, though, when we start generalising through creating trajectories with the linkages we make that we begin to have explanations.

For example, the table can be said to constitute the symbolic heart of family life and its marginalisation over time itself reflects the dissipation of family bonds. We begin to create trajectories because we are introducing the element of time. Categories are static. As such, generalisation is the main means of generating trajectories.

In a trajectory, we have foundations, where the arc starts and ends where it finishes. To understand a trajectory, we can go forwards and backwards along it and work out how it fits together. If generalisation is about making new connections, specification is about understanding the ones that are already there and bringing them to light. Thus, we could study the history of the word table from the Latin '*tabula*', meaning board or plank. Here we are trying to identify the beginning of the word and map its change or use over time in order to understand its meaning. The foundational meaning will derive from its deemed beginning possibly when it came into the language from elsewhere or the point at which it substantially changed its meaning. Yet, much like trying to get to the meaning of a word from getting smaller, trying to get to the meaning from going further and further back seems inherently problematic. There is always a before until we get to a point in prehistory where it was given a fairly arbitrary name which could just as easily have been another. Alternatively, specification when applied to a trajectory can mean we can stop it in order so we can categorise it. We have stopped time, so to speak. so we can look at something in more detail. If we link to another category, we can do this either outside time or in time, to define it or to relate it to something else. The meaning of generalising and specification will always depend upon the state we are currently examining. If we are currently examining a category by expanding its meaning, we are generalising; if we are trying to get to the core of a category, we are specifying. If we are examining a trajectory by stopping it, we are specifying. If we give a category movement in time, we are generalising and we have created a trajectory.

There is another way in which we can tell the story of a trajectory. Let us tell the story of how a chair was manufactured; the place we could start with is trees and wood. Wood is not in the category chair. Something has to happen before wood can become a chair. Generally human beings have to interact with it. A trajectory can be made up of deliberate interventions by actors which change a given course of events. That set of instructions of interactions will be termed an algorithm. What we are interested in with any linked trajectory when we are an actor is to be able to predict what will happen when we identify and interact with it. We want to know the causal links that make up a trajectory and how our intervention will change things. It means trajectories do not exist in isolation but change as the result of coming into contact with other trajectories or categories. From this we can generalise how the self should respond when it comes across a category coming towards us as a trajectory, so we know which algorithm to follow. Generalisation, then, allows us to create algorithms. An example of a simple algorithm would be throwing an orange in the air and moving my hands into position to catch it again. I may believe that when I throw an orange up in the air I can catch it again because I did it before. Yet, we may find that our generalisations are flawed. I may drop the orange this time because I misjudge its flight in the air. The way we describe a category or trajectory does not always predict the best way of interacting with it in the future. We can misapply things when it is not appropriate and this is an example of over-generalisation. In order to successfully generalise we must interact with objects of the same category across time and situations. If I taste one fruit that looks like an orange, I generalise the next time I see a similar-looking fruit that it will be good to eat. If I generalise that the table is the heart of one family, I will generalise this is true for other families. If I generalise that table is good to rhyme with cable and fable, I will do so again.

The best way to see if generalisations about algorithms are correct is to test them. As such we need to collect examples. Collecting could end up being a vast enterprise; yet in generalising there is purpose in our collecting rather than just a sense of aesthetic completeness. It is in finding exceptions to algorithms that we test their predictive reliability. If I catch an orange ninety-nine times but drop it once we need to understand why. If I eat an orange ninety-nine times and it tastes good but on the one occasion it tastes bad, we need to know why. If we come across a white flower that smells lovely ninety-nine times and yet then come across a white flower that smells bad then we need to know why. Only on some occasions will it be that we have placed an object within the wrong category. We may instead have to develop a more nuanced understanding of a category and its behaviour over time, its trajectories, for example that an orange goes off. It may also be that there are different species of oranges and that some are good to eat and others are not. Sometimes, though, it is not about the category but the way we interact with it. Minute changes can lead to very different outcomes. If I throw an orange in the air, I need to be able to track it, move my hands into position and close them at exactly the right moment. This will change slightly on each occasion and may cause me to drop the orange sometimes. It does not mean the orange is in the wrong category but that I have been unable to complete the set of interactions that causes me to catch the object. When we see something happening, we want to know what action we need to take in response. An algorithm allows me to do this. We also need to know what to do when we do something and we get the potential of differential results. Let us say our bedroom lamp does not work. We may want to ensure that it is first plugged in and switched on. We check this but it still does not work. We may then wish to check that the bulb works. So, we change the bulb for a new one. Say it still does not work. At this point we may simply want to buy a new lamp.

Algorithms and trajectories then are linked causal chains in time, where what happens causes the next thing to happen and so forth and it does so in a predictable and regular manner. We believe that in general things happen in a regular manner because of the principle of causality. Causality is the principle that occurrences happen because something prior causes them to happen. This may appear obvious but there are alternatives to causality including that things happen because a supernatural being wills it or because it is random. The picture of the universe that the idea of causality creates is one of perpetual falling dominoes. Our ability to attribute causality is important both in our ability to make predictions of the future and our feelings of security. The idea of causality potentially gives confidence. If we can make regular predictions it makes our influence on other simpler. If, however, something happens that is unexpected, unexplained or random then this could shatter our confidence. There is, though, a problem in establishing that one event actually causes another. If one domino falls it is relatively easy to see it was pushed over by the preceding domino but let us take the example of bad smells and disease. Does the presence of a bad smell cause an individual to catch a disease? Unless there is a good theory, what we are left with are incidents that co-occur. One could cause the other, they both could be caused by the same thing or they may not be related at all. The danger in stringing chance occurrences together into causal chains is ending up with magical thinking. This is the assumption that because two events are co-incidental, they must be causally related. For example, let us imagine that we are medieval knights about to go into battle. Just as the battle starts, a phalanx of arrows is shot and is headed our way. At the same time, I trip over a log and this causes an arrow shot to miss me. I could come to believe, providing I survive the rest of the battle in triumph, that I subsequently must always trip over a log just before I go into any battle. Just because two things co-occur at the same time does not establish that one caused the other.

It is relatively easy to attribute the wrong cause to an event or circumstance. If an object falls to the ground and there is a loud noise, most people are content to attribute the noise to the object falling to the ground. We do so because no other realistic cause can be found and all our sensory impressions point to this location. We also use our experience in that whenever a heavy object falls on a hard surface it will make a noise of some description. However, we often are blind to other possibilities in our attributions of causality. For example, because I got out of bed this morning on a different side from usual, I had a bad day at work and my boss yelled at me. Another way of attributing this would be because my boss is rubbish and jealous of me as a potential rival, he found any excuse to yell at me. A third way of attributing this would be, I am so useless, I had yet another bad day at work and my boss yelled at me. All of these involve attributions of causality. Yet, some such as getting out of bed on the wrong side would almost be classed as superstitious and an example of magical thinking. Some attributions may help self-esteem whilst others undermine it.

The scientific method represents the best way in which we as human beings have so far devised, to establish causal links and dispel magical thinking. This method means being able to hold all variables constant except the thing you are testing for. So, for example, if we want to test if listening to music composed by Bach relieves depression, it is no good testing this whilst people are also receiving counselling, going to the gym and receiving antidepressants at the same time. You won't know if it is the music or the exercise that is doing the trick. Yet, in the complexities of human existence it is very different to hold all variables constant. Science tries to get round this by upping the scale, so, rather than testing ten people, it may be better to get a thousand people listening to Bach. It hopes that statistical probability will then even out things such as a death in the family or winning the lottery as other external influences that could influence outcomes. In science, any experiment must be replicable. This means that it is not enough to perform one experiment and get one result; it must be possible to perform the same experiment repeatedly with the same result. This is in order to prove that one thing really does cause another.

If we have an understanding of causal chains from the past, this in theory should allow us to extend them into the future. Past experience, though, can be a relatively poor guide to the future. We could live for many years in calm and peace only to have our life torn apart by a sudden catastrophe such as a tsunami, an economic collapse, a declaration of war, a freak accident, a sudden change in social taste, a change in belief systems, a brand-new discovery, a disease pandemic, or an asteroid colliding with Earth. History is littered with such sudden and dramatic changes both with consequences for individuals, groups and whole populations. This does not mean that causality has broken down but that there are so many small variables involved when many causal chains come together that mean outcomes can change dramatically depending upon small variations. These are examples of where many trajectories interact with each other. For example, let us take a trajectory where I eat some food and my pancreas releases insulin to transport the energy released into my cells. Let us take another trajectory where my heart beats so that blood pumps blood round my body, thus enabling the energy to get round all the cells in my body. The joining together of trajectories such as these create a system. My whole body is one giant system full of complex trajectories maintaining a relatively stable overall environment. Systems form the basis of theories and models. Although we have improved our understanding of such complex systems, our knowledge is still constrained. We cannot make reliable forecasts of the weather beyond about a week, for example. We can come up with reasons as to why the weather is behaving the way it is the problem is that, given all the vast number of variables in any such system, it is almost impossible to say what will happen when they all interact together. Billions of variables go to make up such complex systems and any variation of just one of those variables has a huge difference upon outcome.

It could be that some of these are luck or have worked in the past for others. So, before you go into battle always fall over a log would be an example of this. The scientific method allows checks on algorithmic sequences to ensure validity. There is though another important issue underlying the construction of causal chains. If everything is caused it is difficult to see how human beings can have free will as all their thoughts will also have been caused. Having free will is usually considered a prerequisite for attributing responsibility for something. If human beings lack free will, then they cannot be responsible and this has the potential to undermine systems of law and morality. We become conceived as a cog in a much larger system in which we can make no difference. The idea of causality demands a causer. The idea of a causer seems to enable us to conceptually place certain beings outside the realms of the causality. We often see ourselves and fellow human beings as causers. If we say that human beings somehow are outside the world of causality this seems to give humanity a position outside reality looking on. Causers can be responsible for their actions that which is caused cannot. How can we hold a domino responsible for falling over when placed next to another domino? Yet, once we have introduced the ideas of causality and causer we end up in a murky and often ill-defined world. We often attribute causer status to some human beings and not to others. We often withhold it from young children, for example, and those who are suffering from severe mental illness. We often excuse poor or stupid decisions as caused rather than those of causers.

The easiest position to hold is that both free will and causality are both true despite the apparent contradiction. One way of looking at the problem is to see that, if causality breaks down, we do not arrive at free will but at randomness, and it is randomness that is the opposite of causality. If a snooker ball moves off in a predictable direction by being hit by another ball at a particular angle and speed, if it suddenly does a loop-the-loop, it is not best described by the ball acquiring free will. Free will is best described as an attribute of something that is conscious, that takes in information that can weigh it up, can make decisions and can communicate that back in some way, which as far as can be seen a snooker ball cannot. The attribution of causer status establishes a locus of control within each individual and helps define them as a person not an object. This matters not just in the ability to make decisions but also emotionally. It matters because it sets up a decision-maker which exists independently. Control is not just something that exists logically but also emotionally. If we feel we have control within the self this gives choices and means the self feels control over the future that decisions are free. If control, though, exists outside the self, the self becomes a domino in the chains of causality. Logically, the more free will is attributed the more responsibility people have. This can be double-edged as responsibility can mean praise as well as consternation. If we are not responsible, we can be excused from either.

At the beginning of this section, a suggestion was made that we have mind which is the ground and from this we manufacture self and other. From the discussion so far, the suggestion is that although there are many ways to get to this other, we can never suppose we can get there unmediated. We have to construct a model of what it looks like. That model will be constructed out of categories and trajectories. These are tested by experience over time, by the self and the community of which we are part, with the aim of constantly improving the predictiveness of the model we have. This enables us through the algorithms we create to have some confidence as to how other appears to function when we interact with it. Algorithms are often interactions we have built up over many years and many we will not be conscious of. It is often only when we enter an unfamiliar environment or something unexpected happens that we suddenly realise our learnt repertoire of reactions isn't working and we need to try something else. These algorithms can result in some complex theories and models. Yet none of this can get us to the reality as defined at the outset of this chapter.

This would seem to undermine the possibility of honesty as linked to reality, if reality is a model of the world around us, even if a fairly sophisticated one. One possible solution to this would be, rather than aiming for a correspondence to reality, we aim for consistency. Thus, although we can never reach a final model because everything is mediated, what we can do is make sure that what we construct makes sense and fits together without any glaring anomalies. This would therefore re-establish the possibility of honesty but as consistency rather than corresponding to an external reality. If I have a picture of the world in which I am a person who is fair and just, but then go on to embezzle millions, it would be difficult to hold these two positions honestly. Yet, honesty is more than consistency. We can establish all the most wonderful and complex theories in the world and could be proved wrong tomorrow. If we have total consistency, our object becomes the formation of a neat and tidy model of how we interact with the world. This could mean that our view becomes constrained in order to make it consistent. This could end up being less than honest. Consistency shouldn't be at the expense of being open. Honesty requires openness to evidence and a viewpoint that is clear-sighted as well.

In terms of the end, if this is what truth and honesty amount to, it is problematic. Truth can only be the end if there is no other greater motivator than it. So, if we are being motivated by self-interest or exploration, survival, happiness or the good of others, then truth is not the end. From the outset, then, there is a problem in that the pursuit of truth always seems to have another motivation behind it. We are constructing a model of reality, made up of categories and trajectories, in order to get us to the end of the day. Truth, when it is motivated for some other end than itself, will be termed 'instrumental truth' because it is not engaged in for its own sake but for the positives that it brings and the negatives it enables us to avoid. Such an instrumental version of the truth, however, if accepted, would undermine all claims of truth to be a candidate for the end. Truth is only being obtained in order to get something else and therefore it will be that something else that will be the end. Instrumental truth is truth with an agenda. This is not to undermine the importance of truth. Truth has come to mean gaining as much predictiveness as possible to enable interactions with other. It means being able to respond to the trajectories and categories coming towards us. As somebody who is a causer, a self we can also make decisions to send out arcs of trajectory and mould our reality. This is what truth can do for us. What it cannot do, though, is give us an end. For that we must look elsewhere.

In order to be able to function in the reality we have created, we need more though than just a model and some ideas. One way we know that we are entering that reality is that it feels different. When we enter such a model of reality, emotions will be heightened and necessarily so. Particularly if we have entered one of those areas where our stock repertoire of algorithms isn't able to cope. We, though, keep an eye on everything in such an environment; our viewpoint needs constraining, to that which looks out of place or is different. We cannot dwell too much in the past or too much in the future. Yet, we need to scan the horizon for categories and trajectories that may be coming our way. Thus, we need to construct our experience of reality as a short-term trajectory that stretches out from the self, just into the future, maybe for a few hours, or days. It is necessarily short term in that our ability to predict reliably what will happen gets poorer as our gaze recedes into the horizon. It also is important that our primary focus is on the present as this is where immediate harms can befall us. If we are not attentive to the here and now there will be no future. This short-term gaze is our paramount reality and it functions much like our home screen on a computer; it is the place where we can get to everything else. Not only is it the place where we can receive trajectories and categories coming towards us but it is the place where we can send out the trajectories and categories we create as well: our ideas, our communications, our actions and responses. How we construct paramount reality will be of considerable importance in how we function and interact with other. Depending on its construction will either give us more or less confidence. Having constructed paramount reality, though, it then becomes clear where the end for the self will be situated. We began by saying the end should be what ultimately motivates us. If, however, we have a trajectory for the self, this will create both a foundation and an end point. By creating a trajectory called paramount reality the end will exist as the horizon point of that paramount reality.

Three

VALUE GOOD AS THE END

OVERLAYING OF GOOD AND BAD DIRECTLY ON THE SELF-OTHER BOUNDARY

Living for the well-being of others could be a better potential end than happiness. This is the 'ethical' good. Being ethical, though, is only one possible meaning of the word good. In the English language, good can also have another meaning, to indicate a comparative judgement as to the nature of something against a standard. This is what will be termed 'value' good. Good does not come on its own but only makes sense when paired with another word, namely 'bad'. By comparison with a standard, we can make distinctions that are either good or bad. In this chapter we will be examining this value good as a potential end. In the next chapter we will turn our attention to the ethical good. In valuing we are transposing good and bad onto the boundaries and classifications we have made in the previous chapter. It could be asked whether we could live without the division into good and bad. The answer is yes, for periods as long as paramount reality is a safe distance away. By no means does everything have to be good or bad but when we are in paramount reality, we do need to be able to categorise things in a potentially unpredictable and not necessarily very friendly environment into things we need and things to avoid.

In paramount reality, we create a boundary between self and other. We also need to be able to add in a distinction between good and bad. One way we can add good and bad to our perception of paramount reality is to overlay another boundary on top of the self–other distinction. In this instance we are taking the self–other boundary, described in the previous chapter, and placing on top of it a boundary demarcating good and bad. The boundary for self and other and for good and bad will align exactly. In these circumstances, we have two possible positions we can take. We can identify the self as good and other as bad or we can identify self as bad and other as good. For the moment we will put to one side the theoretical positions where we identify self as bad and other as bad or we identify self as good and other as good. If we are overlaying the self–other boundary with a good–bad boundary there must be scope for both good and bad. Thus, we cannot have situations where everything is either all good or all bad unless the opposites can be placed somewhere else than on self or other. If these are our only two options, it would initially seem that it would be better to place good on the side of self and bad on the side of other. Our sense of what is good is derived from the self as a starting point when in paramount reality and if good is not with self and goes wrong then this destabilises our sense of value. If we do not see the self as good, this will be called inversion and will be discussed later. Seeing the self as valuable makes it the source of good for everything else and is what gives meaning. Yet, just seeing the self as purely good has the potential to lead to a position of extreme egotism and self-centredness.

Seeing the self as good and other as bad is an extreme theoretical position that is difficult to maintain in practice. Yet, it is useful to examine what such a position could look like. One place it can potentially lead is to the barricaded self. This is where the self tries to shut itself off from other as much as possible. This is a logical outcome of seeing the self as good and other as bad. Other will be seen as a threat to the good of the self. The barricaded self will attempt to defend itself by erecting defences along the self–other boundary to stop anything bad from other reaching the self. This could mean denying the reality of other, trying to avoid entering paramount reality or being as self-sufficient as much as possible. On top of the dual boundary of self–other and good–bad we can often overlay what will be termed boundary descriptors. They help describe what the boundary is in any situation. One such boundary descriptor is pure and impure. Pure will be aligned with the self as to what is good and impure will be aligned with what is bad and other. This descriptor is associated with contamination and the fear that the self will become polluted. It is a descriptor with very ancient connotations. In a world where we do not fully understand disease and illness, avoiding pollution can become a matter of life and death.

Pure and impure applies well to a barricaded self. We can see the self as pure and unpolluted and other as a source of contamination. There is then the constant threat that we will become polluted by other. Therefore, we will want to minimise our contact with other as much as possible. It leads to a desire for self-sufficiency. It is a position that suggests the life of a hermit cut off from the rest of society as much as possible. Yet, it is an impractical position because we know that some interaction with other will be necessary. Things from other will have to be brought into the self. Any interaction with other, though, will have to be carefully managed. Using the descriptors pure and impure, before anything reaches the self it must be successfully decontaminated. Something will have value just because it will be on the self side of the self–other boundary. It is good because it is mine or I am familiar with it. We may need some ritual to purify it first but the valuing schema is relatively simple. So, I may value my hairbrush not because it is exceptional in any way but because it is my hairbrush. It may brush hair no better than any other hairbrush; it may look exactly the same as all the other hairbrushes but I regard it as a part of myself. The only way to make what is other good would be to turn everything into part of the self. Otherwise, it will remain bad.

This leads to an alternative to the barricaded self. We could conclude that we cannot avoid paramount reality and engagement with other is inevitable. The best defence of the self in this situation is to turn as much of other into good as possible. The only means of doing this if we value with a simple overlay of good and bad on the self–other boundary is for the self to expand itself into other. All good means in this instance is that it is part of the self. This suggests, rather than the life of retreat, the self seeks to expand itself exponentially. Rather than a barricaded self we end up with an expanding self. The expanding self, though, will see the whole of other as bad and thus fair game for turning to good no matter what it is. Ultimately, the expanding self leads to somebody who wants to conquer the whole world. At some point this will bring the expanding self into conflict with other. Although the barricaded self and the expanding self can seem diametrically opposed positions, the only difference between them is the confidence the self has in being able to overcome the bad of other. Yet, if we pursue the expanding self, the dualism of pure and impure is most likely to be an unsuitable descriptor. It will tend to encourage a fear of other, whereas if we want to engage with other and conquer it we will need to engage with paramount reality. It is, though, possible to modify the schema by placing alternate boundary descriptors on the self–other boundary. As stated, a boundary descriptor modifies what is understood by good–bad boundary when overlaid on top of the self–other boundary. Another example of a boundary descriptor is controlled and uncontrolled with what is under the control of the self being seen as good and what is not under control as bad. This perhaps can be seen as providing the self a better descriptor to accompany the expanding self. By expanding control as much as possible, the self can view that it gains greater security against a hostile world.

Boundary descriptors, though, must derive from somewhere. They will come from how we have constructed paramount reality. It is from paramount reality that we get both the sense of self and other and the need to have both good and bad. In this case, the other in paramount reality has been mapped directly with bad. In order to enter paramount reality, we need to derive confidence from somewhere and have hope in order to sustain being there. In the case of pure and impure, we have neither confidence nor hope in paramount reality. We see it is bad and polluted and we want to go in and come out again as quickly as possible. The confidence that we have is in our ability to purify what we interact with. If we are looking at controlled or uncontrolled, we must have an ability to feel confident that the good of the self can overcome the bad in other in order to control it. It also comes from a hope: that this control will protect the self. These ideas will stem from a need to survive and make our environment more predictable and secure. Thus, paramount reality will be seen as a dangerous place dominated by feelings of anxiety and fear, that we need control in order to survive. Any boundary descriptor will stem from the way we have set up paramount reality at any given time. We have set up an end of wanting more control and we then create an immediate environment which needs controlling. It is where we place our end that creates this and ultimately creates good and bad. Although plausible, this is not to say this is a good way of constructing paramount reality.

Thus, if we place value through a simple overlay on top of the self–other boundary, we will most likely end up in two rather extreme positions. If we are not confident, our good can overcome the bad of other, we will seek isolation: to barricade the self–other boundary to keep the threat from other out. If we are confident in our abilities, we will seek to expand the self exponentially. Thus, we end up in either extreme grandiosity or extreme isolationism. What could also occur due to variations in our confidence is that we could swing wildly from one position to the other. This leads to a highly emotionally unstable position. It is conceivable, though, we could use alternative boundary descriptors that lead to greater moderation. For instance, rather than control being the predominant theme of the expanding self, we can use different terms such as known and unknown or familiar and unfamiliar. To know something or be familiar with it is often a prelude to getting greater control, yet it doesn't have to be. We can want to know things because they are there. There are advantages this can give us. It allows us to expand the self boundary over vast terrain of what is around us without necessarily directly challenging anybody. Additionally, it may allow us greater accuracy when in paramount reality in constructing helpful algorithms or categories. Yet, there will be limits to what we know. As has been said previously, we can never know anything fully in terms of getting out there. What we are doing by knowing or being familiar with is constantly checking our perception of paramount reality with new information and seeing if it needs adjusting, whether this is new categories or algorithms that need creating or whether new models need erecting. Yet, there is a risk that in constantly looking for new things to know or experience we lose what we have previously known, perhaps to be confined to some backwater of memory. We cannot expand familiarity or known exponentially without limit. There is only a certain amount we can retain or usefully use or be familiar with. It can lead to a sense of the self as a trophy collector of experiences or knowledge. We bag something and then move onto the next thing without properly understanding or digesting the experience. Rather than concentrating and appreciating where we are now, we are constantly craving the next new thing. This is perhaps better than control, but leads to a constantly dissatisfied and shifting self. It also suggests that bad is no longer seen as such a threat as to need controlling. This leads to the possibility that, if all bad has to do to become good is become known or familiar, maybe it isn't so bad after all.

Another way this situation can be modified is if we expand the boundary of the self to include a group that we feel we belong to. The self–other boundary is shifted outwards to include others we feel we are like and along with it the boundary demarcating good and bad. In doing so the self becomes merged into the greater group. This means rather than just the self being good, which can be highly restricted and everything else being seen as bad, we instead expand what is good to the group of people we associate with. So, if I am a sailor on a ship, rather than seeing myself as an individual sailor, I could see myself as part of the crew. I could see the ship I am sailing on as being an extension of the group, owned by all of us. In this case I have merged myself into a group and participate in the extension of the group to an object. This means of valuing may expand what is good but still means anything outside the group would be seen as bad. Having a group around us may allow us to gain confidence that we may jointly be able to impose our good on other, yet it could also create a greater sense of threat to anybody seen as outside the group. They may well then feel the need to form their own groups in response. It will also mean sacrificing the independence of the self to the greater group. Even with these modifications, valuing with the good–bad boundary directly on top of the self–other boundary is a morally dubious way of valuing because everything the self does will be good irrespective of its effects and other will always be seen as bad whatever is done by other.

Yet, there is another possibility. If we value through placing the good–bad distinction on top of the self–other boundary, we could see the self as bad and the other as good. Seeing the self as bad will be termed inversion. It could be said that the normal way we value is to see the self as good. This means we can then value in relation to what the self needs and wants as good for the self. If we see the self as bad, it then means that the self doesn't merit good. This is potentially destabilising and confusing in terms of how we place good and bad on paramount reality. One possibility is that we deserve to be bad and nothing we do will ever change this. We are destined to be bad and what is good is remote and inaccessible to us. We thus become barricaded but in a different way. It is not that we have created the barricade for the self to keep the bad out but that barricades have been erected against us so that we cannot access the good in other. Other becomes a remote and inaccessible place. Alternatively, we can take the view that we are bad but we want to be good and therefore we need to grab as much that is good as possible. This sees that the good of other is almost an entitlement and it doesn't much matter how we get it. We thus will be grabbing as much from other as we can possibly get. This result looks a lot like the expanding self but for different reasons. A further possibility is that being bad is something to celebrate, almost as a means of gaining confidence. We do not try to take the good from other. Instead, we attempt to convert other to being bad. None of these positions is ideal and skews how we value. From this, it can be seen that more complex ways of valuing are required that do not just match the self–other boundary.

PLACING THE GOOD–BAD BOUNDARY ACROSS THE SELF–OTHER BOUNDARY

The alternative to placing the good–bad boundary on top of the self–other boundary is to place it across it so it intersects. This will mean that other will neither be purely good nor purely bad but will have elements of both within it. This perhaps is more realistic than the simple straight overlay. Indeed, creating a paramount reality with targets and ends suggests we automatically create a space with both good and bad. By then overlaying the good–bad boundary on top of the self–other boundary we are oversimplifying the paramount reality space we have created. It is much more likely that good and bad will both exist in other. This makes other a potentially more complex place where it is unclear what our response should be as we need to work out what in other is good and bad. As well as dividing other, good and bad will potentially cut through the self space, which makes it far easier for self to be both good or bad. We said previously that normally the self will be the thing of supreme value but it is possible to feel negatively about the self and let bad in. Yet, in the previous way of placing the good–bad boundary there was a risk that the whole of the self would be valued as bad. In this case we are discussing the proportion of good and bad in the self. When we feel that there is more bad than good in the self, we experience inversion, yet there will always be some good. A question arises as to whether just by splitting other into good and bad this automatically will do this in the self as well. By setting up a good outside the self, what we often do is to create a want for that good in the self. If we do this, then the good will create a deficiency within the self. The self recognises it is less than perfect without this good and often will seek to acquire it. Any good set up this way creates a space for bad within the self. It is, though, possible to either see good in other but not want it for the self, or to concentrate on avoiding the bad and being disinterested in the good. In these cases, the setting up of good will not create a deficiency.

One reason why deficiency happens is because of drives. We all experience drives. Drives push the self to seek what is good in other. Such drives include hunger for food, thirst for drink and the sex drive to find a potential partner. Drives start with indicator alarms that originate within the self as a sense of unease to alert us that we need to get something from other. Thus, drives create a sense of dissatisfaction and push us towards particular targets located outside the self. This allows bad to enter the self. As a result, we learn to identify objects in other that can satiate our desires. Our drives won't be satiated until we either get these objects, or somehow, we learn to switch off these signals. For those that are driven to create a barricaded self, drives are inherently problematic because they push us towards other which is regarded as bad. Thus, for those who want to keep the self good and pure, drives themselves are bad. The very experience becomes painful and something that can be seen as a way for bad to enter the self. Yet, drives are an essential component of what makes us human. They are not in themselves bad and can steer our attention to what in our environment can be good. Drives are a reason we need to create and exist in paramount reality. If we identify a suitable object and decide the self should obtain that object, a drive will initiate a set of actions, a trajectory that will allow us to bring what is desired within the ambit of the self. At the start of these actions, we feel unease but, if we can begin to procure our desire, we will begin to experience a form of happiness that will be termed pleasure. Pleasure is the happiness we experience when we bring something identified as good within the self. This can often be an intense experience of happiness. After a time, though, we will then reach a point where we have had our fill and the object will then cause us discomfort. Drives thus are trajectories that give short bursts of intense pleasure sandwiched between feelings of discomfort. Having been satiated, though, time passes and we will feel the discomfort again. We will become habituated to the feelings of satiation and then feel the pangs of longing once again. Drives tend to create a memory of the time we were happy, yet the memory itself will not satiate us. We have a desire to repeat that experience. Thus, by becoming preoccupied by drives, we constantly feel dissatisfied. There will become a gnawing pain in the self until we can climb the mountains of pleasure again, only to come crashing down again afterwards. Then we are filled to get the pleasure again. Yet often we only see the pain at the time of the pain and pleasure at the time of the pleasure, ending up on a hedonic treadmill of satiation.

Drives are bodily signals that indicate something such as we need to eat or we want to find a potential partner. Yet, because they are so pleasurable, rather than looking at them as a signal, we see them as a source of happiness in itself. Let us take the example of the drive of hunger. We need to eat. If we deny our hunger and its pain, we starve. That is why there is urgency to this signal. We can though if we want to maintain our purity think that other is bad and thus food is a potential contaminant. This is not illogical, as if we eat the wrong thing, we can be poisoned. This can cause us to see the pain of hunger as in itself bad. If we have inverted the self we can end up with the same attitude. Food may be good but we are bad and thus we don't deserve what is good. Either of these attitudes can lead us to concentrate upon the initial pain of the drive. Thus, we fail to experience the pleasure of food. Yet, if we can overcome the initial pain and see hunger as a signal, we can begin to see food as a major source of pleasure. This is particularly the case in situations where we can reliably get hold of large quantities of relatively safe food; we can end up eating to excess, with all the consequent health problems this can bring. We can eat so quickly we fail to spot the signs we are becoming full. Hunger has become not a means of signalling a need to eat but a means by which we can become happy and comfort the self. It does so, though, at a cost. We will always feel this gnawing emptiness inside when we don't eat, the temporary pleasure when we do and then a return to the emptiness again.

If drives can cause the good of other to become bad within the self, it is much the same with the goals we set up for the self to achieve within paramount reality. Drives push the self out towards other. Goals by contrast are something the self sets up to achieve in the future to make itself better. They pull us towards our dreams. Yet, in saying that the self can be better in the future, we are saying it is less than good now. Thus, goals can have the same effect as drives in undermining the current self and mean that good created in other means that bad will be created in the self. Let us take the example of winning a sports tournament. We decide we have the talent to win a race. The thought of running in the race causes us emotional anxiety and discomfort. We train and practise as hard as we can. We then run the race; we either win, in which case we experience heightened pleasure for a short time, which results in euphoric pleasure and then this will dissipate. Alternatively, we lose the race and feel crushing disappointment. Either way we end up with the evaporation of the pleasure we sought. Having evaporated, though, we then replace this goal with another one in order to fill our emptiness. This is not to deny the importance of hope but that setting up particularly personal goals will set up good in other but at the expense of allowing bad into the self.

Yet, it could be argued that having a small amount of bad in the self is a price worth paying for having large amounts of good in other. It also acknowledges that drives and hope are inevitable but that we need to be able to contain their signals appropriately. They after all are an integral part of being human. Yet, we must choose to act on them only because it is appropriate and not as a primary means of happiness. Targets provide hope and this is a necessity to sustain us when in paramount reality. They enable us to look forward to the future and inspire us. Our end is ultimately what targets point to so, without targets, there is no end. It matters, though, what we hope for and this will be discussed later. Some goals will end up opening up a greater amount of need and bad within the self. This becomes an issue when the small amount of need in the self gets out of control and we primarily crave the good in other leading to the self being seen as largely bad. If the good–bad boundary is a straight line that intersects the self–other boundary, it suggests that the more good we create in other the more bad we get in the self. Thus, the more we desire from other, the less good we feel about the self. The less we desire from other, the better we feel about the self.

This, though, doesn't always hold. There are examples of where we can have both a large amount of bad in both the self and in other. When we think of the self as bad, we can be apt to think of other as everything from bad and good and somewhere in between. There is no correlation between how other is and the bad self. Thus, inversion plays havoc with how we value other. There are also examples of where we can have a large amount of good in both the self and other. If it was just goals, wants and needs that determined the good in the self, the good–bad boundary would be a straight line. Yet, what determines good in self isn't just the desires and goals we have. The amount of good in the self is determined ultimately by the confidence we have. If we derive our confidence from either having goals or the satisfaction of our drives, it is right to assume that the greater our needs then the larger the amount of bad that will be left in the self. This can be offset, however, by replacing this good by alternatives. It thus becomes possible with a confident self that isn't too dependent upon drives or goals, to have both a self that is largely good and other than is predominantly good. This will be explored in more detail later on but means the simple linkage between increasing good in other and bad in the self doesn't hold.

The same is also the case for good in other. Good can be derived from goals and drives we have, which will also shape what we find good. A goal to achieve status in life will mean what is good is that which helps the self achieve this goal and bad is what frustrates this. If we want to achieve companionship, then likewise what is good will be that which helps this and bad will be what frustrates this. As our goals change and alter over time, so what will be good and bad will be adjusted. If the good and the bad in paramount reality is only determined by goals and drives then all good will be related to where we are in achieving these goals. Yet, if all good and bad solely come from drives and goals then we turn paramount reality into a stage for our ambition. In doing so we will create a large space for deficiencies within the self. Alternatively, if the self does not depend for its confidence on the outcome of its ambitions and instead can make its own good, then it will not crave the good from other. Instead, the good in other can come from alternative sources and serve other purposes, such as an appreciation of complexity and how everything connects together. Good no longer then is a signal of something we need to control and bring into the self but something that is good in itself. To achieve such a position is connected with how the self feels confident. The self must be able to identify what is bad for it but must try to keep this as small as possible, then by a process of elimination the bulk of the rest of other will be good. That good, though, will not be a signal for acquisition for the self or related to a goal. We can know about it and be familiar with it and leave it where it is within other.

In the previous section, with the overlaying of the good–bad boundary on top of the self–other boundary, two possible positions were considered. These were that the self is good and other is bad or that self is bad and other is good. If the good–bad boundary is placed so it intersects with the self–other boundary and that neither is wholly dependent on the other, it means there are other possibilities. All of these possibilities will have combinations of good and bad on both the self side and in other. Thus, the self is never entirely good or bad but it will be predominantly one or the other. Likewise, other will be either predominantly good or bad. This makes possible the self being seen as predominantly good and other as predominantly bad or that the self is seen as predominantly bad and other as predominantly good. These are slight variations on what was previously discussed. Yet, other configurations also become possible such that we regard most of other as bad and most of the self as bad. Good will exist in both, but only minimally.

This, though, will lead to a sense of despair and hopelessness and would be best avoided. It is only where most of the self is good and other is also mostly good that we get to a point that we can feel everything is all right. Seeing predominantly good in other allows us to go into paramount reality positively. It is better that other is regarded generally positively as long as this is safe, but some acknowledgement is made that there will be bad elements we need to deal with. Although in order to want things there must always be some bad in the self it is also far better that the self is generally held positively. Happiness is our detector of what is good and the position where good is maximised in both self and other will lead to a greater feeling of happiness.

It is possible we can see other as good and not let bad into the self. As stated, if we identify good in other but are content to leave it where it is, we do not create a deficiency. We could be content to leave something good where it is as the self is sufficiently good already. It doesn't need to be brought into the self. Thus, we may only be concerned with identifying bad. This could be that we identify so much bad in other that we become fearful and want to avoid paramount reality altogether. Yet, as long as we are valuing with the good–bad boundary lying across the self–other boundary, there will always be some bad in other, even if this is minimal. The point is to be able to identify this accurately and develop strategies so that harm is minimised. It means, though, that we do not mostly desire what is good in other but appreciate it so it doesn't become part of the self. We then have no deficiency. In this way, we can maximise the good in self and in other. We do, though, need to still have some acknowledgement of drives and goals, even if we minimise them. Thus, we will have some temporary deficiencies in the self.

We have previously referred to boundary descriptors, such as pure and impure or controlled and uncontrolled. They were used when describing the situation where the good–bad boundary was overlaid on top of the self–other boundary. It is also possible to consider them in the situation where the good–bad boundary crosses the self–other boundary as well. Here, though, such boundary descriptors will need to sit over one boundary or the other. When they are placed over the good–bad boundary they will be termed value descriptors as they elucidate what good and bad mean. So, for example, instead of mapping pure and impure onto the space divided by the self–other boundary, we place it on the good–bad boundary, which is tangential to the self–other boundary. If we do this, we are evaluating other by how clean or pure it is or how contaminated it is and will usually be more concerned about keeping out the bad and contaminated from the self rather than the acquisition of the good. Therefore, if this is the case it does not automatically create a deficiency in the self. We can keep the self as good, as we are not using the evaluation to identify good which we then want to bring into the self. Instead, we are seeking to defend the self from bad. It is difficult, though, with this use of descriptors to see how the bulk of other will not end up being seen as bad or impure, which is something we are trying to avoid. If, however, we are using pure and impure to identify the pure that we want to bring into the self we are then creating a deficiency.

Another example of a boundary descriptor that was applied previously was controlled and uncontrolled. When placed solely on top of the good–bad boundary, we will identify in other that which will give the self more control and that which will give us less control. So long as our overall aim is to have more control this is a schema that will create a deficiency because it leads to an acknowledgement that we need to have more control than we already have. That which gives control will be good and that which doesn't will be bad. In order to increase the amount of good, we need to expand the control of the self. Once value becomes involved with controlled and uncontrolled, this leads to an expansionist self that seeks to colonise as much of other as possible, which will inevitably lead into conflicts. The corollary for the self is that control and self have no relation. Just because we control something doesn't make it any more part of self than if it wasn't. Instead, control is linked to good and bad. Thus, there will be parts of other the self controls but which are not part of the self. There will, likewise, be elements of the self we don't control, resulting from the created deficiency. This runs counter to how we usually see the self as the seat of control. If the self has no control, it means it is determined by outside forces with no free will and ceases to be an agent of choice. In other words, placing controlled and uncontrolled as a descriptor on top of the good-bad boundary doesn't work well. Alternatively, controlled and uncontrolled can be left to describe the self–other boundary. It then describes what we are responsible for but without seeking to see this as either good or bad. We become responsible for the self, how it reacts and the decisions it makes. It, though, cannot be responsible for other and what happens there. Neither is in itself good or bad. Thus, it can be concluded that controlled and uncontrolled will inevitably be best placed along the self–other boundary and we will have to rely on other ways to elucidate good and bad.

The other pairs of boundary descriptors discussed were known and unknown, familiar and unfamiliar. These behave in a very similar way to controlled and uncontrolled as value descriptors. The main difference is that known and familiar give the possibility of knowing about something without necessarily the need to control it. Even so, knowing about something can lead to control down the line. If we place known and unknown on top of the good–bad boundary, what is good becomes what is known to us and what is bad is unknown. Yet, there are many things we can know or be familiar with that can be bad. There are also many things we don't know or are unfamiliar with that can be good. It also leads to the detachment of the self from being known or familiar. Thus, it makes possible that parts of the self are unknown or unfamiliar. Alternatively, if we overlay known and unknown on top of self–other, what is known becomes the self and what is unknown is other. Good and bad attach to neither, so it can be good that something is known or unknown. There may be times it is good to be somewhere or in something that is familiar but this continually can be dull and unchallenging. There may also be times when being somewhere unfamiliar is good but we may yearn for what is home and familiar. Yet, whereas, control seems to be a prerequisite for having a self, it would seem possible to know or be familiar with things and leave them in other. We know the capital of China is Beijing but this doesn't make Beijing part of the self per se, just that we know this. Knowing or being familiar with something would be a way by which we could see something as good but leave it where it is, as a means of appreciation of other.

None of the boundary descriptors examined seems to sit well on the good–bad boundary. It was mentioned in the last chapter that not only can categories exist in hierarchy to each other but they can also exist as opposites. Let us take the example of cat and dog. Cats and dogs are both mammals and animals and can fit into the same supercategories. They are different classifications of animal, therefore they would not instantly appear as opposites. It is just they are commonly paired as pets which compete for their owner's hearts. For categories to be opposites they must be underscored by the values of good and bad. By placing both good and bad within the field of other we now make possible the existence of opposites. So, if we look at cats and think they are wonderful and dogs are from the Devil, we have underscored the categories with value. It is not that the categories in themselves are opposites; they have been made opposites through the addition of good and bad. In placing good and bad within other we are mapping positive and negative upon categories and trajectories that come towards us and situating the self in relation to them. It is also possible, by valuing cats, I come to believe I am deficient without a cat companion and want a cat to fulfil me. I am also repulsed by dogs and become fearful whenever I see one. So, we can either use these values to identify objects we want to bring into the self or as a means of situating the self in relation to other. If we value by opposites, half our world will be good and half will be bad. We find two things that seem to be related and emotionally align ourselves with one or the other. Although human beings are capable of sophisticated use of multiple boundaries, categories and trajectories in their putting together of reality, it is easier and simpler to place one boundary onto a situation rather than many. Dichotomies of good and bad are simpler and match emotional equipment.

Yet, these dichotomies are fluid and impossible to anchor 'out there' in the same way truth could not be anchored. There is nothing with a cat or a dog that makes me choose one over the other. I could just as easily reverse this dichotomy. It is a matter of personal preference. Most people, though, manage to get along with these fluid dichotomies. If I argue I could not choose between different cars to buy having been given all the available information because there is no universally agreed standard on which to base a choice, many would greet this with frustration and perplexity. This judgement is arrived at through having built up a matrix of different values over time. If something is seen as positive there must also be some idea as to what the negative is and vice versa. So, for example, if I see a hairbrush as a good hairbrush, I must also have an idea as to what a bad hairbrush is. It may be because the hairbrush brushes my hair well or is a particularly fine-looking hairbrush. It may be a well-tested hairbrush. This makes this judgement relative. Human beings have a particular wish to standardise their judgements, so we invent many ways of doing this. We could define good hairbrushes through the materials they are made from. This would create a binary value pair of flimsy or long-lasting. It could be through how the hairbrush looks, which would be underscored by a value pair, beautiful and ugly. We could hold competitions in how well they brush hair, which would create a value pair of effective or ineffective. Value is formed by the person or persons imposing the idea of positive and negative on what is other. Those rules are derived from the distilled wisdom of people making judgements about hairbrushes or whatever else is being judged. These are examples of algorithms discussed in the previous chapter, rather than rules for changing light bulbs though these are rules for making judgements about hairbrushes. Being able to value enables us to make choices with a view to bringing what is good within the ambit of the self and rejecting what is bad.

Although positive and negative values can be mapped onto objects such as hairbrushes, these values will come from somewhere. Some value descriptors are fairly clear where values should be placed at the outset, such as effective and ineffective. To use these values, we just have to have a notion of what effective looks like: what it means to brush hair well, for example. These direct elucidations of good and bad are either used or not. Other value pairs are less clear. For example, we could use pairs such as old and new, fast and slow, work and play, male and female. In the case as to where value is placed in these distinctions it is less clear cut and often can depend where the self starts off from, assuming we regard the self positively. With a male and female distinction, for example, things often depend on which gender we identify with in the first place. Yet, undergirding all these binary pairs is some idea that we favour one or the other of these distinctions. We see one side as positive and the other as negative. As there are a multitude of these binary pairs it is easy to see how a matrix of value can become complex. Just forming a binary pair, though, is not sufficient to create value. Without the associated positive and negative emotional feelings, we are not really valuing but merely observing. Valuing therefore is an inherently emotional activity. If we feel nothing about something then it has no value, positive or negative. It is therefore possible to regard male or female as an unimportant distinction in how we approach or interact or make judgements. This is an example of a non-value-laden duality where we have placed ourselves outside this duality, as an onlooker. Alternatively, we could associate positively with our own gender or associate negatively. So, a male self could see men as negative and female as positive, or vice versa.

Valuing, though, can be even more complex. It is possible to take value dualism and feel positively about both of the values or negatively about both of them. What we do here is create a continuum of value with the two values at either end. For example, we may see pure unfettered capitalism as a bad thing; I may also see pure centralised socialism as a bad thing and instead seek to tread a path in between these two poles. What we want to suggest is that there is a path of moderation between two poles of value. The path of moderation represents good whereas the extremes are both bad. In this example, I am still valuing, I am not taking up an onlooker status but I am choosing to value both binary distinctions negatively. This is because I may value individual freedom but I may also value equality. I may see that socialism may seek equality but at the expense of freedom and capitalism allows freedom but undermines equality. As I value both equality and freedom, I choose the middle course. Alternatively, I may value equality as a good thing but not if it means ending all freedom, thus, I may place freedom above equality in a hierarchy of value. Equality and freedom do not exist in isolation here but as dualisms in themselves. Equality will be in a dualism with inequality and freedom in a dualism with slavery. Underpinning value continuums will be other value dualisms of some description. It is therefore possible depending on the values we use for us to value both equality and freedom but in some situations, we may have to choose one over the other.

The value continuum though can be changed, so that both ends of the continuum are seen as good. Let us take the example of old and young. We can associate old with being experienced, well-tested, mature, wise, as part of history. We can associate being young with being fresh, enthusiastic, innovative and dynamic. All of these positive values will also be part of value dualisms such as mature and immature, wise and foolish, fresh and stale, enthusiastic and staid, for example. Yet, we take the positive parts of the dualism so we get a position that whatever we see along the old–young continuum will be regarded as good. In this latter example, we are not forming an onlooker status to old and new as we still value both sides but we have not got a simple value dualism either. We are taking one value dualism and undergirding it with the positive sides of other dualisms in order to get universal positive value and managing to find good on both sides of a dualism. This position will maximise the amount of good. In this continuum of value, we are maximising the good around us, even if it is underpinned by other value dualisms. Since the aim of valuing is to have as much good in other and in the self as possible whilst not placing the self at risk, then the constructing of these continuums is a good way of valuing. We are not creating preferences to bring into the self but seeing why what around us might be good in itself.

HAPPINESS AND VALUE GOOD

If our values carve up other into good and bad it will be our emotions that alert us to their immediate presence. As stated, carving up these spaces into binary pairs tends to match our emotional equipment. We often prefer drawing the fewest number of boundaries we can get away with in any given situation. Although human beings are capable of sophisticated use of multiple boundaries, categories and trajectories in their putting together of reality, it is easier and simpler to place one boundary onto a situation rather than ten, fifty or thousands. Such dichotomies are simpler and tend to match emotional equipment. This can lead to issues and problems, however. Extreme thinking is where we think only in terms of one

or two possibilities rather than seeing many. When we have over
-simplified boundaries this is likely to lead to extreme emotional
responses; so, for example, seeing other people as either friends or
enemies or seeing any given situation as either good or bad. We
often fail to see that people can be friendly sometimes and hostile
at others, or that situations and things can have elements of both
good and bad in them. Dichotomised thinking often fails to pick
up on the subtleties of life. One version of intelligence could be
the number of boundaries being used to map any given situation a
human being finds themself in.

There are other ways of looking at intelligence, which mean
we try to build as sophisticated a model of paramount reality as
possible and thus avoid just seeing positive and negative. These
include the ability to see new and different connections between
categories in the form of generalisations, exceptions to cores of
categories and the ability to see new amalgamations of previously
separate categories. It also means ensuring the stability and
consistency of boundaries applied over time. It is often fairly easy
to apply a boundary on the spur of the moment and then change
it when circumstances change. This means we will be carried along
by emotional circumstance. It is less easy to commit to maintaining
boundaries over time. It is only when we examine a task or an
attitude in detail that we begin to realise how easy we can tangle
ourselves in contradiction. In much of life, we proceed by making a
lot of assumptions or things assumed as common sense. Things that
are assumed may be so taken for granted amongst a community
that we don't see them at all. Another version of what intelligence
could be is to make explicit what people otherwise would simply
assume. It could be that by doing this we may question the validity
of our common sense or accept it as correct. All of these are
examples of how we build a greater, more accurate model for our
paramount reality when it becomes underscored by good and bad
and prevent us swinging wildly from positive to negative emotion.

Happiness is the key detector of positive value and stems from detecting good, wherever it is. If we can identify the maximum good in other and in the self then we will de facto feel happier. This need not be about getting good. If we are about identifying good in other to bring into the self that happiness will be pleasure. This, though, creates a sense of jeopardy; we may fail to bring the good into the self and now feel we need the good in order to feel better. By actively seeking out good for the self, though, we undermine the good within the self that is already there. Happiness, though, can also be experienced when we see good in other, appreciate it without the need to bring it into self. Seeing as much good in other as possible enables the self to feel more secure and less threatened. The more we can do this, the happier we will feel, so long as we don't undermine the happiness in the self but also don't ignore genuine threats. If we identify little or no good in our environment then de facto we will feel worse. Value good is intimately bound up with happiness and therefore cannot be a suitable rival to happiness or a basis to critique it as a candidate as the end. How we structure the self and other in relation to value good will inherently alter our experience of happiness.

Four

ETHICAL GOOD AS THE END

THE INVENTION OF SPECIALNESS

Having discussed value good, another possibility of what 'good' means is to live for the well-being of others and from this comes ideals such as universal peace, justice and prosperity. This idea of 'good' has the appearance of being less selfish than living for individual happiness and appears morally superior. Not only does the idea of what is ethically good potentially undermine happiness as an end but it can be argued it can provide a suitable rival candidate to be the end. When mind has been split between self and other, living for the ethical good would mean living for that which is other within the mind. Yet, other can mean anything that is not already conceived as part of the self. We would find living for the well-being of everything that is not self difficult. Even within the confines of our relatively narrow appreciation of other, this is potentially a massive space within our mind. It is therefore wise to make distinctions in regard to other. An important distinction is between that which is other and can be potentially property and can be bought and sold and another which can't. One reason that other cannot be bought and sold is that it possesses 'specialness'.

The archetypal possessor of specialness is another human being. The term here will be used as primarily an emotional one derived from the ability to attribute personality or personhood to somebody or something. Although therefore the archetypal possessor of specialness is another human being, specialness could be withheld from some people or personality could be granted to some non-humans. The attribution of specialness means the person is allowed a moral status from which rights and responsibilities are drawn: an ethical being. It also means that the person is regarded as an independent attributor of value, to have causer status. Even restricting the ethical good to possessors of specialness means we will have a potentially high ethical debt. We will often not have the same concern for all we consider having specialness. I may for example have greater ethical concerns for my partner, my family or my friends and prioritise their welfare accordingly. Ethical people, though, are often those considered to have the widest possible concerns the greater community, non-human subjects and the whole planet, in an ever-expanding sphere of concern. The problem is that the greater our sphere of ethical concerns the greater potential for ethical conflict to arise.

For the most part, we intuit who others are through habit or education, often concluding that those with specialness are predominantly other human beings. We give them existence from the snippets of evidence we have. We may not spend much time as to why we regard other human beings as moral subjects. To regard the whole of humanity as worthy of specialness, though, is something comparatively rare in world history. Empires have been forged on the belief that others who do not belong to a particular population group can be turned into property to be exploited and conquered. Many societies are stratified such that whole groups, defined by things as work or gender, can be afforded little or no status and deprived of their personhood. Sociopathy is a failure to recognise others and their needs. In such circumstances the attribution of specialness is virtually absent. By contrast, it is also relatively easy to say we regard the whole of humanity as having specialness but to make this meaningful can prove a lot more difficult. Specialness is not a commonly held term but we need something like it in order to understand morality and why we owe an ethical debt towards others. It is the attribution of personality that is at the heart of specialness and makes a person an emotionally alive being that engages our imaginations both positively and negatively. Our emotional landscape is often very sensitive to those with specialness. It could be possible to imagine giving an object an ethical status without the attribution of personality, through habit or following a law, for example. Even if unacknowledged, however, the moral debt is always owed due to the potential of personhood.

Although often confined to humans, we can project personality onto anything, including animals, plants, buildings, an imaginary character or being, toys, volcanoes or stars. We can give old buildings a history and personality. We tend to speak of whole nations having certain national characteristics. Football teams often take on aspects of personality for their supporters and followers. It isn't too far from this to a view that everything has its own spirit within it. Pantheists see the whole of creation as a form of giant personality. By way of further example let us say we discover a smooth pebble in our garden. Let us imagine turning that pebble from just any old pebble into our best friend. Perhaps the first thing we would want to do is give the pebble a name, maybe Eric. Attributing a name which is associated with personality is a very strong way of attributing recognition of personality. If we want to dehumanise somebody, we refrain from naming them or name them in a way that demeans them, say giving them a number or calling them by a derogatory nickname. In naming we begin to create uniqueness for the personality. We may then want to give the pebble a back story, how Eric came to arrive in our garden. Maybe Eric is a pebble from another country but somehow got lost. In attributing a narrative to the personality, we can extend our sympathies for the personality and actions become more explicable. We may want to create some friends for Eric, maybe Eric has some pebble friends who he has lost, maybe Eric has a pebble family who are far away. In socially situating any personality, actions become explicable that may not be otherwise and in so doing we more easily identify with the other person, imagine what we would do in their situation. We will want to create for Eric an inner life of thoughts and feelings; Eric may be lonely being a pebble far from home. From this inner life will come an understanding of a web of preferences and dislikes as well. Eric likes rain and being in water because it makes him shiny but doesn't like being in dirt. We will want to create a desire for future action for Eric. Maybe Eric wants to find his way home in order to see his pebble friends and family again. Eric is able to make choices but also constrained in those choices as well. We will want to create a relationship with ourselves, an engagement with Eric. We can find things we can do together. Eric can have opinions about me as well as I have opinions about Eric. That relationship should be founded on the explanations we find for why Eric is Eric and as we have had our sympathies extended to Eric. We will want to give boundaries to Eric: what does Eric own, where does he live, what does he know?

Suddenly we have turned a pebble into having a personality simply by a few imaginative acts. This is one of the greatest skills we possess and it is at the root of much that we do socially. We may well feel the rush of excitement as our imaginations introduce us to the creation of a possible new friend and, yet, we may think this childish. Yet, this capacity enables human beings to denote specialness and therefore is an important stepping stone to moral behaviour. If we cannot do this, we will be at best morally stunted as we can have no real appreciation of the existence of another. In creating specialness in this way, we are creating a specially labelled object within our minds within the space of other. It is however equally easy to refrain from attributing specialness; we only think of treating a person as part of a group labelled with a pejorative title, often a negative moral term, and it becomes easy to dehumanise. It therefore becomes possible to deny specialness to beggars, drug users or prostitutes or to limit it. That being said, we generally don't ascribe personalities to pebbles either as they exhibit none of the properties of personality we are imaginatively ascribing to them. There is no sign of an inner life; there is no sign of motivation to do anything. The pebble just is and that makes it difficult to have a relationship with. Often, the ascription of personality is not something we feel we have the freedom to ascribe simply from imagination. For although the other is always something that is beyond total knowing we find a constant stream of evidence from what another person says and what they do. From this we can deduce what their inner life might be like and what important things may have happened to them. We can do this from our own experience and whatever psychological generalities we have learnt to model from. The ascription of personality then is not just a one-way street and specialness is not something we tend to freely create. Specialness is usually something we have to interact with and is part of other within the mind, but not in the control of the self. Any interaction with other opens up the possibility that interactions may not go as intended. Specialness therefore is something we have to go out of ourselves to appreciate and risk coming back changed from.

It is though possible to stunt specialness. We often meet people in fairly narrow contexts. It is then possible to know only a small amount about the other person. If we see specialness as primarily being in relation to what we can know about a person, this could limit the specialness we ascribe. In these circumstances, we could project assumptions about the other through intuition and clues that we have. These though may be inaccurate and the result of prejudice and bias. This in turn implies that what specialness requires is more information and knowledge about the other in order to make accurate attributions. The consequence of not having full or accurate knowledge is that we reduce the specialness of the other. There is a problem, though, in assuming the ascription of full specialness equates to having full knowledge about another's personality as we cannot know the other's direct subjective experience. We should try to be honestly aware of another but we will always have aspects of the other we will not know. Therefore, if we rely on knowledge about another, full specialness will always be impossible to attribute as we can never fully know the other. We can only have a partial ascription based on what we know and will always be making assumptions, even with somebody we know well. It is also possible to see some people as lacking aspects of personality. For example, when somebody suffers from advanced dementia, intentional considered action following the processing of information becomes difficult. Does this mean that, because we can access even less of the person's story, or ability to make decisions, we should deny them specialness? To do so suggests that we may have to differentiate between attributing greater and lesser specialness, depending on circumstance, depending on what we know and find out but also how the other person is.

In the last chapter we spent time discussing the attribution of value to objects and we can also do the same with possessors of specialness. We can spend time imagining another with personality and then proceed to compare that personality with others we have come across. Specialness is positive, but aspects of personality can be underscored with good and bad. That may be because we see the person as a good or a bad person, making a moral or ethical judgement about a personality in some way. Alternatively, giving time to another person can be costly to the self and if we are looking to bring them into our ambit. We will be keen to work out whether this would be a suitable emotional investment; whether the person would be good or bad for us. Ultimately this rests with passing judgement onto the nature of the aspects of personality they have as either good or bad. One way we can ascribe personality is to see the other as a possessor of fixed globalised personality traits. This could be in relation to how trustworthy somebody is, or what skills they possess that might be useful to us, or whether they make us laugh, or what resources they bring to the table. It could be that the person is like me in some way and I feel I can share something of myself and they will understand me. Therefore, what interests many when they meet another is not that they have personality but what sort of characteristics they have. Categorisation of personality thus has become a common enterprise. Extraversion and introversion are common distinctions, with extraverts being seen as more sociable and gaining their energy from being with others, whereas introverts are perhaps more wary of others and find sociability an effort. I may value extraversion positively because I myself am extravert, or I may value extraversion because I associate it with other traits I value positively, such as being chatty and fun to be with.

All these traits can be judged in the same way as we would judge any object in valuing from other, whether they are good or bad and any attached value fields. This way of looking at other tends to limit specialness making other more like property. Property can be defined as an object, skill, idea or event that is positively valued for its utility, has a relationship with a person or group and can be subject to their control for a time. The act of valuing therefore is one of the ways property is created. Valuing per se cannot reduce specialness to property on its own as this also involves utility, control and tradability. Yet once personality has been defined and categorised, much of the reason for valuing is for reasons of utility. Utility is a potentially vulnerable reason to be valued. I may value somebody because I like their company or because they are a good electrician. Both examples represent a valuing due to utility. If I am unable to perform as an electrician, I will no longer be valued and if I am valued because I am good company, we can imagine what would happen if this were no longer the case. When our use has been fulfilled, our value also will disappear. It indicates our disposability. Control similarly indicates that our value depends not on who we are but on our compliance with the wishes of another.

Specialness that contains evaluative characteristics or traits will be termed a reputation. Holding another's specialness is like keeping a bit of another within the self. We can hold specialness through keeping a reputation of the other, with evaluative traits, either positive or negative determined by another's utility to the self. How our own reputation is held can often be of great concern and we will then seek to influence others to hold a positive reputation of us. Our own reputation can appear as an extension of the self and we can feel intensely threatened if others appear to treat our reputation badly. Yet, we cannot ever really know how others hold our reputation and seeking to control this is often futile. What we can control is how we evaluate others and hold others' specialness. It is questionable therefore in holding the specialness of another should be done by giving traits and underscoring this with value. Personality is not fixed but changes over time and will include the accumulation of learnt responses and predispositions. Behaviour changes as we age and our personality will change as well. We may suffer greater shyness when we are younger as opposed to when we are older, for example. Personalities can be differentiated through tendencies, for example that somebody is frequently angry or cracks under pressure or is shy and withdrawn and yet there will be instances where this is true and others when this is not. How often does somebody have to be angry to have an angry personality or how shy to be shy? Gosling (2008) suggests that, when we get to know somebody, we first get to know them through traits but it is only when we appreciate their inner story, the dynamism and change, that we really come to know them well. We may need to evaluate the behaviour that derives from the specialness we observe and even seek to advise, correct or change it but specialness itself should be beyond evaluation. It is beyond being property and is always positive. This means that specialness is not given solely on the basis of knowledge about somebody and the categories we place them in.

THE DETECTION OF SPECIALNESS – EMOTIONAL IDENTIFICATION

A way out of these dilemmas of evaluation and knowledge is to argue that the ascription of specialness does not rely on either evaluation or full knowledge. What we can do is emotionally identify with the other. Identification essentially means using the imagination to place oneself in another person's position. If we fail to identify, we risk turning other directly into property and just evaluate them as such. Having identified, we can then either add in the step of relating this to the needs of the self or stay with the person. If we relate the identification to the self and its needs we evaluate other and form a reputation. We only don't do this if the person either threatens the self or other people. If, however, we stay with the other person and focus on them, we keep them as special. Clearly a fair degree of knowledge of the other person must be had in order for this to be done accurately, so knowledge as well as feeling is important. Unevaluated identification emotionally lets the specialness of the other live within us for a time. We can do this by projecting ourselves into a situation and think how it would feel to be in this situation ourselves. Alternatively, we can, much like we did for Eric the pebble, find out about another's story and then imaginatively simulate each situation as the other. Unless we can do this, we are likely to see other personalities as utilities, for what they can do for us and at constant risk of becoming property.

Yet, as with knowledge alone, there also appears to be scope for degrees of identification; for example, I may be able to identify enough to tell that another person is upset or I may identify so much that I cease to have my own self and believe I am the other person. It is perhaps also worth comparing the identification continuum with a selfish and selfless continuum. If total selfishness represents an inability to recognise the needs or existence of others, a total selflessness represents a failure to recognise one's own needs and heightens the importance of meeting other people's needs. Identification and selflessness are clearly related. If you identify with another person this is likely to lead to selfless behaviour. The more you identify with the other person the more selfless the behaviour is likely to become but the selflessness could result for reasons other than identification. I could be selfless because I hate myself and believe I deserve nothing. I could be selfless because I believe I am in permanent debt to a god that manifests itself in the existence of others. I could be made to be selfless through coercion, bullying and threats. Selflessness is more defined by action towards others whereas identification is about a certain imaginative state that leads to those actions. Selfless actions, however, could result from different imaginative states. Yet, both an extreme identification and extreme selflessness are likely to lead to states of excessive self-denial which seem to go way beyond a simple recognition of other's specialness. It would seem to be fair to conclude that extreme identification and selflessness would need some form of qualification due to the risk posed to the self. Having removed the evaluation of other to the self, there is a risk that we fail to detect the risks posed to the self. Thus, unevaluated identification needs to be qualified. That qualification seems to be twofold, that the recognition of other's specialness should not come at the expense of the specialness of self or the specialness of others around either.

A distinction can be made between sympathy and empathy on the basis of the degree of identification. Empathy can be seen as identification without losing sight of our own specialness and the specialness of others. In a state of empathy, we identify enough with a person to know how they are feeling and to be able to respond accordingly but not identifying so much as to be overwhelmed by another's emotions. We can appreciate emotionally what the other is experiencing but never so completely as to be overwhelmed by contagion. As such the emotional life of another is understood but it does not mean that we necessarily experience the same emotion. So, for example, if you tell me you are happy because you have got a new job I would have to know what getting a new job means and what it feels like in order to be empathetic. It does not mean I experience the same thing that you feel; I may experience happiness for you that you now have a new job. If, however, I find out the new job is unsuitable, instead of happiness I may feel concern or anxiety. Empathy then is not just a reflection back of emotions felt. This is because in empathy contact is maintained with a larger view than just the person in front of us. In general, if you are happy, I will be happy, but if that happiness is short term and a possible prelude to unhappiness then I may be concerned. If your happiness is predicated on others' own unhappiness and I also feel empathy for them then too I will also feel concern. Some forms of happiness can be shared around with the intention of making others happy, whereas other forms of happiness can be at others' expense, including our own. To the extent that you are happy and that is not causing anybody else unhappiness then I too will be happy.

Sympathy by contrast is identification that goes further into selflessness and begins to lose sight of our own specialness and the specialness of others. In sympathy, I will feel as an echo of whatever the other is feeling, whatever the circumstances. This is because imaginatively I am identifying with you and imagining what it is like to be you. This is likely to be reduced in intensity as I am still living my life and you are still living yours. Yet, in theory, if I can fully identify with you, I will experience emotion of the same intensity or more. Unevaluated identification, when taken to its logical conclusion, suggests we become the other. It is of course a faintly surreal possibility because we can never actually become another person. Yet this is what unevaluated identification can lead us to. There are though attractions to this possibility. If our life is dull, hard or a frightening place to be, imagining we are somebody who has a glamorous or powerful life offers a route of escapism. This exercise in imagination can be bolstered by our own real-life predicament and incentives to escape from it. In computer games, alternative realities have been devised where we can create other characters and can spend much of our free time living and feeling alternate lives. Although escapism may be a reason we would want to indulge in sympathy, our main concern, though, will be as a means by which to emotionally identify with specialness. It could, though, be seen that, if sympathy goes too far along the selfless continuum, empathy whilst useful only gets us to the start line.

LOVE, RESPECT AND COMPASSION

Many emotional states lauded by humanity as ways to be moral and elevate our emotional relations to other can be seen as problematic when examined in relation to empathy and sympathy. Love, respect and compassion highlight different issues with identification that ultimately undermine specialness and lead us towards over-expanding or contracting identification. It is love which is often seen as the state which most fully echoes the full range of emotions of the other. Within Christianity, love has traditionally been prized as the most important of emotional states; God is even described as being synonymous with love. Love is often seen as central to the most important of human relationships whether it is the infatuation of romantic lovers, the companionship of close friends or the bonds of caregiver and receiver. Identification is central to love but the experience goes beyond this and can end up in total self-giving or possessiveness. Love is generally regarded as a positive feeling strongly linked to happiness. People enjoy the experience of falling and being in love. Yet, it is also widely acknowledged that love can be immensely painful. We only need to think of unrequited love, feelings associated with the loss of our beloved or when we fall out of love. Love is best understood not as an isolated feeling but as a journey of strong emotions that result from the attachment to an object of our affections, our beloved. The romantic ideal of love runs right from the first meeting where we feel the first pangs of attraction, to the falling in love where every gesture and action of our beloved takes on huge significance to the final consummation of that love. Most love stories are ended on this emotional high. The full journey of love, though, is rarely like this. We can jump into the journey of love at many points and also jump out again. In addition, this sort of love only tends to apply to romantic relationships and not to other forms of love. The journey of love a caregiver feels for their child or a child feels for a caregiver is likely to be different but also equally centred on attachment. The idealised story of love also fails to grapple with what happens after the consummation of love. Love is rarely just a story that ends happily ever after.

Although we can use the term love for anything that we strongly positively value, such as ice cream, football or watching television, because these things share with love the feature of a strong attachment, love here will be defined as needing to attach to at least an aspect of another's personality. In other words, we can only feel love when we imbue specialness into another. We cannot love a wall, a garden or a house in the same way we love a person unless we consider the object as having aspects of personality. This is possible, as the example of Eric the pebble shows, but for many this will be a leap too far. We are often fairly discriminatory as to whom we offer love to. It is often based either on perceived similarities and therefore we value the object of love from the self and bring the other into our ambit as an extension of us. This could be by devoting our affections to a blood relative, a member of our group or tribe or somebody with similar interests or dispositions. Alternatively, we may believe we are lacking in a valued characteristic and to compensate for this we find somebody else who we believe has what we are missing. By loving that person, we are attempting to incorporate this compensatory element into our self. One compensatory reason for love could be aloneness or a feeling of isolation, where we look for somebody who is similar to hold up a mirror to ourselves. This combines themes of both similarity and compensation. Love then can be rooted either in similarity or difference but must have a strong positive attachment to other to be called love. We often rule out vast swathes of potential love objects according to gender, looks, age, social status, social skills, levels of assertiveness, relatedness, locality, opportunity, culture or interests. This highlights an issue with love in that our affections are often narrow and although love is supposed to be our most selfless experience it is often rooted in the self. The issue of valuing people for their purpose and utility has been highlighted previously. Love will often add in the extra step in identification of evaluating other in relation to the needs of the self. A person who is our love object will usually want proof that they are not being loved for these reasons. Yet, if we are valuing on the basis of looks, age, social status, to compensate us for our isolation, or to extend my sense of self, there is an issue as these appear to be about utility. If this is the case any positive valuation will tend to be heavily disguised. This is often done through demonstrations of selflessness. Despite this, however, it can seem difficult for love to escape its utilitarian roots.

Love is demanding and time-consuming. We can only genuinely offer it to a few people in our lives and therefore it relies on us constraining its scope of whom we accord this heightened relation. In a viewpoint dominated by love, others will remain in the background of our awareness with limited acknowledgement of their specialness. This is problematic if specialness were to be determined by the feeling of love. The initial movements of love represent a deficiency in the self. This is because love represents finding something in the other that could improve the self. The starting point of love therefore is a feeling of negativity about the self that can be improved by another. If the self is perfectly good then the self could not be improved by adding any more good to it. Yet, even if we positively evaluate somebody and persuade them and possibly ourselves that the basis of this positive evaluation is free from the taint of utility and control and we attach ourselves to them, we often still want more from love. Most people, objects or things, will end up passing quickly through our imaginations. Love, however, is grounded in preoccupation, for a person through the ascription of a personality can come to live in our imaginations existing when they themselves are not physically present. Preoccupation is more than attachment. In attachment, we acknowledge that habituation can occur but we remain together emotionally, even if this is of lessened intensity. In preoccupation the love object is continuously psychologically present in our imagination even when our beloved is not. We can be preoccupied by anything and the experience of being preoccupied encompasses both positive and negative experiences. I can be obsessing about how great my new Ferrari is or worrying the night before about what I do now I have failed my exams. If we are in love with another, though, we long for their presence when they are absent and continually bring them to mind when they are not there. We worry about them and their welfare. If we are preoccupied about our object of love and they are not present to us or don't do as we think they should for their welfare, this can cause us great distress.

Although the experience of love includes preoccupation, being preoccupied does not equal love either. It is difficult, however, to imagine how we could be in love without being preoccupied. If our supposed beloved only came alive for us when we met them and then forgot about them the rest of the time, including all their wants and needs and those tell-tale anniversaries, we would be suspicious that this is not love. If my beloved had a serious illness and the relationship became difficult it is hard to see how love can remain enduring without some preoccupation. It is a requirement of love that a part of our beloved should live within us and that we should be preoccupied with them. Preoccupation leads to the enduring nature of love. One of the distinctive characteristics of feelings of love is its persistence over time. If I were to declare my love one day only to revoke it the next, most people would see my initial declaration as false. There are two commonly used words in English for feelings emotions and mood. Generally, emotions are associated with short-term feelings. If I buy a new object for the house or my sports team wins a match, I may feel happy but that feeling will soon dissipate; we habituate to the event. There are several meanings to mood which will be discussed later on but one important meaning is that, in some emotions, habituation delays. Some feelings have great persistence or endurance over time including many negative ones such as jealousy or anger. Family feuds based on feelings of anger or resentment can last a lifetime or even be passed on from one generation to another. People can be in a depressed mood over many years. It means that rather than objects or people passing quickly through our mind they stick there being constantly present to us even though they are not there. This will be termed elongation. Love represents an experience of the elongation of emotion.

There is another experience which has much in common with both preoccupation and elongation which merits further discussion. This is the experience of addiction. Many would see preoccupation and elongation as part of love but we could equally see it as a sign of addiction. Addiction has a quality that we become psychologically dependent upon an object or experience, whatever it is. We take the object in whatever form it comes and it makes us feel good. As with many objects, the experience we have is fleeting and soon ends. We are left with its aftermath of emptiness or worse. To compensate for this emptiness, we try to get the experience again and again. It is as if we have dug a happiness hole in our memory and we then feel dissatisfied until we can fill it up, only to find the experience doesn't last. We become unable to give this habit up without distressing withdrawal symptoms and more of it is required to achieve the same effect. The usual objects of addiction are drugs of various sorts and gambling but other things such as food, exercise and sex have become candidates for addiction. Yet, as indicated, if this is the sole definition of addiction this could include much that also passes for love, for love induces a kind of psychological dependency upon our beloved to the extent that we can put our beloved's needs before our own. It is also possible to conceive of being addicted to love, meaning often an addiction to either falling in love or a craving of affection. It is possible that one way of making the distinction between love and addiction is whether the object of preoccupation is socially approved or not. Is there so much difference between being in love and being an alcoholic? To the alcoholic the love of alcohol consumes their life. It comes ahead of all other selfish pursuits and indeed may end their life. Yet, alcohol hardly counts as another person to whom we can perform good things to, unless we can attribute to it personality.

To explore the nature of love and addiction we need to examine the experience in more detail. Happiness is our detector of good. One way happiness is experienced is when we have something we identify as good brought within the ambit of the self boundary. When this happens, it will be termed pleasure. We have already explored some of the means as to how we establish what is good and what is bad. This is not to say though we could be mistaken. Something could appear to us as good outside the self boundary but, when we bring it into the self, we may realise all may not be as it seems. This is probably a fairly common experience. Many objects, experiences and ideas that we can bring into the self will have elements of both good and bad. Potentially addictive objects will tend to appear as very good to us and only after we bring them into the self do we realise this is a disguise, by which time it is too late. We may already have consumed them or then expelled them. The thing with addictive objects though is that we are then apt to forget that they had these bad elements. We will then go back to them again and again seeing them as good. Let us now compare this with the experience of love. This may be our experience of love particularly early on in the journey. We may meet our beloved, they may excite our passions and we may feel happy about being in love. Yet, at the time, we cannot fully bring into the ambit of the self for some reason. When parted we are constantly craving our beloved and thinking of them until the next meeting, when our cravings are assuaged for a time. We then have to leave and are pining until the next time we meet. Maybe within these besotted feelings we notice that our beloved occasionally slips from their pedestal and they have faults but we choose not to pay too much attention. The love could be illicit and we fear others would disapprove. We expel the bad for a time only to crave the good in the future. This form of love looks a lot like an addiction and is more often reflective of the beginning of the relationship. Assuming we do manage to cement the relationship, we then habituate to our feelings and it matures into companionship, where love turns to fondness. We may care enough not to leave and we may develop habits that include the beloved but the preoccupation that is such a hallmark of love disappears. It becomes much like any object we incorporate into the self; we would only notice it matters to us emotionally if the other were to leave us. This means that habituation can only be delayed through not yet feeling we possess or by fear of losing the other.

We can contrast preoccupation with another idea, that of familiarity. We have already come across the idea of familiarity and its opposite, unfamiliarity, when discussing valuing. When looking across the self–other boundary it can be experienced as something comforting. Yet, familiarity can be double-edged. We also can experience familiarity when we have got used to an object. It can cover everything we have and do in this fog of the mundane. When this happens, we tend to only recognise objects when they are gone or something happens to make them unfamiliar again, for example giving an old cupboard a new coat of paint. We do not tend to see those objects until strangeness throws them into relief. The tendency for things and people to become familiar is an example of habituation. When the object of our attachment is around, we almost fail to notice but when that same object leaves us we feel gut-wrenching pains of separation. This is not so much as renewing an object through a new coat of paint. All we need to be reminded of an object is to experience separation but this is a relationship defined through pain and not through positive emotions. When the object is around, we tend to feel nothing. The object has been so incorporated into the self that we barely notice it, like a well-fitted jumper. Yet, when it is wrenched out of our self space, only then do we feel as if we have lost our own arm or leg. This attachment is a potentially very painful form of love with little emotional reward. Habituation is a problem for love which so far can only be resolved by expelling the beloved and then pursuing them again or constantly worrying they may leave us.

Yet, the romantic dreams of a love that doesn't die. Love in its idealised version is positive and remains positive. Love idealised represents a failure to habituate to an object and a failure of the usual processes of degradation. It is precisely the enduring nature of love that distinguishes it from like. Previously we identified two forms of identification, empathy and sympathy. Love can appear to have much more in common with identification in sympathy than empathy. Empathy never loses sight of our own specialness and the specialness of the wider population but sympathy tends to identify with the single person for whom we lose all other perspective. In other words, empathy seems to hold something back, whereas sympathy gives ourselves entire to the person in front of us. Love, though, potentially goes even further than sympathy, as sympathy is often confined to negative emotional states and does not have the same connotations of preoccupation and persistence. This means we are likely to be able to be sympathetic to more people than we love. If we are sympathetic to lots of people, we are likely to have to take up highly contradictory positions that will end up pleasing nobody as our sympathies swing from one person's point of view to another. We are then left narrowing our sympathies or presenting different selves to different people in a highly self-contradictory way. In love, this is less likely to happen because our sympathies will be further narrowed.

There is a common metaphor concerning self boundaries when two people fall in love, which is to describe self and other as being of one essence, as having merged into one body. This metaphor can ironically lead to selfish behaviour being seen as justified as the other has been imaginatively incorporated into the self to be controlled as much as we would our own arm. Therefore, anything done for what was once regarded as other is now being done for the self. I regard my arm as my own and if I choose to cut it off that is my right, however foolish; my actions will only hurt myself. If another person, however, is regarded as part of me this reconceptualisation would allow me to cut off the other person's arm. The other can be treated as an extension of self and as property: not respecting otherness. This love, if we can call it love at all, occurs because we imagine we can incorporate the other fully into the self. We then become threatened when the other still behaves as other and live in constant fear we may lose our beloved. This ironically can mean we fail to habituate to the person because we are in constant fear we may lose the other. An alternative reconceptualisation of love, though, could shift our own boundaries and instead of incorporating the other into our self we project of our own self into the other. This is the form of sympathetic identification in which we become the other and try to experience as they experience. We live our lives as if we were the other person and experience pain when they feel pain and pleasure when they feel pleasure. In doing so, we deny our self, seeing it as insignificant compared to the emotional needs of our beloved. The self becomes inverted and bad compared to the other, which is good. Although sympathetic pain can be part of love, love is ideally rooted in positive attachment. It is theoretically possible that such self-giving could be reciprocal in a loving pair, so each denies the self and attempts to live for the other. This, though, would result in each of the lovers in a labyrinth of mirrors as each appeasing the other who is also appeasing the other in an endless regression. More likely, though, is that it leaves one of the pair of lovers open to exploitation and manipulation by the other.

We could accept we cannot give ourselves entirely to our beloved and must accept their otherness as well as accepting our own independent specialness. We can, though, be concerned with our specialness and that it is held well. The goal in life can seem to be to have our reputation held as positively as possible by as many as possible. That it isn't turned into a stunted negative reputation that can easily be disposed of. In such a scenario, the beloved who knows us deeply and holds our reputation can be set up as a sort of refuge from the judgement of others. Ideally, such imaginative reputation-holding will be reciprocal, each party keeping a part of the other inside of them. It can be important to us that our reputation is held come what may as an extension of self. It can then come as extremely painful if we find that our beloved isn't holding our reputation well but judges us just like everybody else. That we cannot escape the eyes of the judgement of utility and we are still having to put in the work to manage how we are seen.

Reputation is still a utilitarian evaluation, even if a positive one. Thus, although there are techniques which delay habituation, all come with warnings attached.

Love is often rooted in compensatory needs of the self and leads our identifications to be too confined. If it doesn't habituate, it will be maintained either because we want to live entirely for the beloved and take on their identity, which is impossible. This leads us too far along the selfless continuum towards over-identification. If we do not do this, we can give our beloved our unedited self to look after and feel crushed if they don't do this well. Alternatively, we stave off habituation by treating the beloved as a possession which we are in constant fear of losing. Apart from the risks to the self from such over-identification or possessiveness, if we identify love with the attribution of moral debt, ethics would be confined to the welfare of very few. Other emotions may offer more scope to extend our ethical concerns. Yet, love would not be so lauded an experience if it did not have positive elements. Love can lead us to loyally give of the self to those around us in generosity. Other emotional experiences, though, may be able to achieve this whilst still accepting otherness, be less over-identifying and more accepting of the self.

The next lauded emotion to be examined is respect. Respect is what is returned by somebody in an unequal relationship of status and power, when somebody does not adore the person but admires their skills, attributes and abilities. A common historical and cultural means of achieving respect was to be born well into the right family, with the right connections. This offends many modern sensibilities, however, as there is little one can do about the family you are born into. It is often felt better to give respect for something that has been earned through dedication and hard work. Respect is clearly related to a form of love that we give to our heroes and role models. Thus, respect appears as a slightly stunted version of love. As such it is sometimes proffered an acceptable form of relationship where full intimacy would be socially or emotionally problematic. We can give respect to large numbers of people, whereas we would find it difficult to love too many heroes. Respect requires less emotional investment and does not require the ongoing emotional commitment required in love. Yet, respect is founded on evaluating other, defining people positively by their skills, attributes and abilities. To have respect there must be evaluation and the holding of reputation. That evaluation is deferential in the case of respect. Respect is humility in the face of talent. Consequently, wonder and awe are present in respect. These emotions are the basis for worship and a surrender of the self to something greater. Respect requires identification, to the extent that we look at somebody's achievements and want to understand the person to see how they got these desired attributes. Identification becomes the means by which we can learn to emulate. Respect, though, can be grudging in a way that worship or love cannot. We can admire somebody's skills, attributes and abilities but not like them very much. We might respect only an aspect of who they are, for example admiring a particular ability but disliking their character. Respect also places the self in a position of inferiority and lower status in relation to the respected. The self becomes relatively bad in the presence of other. Yet, it is precisely this ability that allows us to offer respect to large numbers of people, for most people will be better than us at something.

It is precisely this grudging nature of respect that can make it like politeness; it can smooth the wheels of social interaction rather than having deep emotional significance. This can lead to generalised respect and to people saying what is expected rather than what they believe. In societies where macho self-assertion is the norm, respect can provide a useful brake on excessive antipathy. It is why respect is of such heightened significance in codes of chivalry. Yet, mutual deference can mean the person left at the top of the pile owes no respect to anybody and can do as they please.

If respect is genuinely based on skills, attributes and abilities this moves to a metaphor of an audience judging a performance. This metaphor allows people to have two perspectives, one of the performer or the actor who gets up on the stage and gives a performance and seeks respect. The other perspective is to sit in the audience and act as judge and offer respect where appropriate. In return, the performer can return that respect back to the audience for their wise words. The self can identify with either or both of these roles. Much depends, though, upon the skills and attributes that are deemed worthy of respect. In modern culture where economics and markets are predominant, it will often be those skills and attributes that can command the highest price that are often deemed most worthy of respect; in situations where brute force is what tends to determine outcomes, respect may be more dependent on fighting abilities. If you are ill, those who can give care will often be deemed far more worthy of respect than those with money or muscle. When we have enough money, it may be those who can give us the most pleasure that are deemed worthy of respect. This more specific form of respect, though, means we can be in constant fear of losing esteem and there will be sections of society who feel they are not respected at all.

Sometimes we will choose situations to be judged but at other times they will be chosen for us. If only parts of life are being judged by others as important, life is broken up into critical moments, interspersed by long tracts where it doesn't matter what is done. What are seen as critical moments can become very scary places to be due to their importance to the self and the lack of control we have over them. It is also possible that we can be unaware of critical moments when we enter them. Sometimes moments can be designated as critical only when something goes wrong and investigations start as to what happened. Respect is something that we can have that can be taken away just as much as something to be earned. If what matters is the applause then it may lead me to try and manipulate my audience to get the desired result. For many people it serves them to feel good to maintain an inflated and grandiose opinion about their own competence; however, if this leads them to enter critical moments it can mean people are surprised when they are judged harshly. If I believe I am a highly talented athlete and this leads me to enter the athletic competition only to come last by some margin, I will be very disappointed. It can also mean we underestimate our own abilities, though, and don't enter critical moments we would be judged favourably in. We therefore need to have an accurate picture of our own abilities and sometimes the only means of doing this is to test them in some way. The other strategy around our own skills and abilities is that most will tend to improve with some kind of work, practice or rehearsal. It can help to improve a skill to be able to act and correct it from negative feedback. Many performances therefore are only the result of hard work and practice, but sometimes this takes judgement to work out. The outcome of many performances is also dependent upon our competition. It is not always the case that critical moments have direct competition but they will be judged against some kind of standard. Sometimes that standard will come from other competitors. Yet, the fact that the result of a performance can be judged against others may tempt some to influence the outcome by tampering with the performance of our competitors in some way. We do not necessarily win a competition by putting in a strong performance but by being better than our competitors. Yet, in employing underhand strategies there is a risk of being found out by our audience and exposing our performance as a fraud. Such are the risks of performance, which can result in us shying away from it altogether. Therefore, it is not always an audience who chooses who we are judged against but there is an element of self-selection. Who we define ourselves against in these situations will be called our referent.

This leads onto the idea of role. Role is built around a skill and can be defined by a socially sanctioned standard of performance which people have been judged to be suitable to occupy. For a performer if they are perceived as being successful in a role this allows a certain status to be gained. For example, I may define myself through being a police officer or teacher and this will allow me to feel valued and have a certain status. Titles, though, can often be provisional with role and person being conceptually distinct. For example, it may be common to remove a person from a role and then have a succession of others perform it. This is particularly true of work-based roles. It is possible, however, that role and person become so entwined that they become one. People can go on trying to perform a particular role long after they are capable of performing it. The problem with having role and person too entwined is that people's capacities change over time. The person may never have been up to a role or something may happen that means the person cannot perform the role. It is also possible that roles need to change and the person may stay the same. Often social situations are such we see a role rather than a person. Roles, though, can be both positive and negative. In fact, to throw off a negative role such as a criminal, waster or fraud can be far harder than to keep a positive role.

Being in a role provides an audience with a means of evaluation of a performance. Different cultures and economic systems will afford and applaud different roles. There are roles that are provisional on a particular performance but there are other roles that are not. Let us take for example the role of son or daughter. Whatever I do, I will remain in this role. Yet there is skill and performance at the heart of even this role that is evaluated. It is perfectly possible to be a good or bad son. It is possible that if I am judged to have performed poorly in this role I may be cut off from my inheritance or even cease to be recognised socially as a son. Roles may also become entwined with group membership. So, role can become about being a good member of a particular group.

Being in a group does not automatically lead to role performance but when a person is evaluated and subject to judgement according to the rules of a given group then that group will have designated roles. Roles therefore can be seen as provisional or permanent or as stemming from an individual performance or as part of a group.

The idea of performer and audience is intertwined with status. Generally, audience will have status over a performer as the audience has power to reward and punish. Specialness can become stunted when on the stage of performance, reduced to whether the performer can meet the required expectations, with the risk they become a role and risking being reduced to property. Rather than identifying, the audience only sees a performer and judges whether that role is being done well. Personality is most likely reduced to an evaluation and a reputation in such circumstances. Yet, at the point that the reward is given it is the performer who seizes status and gets respect. Respect is given to those who rise above the chorus line to distinction. Only at that point does the performer become worthy of having respect: the immediate prize of the applause of an audience. This, though, will be fragile and could evaporate the next time we get on stage. We could imagine a time when that status inversion is made permanent. That we become adored to such an extent that we no longer need fear an audience. This marks the achievement of ultimate status, which many build their lives around, the achievement of the respect of others. It is, though, a fragile and contradictory position. It represents having both an audience of infallible judgement and a performer who is constantly adored. In other words, it is an impossible position to either achieve or maintain. Instead, it is possible for many to seek to influence their audience by underhand means or determine those who make it up are well rewarded to give the judgement we want. It is possible for some performers to want the power to determine who should be their audience. Yet, such actions ultimately render any applause worthless.

Many, though, would like to feel less subject to judgement. It is us as performers that gives an audience power over us and the ability to reward or punish us. As was previously stated, the other exists within our own mind and within this we give the opinions of particular people status to judge us. If somebody smiles and says we have done well and we feel good about this then we have given them an ability to judge us. We have given them the ability to determine our respect. On the same score, if somebody says we have not done your job well and we feel angry or upset then we have given them the ability to judge us and remove our respect. In both cases they have become our audience. When people have this power over us to make us feel either good or bad because of judgements they can make of us, this will be termed their rewardingness. The term rewardingness is here meant to designate both positive rewards and negative punishment and reflects the recognition of the power to give or take away respect.

Rewardingness is defined by the feelings we get when somebody either approves or disapproves of what we do and this matters to us. It makes possible both strong positive and negative emotion. Respect is primarily about the rewarding of positive performances. Yet the corollary of this is that there must be negative performances which are rewarded by negatively. This makes the seeking of respect as a performer inherently risky. We give others the power to shape our emotions. Reputation is also intimately bound up with the metaphor of performer and audience. When we perform in what has been judged a poor way, especially when this affects others negatively or sabotages a valued goal, this can mean blame is attributed. The justification often cited is that in order to learn the correct and acceptable performance we must be disciplined. For an audience, finding a performer responsible then gives us a target. If we see ourselves as being in an audience most of the time and set our standards very high it can mean we are dispensing a lot of criticism. It then becomes possible to reduce personality simply to a reputation and not to identify at all. For a performer it means we can be on the receiving end of another's rage and anger much of the time. Respect can thus lead as much away from identification as towards it. Even if we, as a performer, are recognised as a person with exceptional talent or genius, we will need to continue to exhibit this in order to maintain respect and it can make our social existence and any confidence attached to this extremely fragile. Liable to collapse at any moment if the fickle audience changes its opinion about us.

There is an option for the self to try to live without an audience. One problem in having any kind of audience is that it can be unclear what the audience wants of us. For one thing an audience may be far from uniform in a response. A performance could be treated by some with adulatory applause and by others by boos of derision. Audiences can be changeable; we may do one thing and be treated as a hero one minute and then do the same thing and be treated as a villain. It can also be very unclear what audiences are judging, whether they are judging our performance itself or a minor aspect such as our appearance. It may be that we are being judged simply because we are seen as part of a particular group and we are not given a chance to perform. In addition, audiences may not be qualified to tell whether we are giving a good performance or a bad one or may be motivated to give a particular response other than the quality of the performance itself. This is not to mention that performing in the spotlight with an audience is stressful even if that audience is relatively knowledgeable and fair-minded. We can always slip up and do something wrong. Sometimes it is unclear what the audience response is and we end up reading things into reactions that simply are not there. A negative reaction may be not directed towards you but towards a fellow performer, for example. Some audiences react only when things go wrong and this can be very unrewarding. For all these reasons it can appear attractive to live without an audience sitting in judgement. I would no longer have to worry about my appearance, what clothes match; I would no longer have to watch what I say, I will just say what comes into my mind.

Yet there are issues in trying to live without an audience at all. Taken to extremes this attitude could end up in psychopathy and sociopathy. Knowing what others may think of me provides a potential check upon my behaviour or desires. However, to become a psychopath or sociopath there also has to be an inability to identify as well. Identification provides positive reasons to treat others well, whereas an audience instils fear that we will either not gain or lose respect. It is possible that rather than relying on fickle and unfair external audiences, or doing without audiences entirely, we become our own audience. The problem with this is one of perspective. Although many external audiences are not consistent, fair or honest, having the self as its own audience is no guarantee of this either. We have an automatic tendency to attribute what is positive to the self and what is negative to external sources. It is easier for the self to applaud our own weaknesses. It is arguable that we don't need the reward and punishment that audiences offer but we need an ongoing dialogue with our environment and with other to better shape and hone the skills we have.

The successful building of an internal audience will be termed conscience. To build conscience, we use imagination to construct what we believe people might say before an event rather that what they actually do say after it. This act of imagination is similar to identification. Rather than imagining what the person in front of us might be thinking and feeling on their terms we ask what a particular person thinks of me and what I may do. It is reflexive, meaning about the self and it is also future directed. The answers reached will help guide our behaviour. Yet if we try to derive conscience from everybody we would probably end up in as much of a muddle as relying on real audiences. We often derive conscience from important people we have come across. These will often be people we have met in our formative years such as our primary caregivers, a favourite relative, teacher or best friend. The problem often is that we take for our voice of conscience people who are likely to have a strong positive bias towards us. Many external audiences won't have these biases and our actions and beliefs will not have much importance to them. We are also likely to adopt any moral or performing framework from our imagined individuals who themselves are likely to have strengths and weaknesses. If we simply incorporate these uncritically then we ourselves will end up with the same blind spots. We will more than likely get it wrong. Yet, if we take enough selected voices and we learn from our mistakes, small voices can become one and sound a lot like me. Conscience eventually becomes the voice of our own learnt judgements over time.

Conscience though is often not considered as just any internal voice but is something connected to morality. If conscience is merely about the performance of a skill, this could well be about anything. A skill is a morally neutral act we could be a very good code-breaker, for example, but we can put this skill to use in many ways including for underworld gangs. Conscience is that small voice that tells us it is wrong; our sense of what is right and good. It is though possible to become far more critical of ourselves than any normal audience would be, to have a constantly chattering inner critic in our head. This voice can undermine confidence and paralyse us with fear. When allied to morality, conscience can be easily viewed as synonymous with the emotion of guilt. This is the feeling we experience when we internalise traversing a moral code. This is opposed to shame, which is hearing from others that we have traversed a moral code and accepting this. Historically guilt and shame were often associated with sexual mores. Sometimes conscience is not seen as our own voice or that of other people but as the voice of God. Getting rid of religion can be about throwing off the shackles of that voice and refusing to listen. Freeing the self from the restraints of conventional morality, being free to innovate, be creative and enjoying life. Yet, we still need the whispers of conscience. To not have such a voice altogether would be to live without concern for morality or for anybody else. It is just what preoccupies the voice can sometimes focus on how we are perceived by others and cause others to look down on us or it can be based on a genuine concern for the welfare of all. Although getting conscience right is often a delicate balancing act, by setting up an internal audience we no longer become dependent on the approval of others and this can be liberating. We no longer crave the respect of others. Yet if we have no constraints and don't have any internal audience at all this can leave us solely concerned with maximising our own pleasure and, with a lack of suitable identification, can lead us on a path of immorality. It can be seen that perhaps respect is something we should learn to be able to do without and not build our confidence around but in order to do so we need to be able to build our own internal audience. We shouldn't remove the disciplines of respect until we have managed to successfully do this. This internal voice will become a temporary self above the self.

Compassion is another lauded emotional experience and is rooted in the skill of identification. To be compassionate is to be charitable to those less fortunate than ourselves for whatever reason. A precondition of compassion is the previously discussed feeling of empathy. Unless there is understanding of distress it is difficult to imagine how compassion can be shown. The focus of compassion is to alleviate the distress of the other, not to share it. Compassion is more than just empathy, though. It is rooted in feeling the pain of the other and therefore starts in negative emotions but has the desire to remove them. Compassion calls forth a requirement for action. We can be empathetic by just understanding the emotion of the other. In compassion we identify with the other in their negative emotions to such an extent we need to act. We evaluate the other negatively, defined as in need and wish to move them to a positive situation, which the self is seen as the main actor. Compassion, though, also needs to be differentiated from sympathy. Sympathy and love are the emotions which get us close to as full identification as possible. Yet, in fully identifying we can lose perspective and be unable to help. Therefore, we must not identify so completely with another person as to be incapable of doing something different to what they themselves are capable. Compassion is also different to love in that it is generally shorter term. Love had important facets such as endurance, preoccupation and a failure to habituate, none of which need be present in compassion. It is enough, in compassion, to act to sort out the difficulty and the relationship to end at the point of resolution. Compassion only becomes a more continuous relationship should the need to relieve suffering be seen as ongoing or there is a closer bond which morphs into a form of love. Those who permanently seem in need risk being the victim of compassion fatigue. In the discussion on love, one archetypal relationship was between a caregiver and cared for, between parent and child. Compassion clearly has a relationship to this form of love. For in both there are status differentials between the caregiver of either compassion or love and the recipient. The act of giving places the receiver in debt. If compassion were to become the basis for a longer-term relationship it would become the basis for this kind of caregiving love. Compassion requires something practical to be offered. It is possible to skip demonstrating identification and empathy when you are sure you can solve a person's distress. If you do this, you had better be sure you are right or the person can be left feeling not only that you have not helped but you didn't even bother to understand them either. Yet, if somebody is dying from a heart attack you get on and apply first aid, the reassurance can come later. It does leave the possibility, however, that if compassion becomes primarily about the act, then we could feel nothing for the person we are helping. There must be a degree of empathy otherwise we would be unable to identify a person in distress but it means feelings could be secondary to the act. There are times, though, when faced with overwhelming suffering we can do nothing except offer faint empathy.

Compassion then without ulterior motives is initiated by feeling pain at seeing somebody else suffer and is resolved when there is relief of that suffering. If love is founded on a feeling the self is deficient in some way, compassion is founded in our own empathetic pain. This is also true of sympathy but compassion holds the perspective of empathy in order to be able to do something about it. The ability to relieve this pain through compassion, however, usually provides a great deal of satisfaction and joy and therefore the ability to give compassion is overall a positive experience. Yet its success or otherwise is dependent upon the gratitude of the other. This makes compassion a potentially vulnerable way of achieving happiness. It is rooted in seeing what is bad and being able to turn that into good, but that good is dependent upon other acknowledging their indebtedness. If we define others through the lens of compassion, they are defined solely by their need. Some world views attempt to define everybody as being in need but try not to appear patronising and demeaning. Compassion is often considered one of the most important emotions within Buddhism, in which most living beings are viewed as living in delusion, which then adds to their suffering. They are therefore worthy of compassion from more enlightened beings that see things as they really are. Compassion within Buddhism stems from passing on this wisdom to all. If through a broader philosophy or intellectual framework everybody can be classed as being in some kind of need, this broadens the scope of compassion. It is therefore important to have some definition of need as this will define the scope of compassion. If everybody is in need then compassion will be expanded exponentially. It also potentially casts the recipient into a position of continual weakness. Some would see that they do not need the compassion of benevolent superior beings.

By contrast, the giver requires self-confidence that they have something to give. This confidence, though, will be tested by the results of compassion. If it is found wanting by recipients, that confidence may be undermined. Confidence can be found in problem-solving, having a truth to impart or access to resources. Often compassion is necessitated when a person is in difficulties but when those difficulties keep happening it can look as if our compassion was inadequate. The temptation here is to blame the recipient rather than the inadequacy of the compassion. A failure of compassion can challenge our confidence and make it vulnerable and then damage our view of our self. Confidence, though, can be problematic to compassion as it is related to status. It is a status, though, that reverses the usual audience–performer relationship. It is the performer who has the power of the help they can offer; it is the audience that must judge whether that help actually aids them. This can lead to a questioning of motivation. The same questioning can also be made for all emotions which prompt us to give but are based on differentials in status including caregiving love. To demonstrate empathy to a person means showing them you have understood their emotions and this often requires humility and openness. Confidence based on a belief in superiority can therefore undermine empathy, which is at the root of all emotions of identification. Compassion can be done with dubious motivation. For example, a despot can use compassion as a means of looking powerful and enhancing his image, but that does not necessarily make him compassionate. Yet those in need can be so desperate that they will accept help from any quarter not caring about such niceties and be placed into the debt of those being compassionate. Compassion then can be a weapon of persuasion and a means of placing others in your debt, which can render it suspect and undermine the very empathy which brought it forth in the first place.

Earlier, we said that one way to detect specialness was through emotional identification and yet there was a risk that we could either over-identify or under-identify. We have now examined three emotional states that over time have been lauded culturally as being a potential basis for ethical behaviour. All though have issues if we use them to help identify specialness. Love is a broad term and must include some level of attachment to other that makes it restrictive and ties our emotions to that which we cannot control, although it is the only one that potentially offers parity of status. Compassion defines people according to need and encourages others to see themselves as requiring help. It only works when we can assuage that need. Respect is the emotional state that seems to most oil the wheels of politeness. It is perhaps respect, we often crave from those deemed qualified to give it and yet respect because we can lose it so easily, can be a hard task master. It is probably better that we learn to give our own respect. Yet at the core of identification is empathy, which is without status or over-commitment. This is attractive because it is relatively easy to apply empathy to wide numbers of people and yet because it is not tied to getting anything there is little point in faking it. Yet, it would be easy to see how empathy could be perceived as relatively useless. Empathy is emotional identification without individual action or commitment. It then becomes possible to see empathy and identification as core to our relationship with specialness. Empathy becomes the means by which we can detect that another possesses specialness, without either over-identifying or involving status but to be ethically good we then must aim to give the good of the self to other, without precondition.

THE HAPPINESS OF OTHER AND THE GOLDEN RULE

The ethical good is primarily concerned with the happiness of the specialness imbued other. Not the happiness of self. Thus, if we are looking for an end in these circumstances, when we enter paramount reality, this would mean being concerned with the happiness of the other. There are though immediate issues with this target. If all ethical action amounted to was making the other person in front of me with specialness happy, it shouldn't be possible to conceive of exceptions. Yet, we can conceive of times when actions that result in making another happy would be unethical. Some of those issues are the same as for other as they are the self. Happiness could be at the expense of others, doing others down; it could be at the expense of the future self, or it could lead us away from reality. There are though additional issues when it comes to making another person happy. In the discussion on compassion and respect previously, we were concerned with identifying emotional states that can identify specialness. For compassion and respect, one problem lay around the status differentials they tend to promote. These issues around status differentials remain a problem when we are then attempting to behave ethically. Thus, when attempting the act of making others happy, if this leads to a power imbalance, it can then be ethically problematic. In an act of compassion, if that party is seen as being in genuine need, the act should aim to restore status to parity. If this doesn't happen, though, it can lead to a situation where one person continually gives and the other receives. To a dependency by one party on the other for happiness. This can lead to issues where the act of intending to make the other happy can also become a demonstration of one person's superiority over the other. The other person can also take the gifts for granted and not really appreciate them, as an amusement or an entitlement. In addition, what we may want from giving to the other is favours. An expectation of payback in the future. This is particularly risky when status differentials are involved, either because the gift is from somebody with power and is to demonstrate that power or because it is a supplication because of a want for something. There may be happiness now but it should be returned with interest in the future. This is happiness with an agenda.

Further, perhaps even more significant issues arise because the self cannot control whether somebody else is happy or not. This is something the other person must choose for themselves and take responsibility for. It means that, if we have an end which is to make the other happy, it is an end we cannot control. It is also an end we can never fully know we have achieved. We can see what the other tells us, we can see their reactions but we can never fully know their subjective experience, their experience of being happy. We can get clues as to what the other is feeling but we can never fully know. Yet, this is not an argument for saying being ethical is impossible. It is not an excuse to be unkind. Besides, if we had no interest in the welfare of the other, we wouldn't be bothered to create and hold the specialness of other in the first place. We would just need to hold reputations and evaluate them according to their utility. Happiness is the way we detect good from bad. This is the same for other as for the self. If the self gives out what it considers to be good there is a greater chance that the other will take this as an indicator for happiness compared to giving out bad or deliberate acts of harm. To be ethical, what is needed are a set of principles or rules, which can be readily understood, by which we can give good to the other, increasing the likelihood they can be happy.

Let us say we have a random individual in front of us to whom we have imbued specialness. An obvious means to do good, and thus increase the chances of another's happiness, is to do whatever the person in front of us says they want. So, if a person asks for food, new clothes, a car, some money for drugs, or justice we should endeavour to give them what they ask for on the understanding that this would make the other person happy. Yet, this complete selflessness, synonymous with some of the examples of sympathy or love mentioned previously, means there is no boundary to the potential giving we may have to perform. This form of giving however could be suggested by a reading of some ideas in the Christian tradition. Rather than traditional punishing ethical responses to violations we are encouraged to shock people out of unethical behaviour by loving them even more. This could mean, though, we sympathise with the person in front of us to such an extent we meet their whims and needs over our own, even when some of those wants are spurious and frivolous. One way people can realise that certain things won't make them happy is for them to actually get them and then habituate to the experience. The trouble is that, if somebody is addicted to pleasure, they will move on to the next demand and the next, continuously. For giving a person what they say they want is no guarantee of making them happy; they may quickly become bored or be getting us to perform for them as a demonstration of their status.

Another issue therefore is to be able to tell if we have succeeded in making the other genuinely happy. This may be as simple as asking but people lie for all sorts of reasons and that includes to themselves. People may not even know what makes them happy. Such unlimited self-determination of happiness is therefore problematic. It is more so when what is desired negatively impacts either on the self in the longer term, on others, or is delusional. We can imagine if the random person in front of us is a multi-billionaire who can potentially reward us well if we please them. We find ourselves in a scenario where there is great inequality of power and where we could be incentivised to meet every last whim. This suggests that an individual cannot solely be left to determine what they need to be given in order to make them happy. Besides, there seems little point in substituting my own happiness as end for somebody else's if their end is equally as troublesome.

The undifferentiated happiness of other as a measure of ethical action can be problematic for other reasons as well. It is possible for somebody to be happy and for me to intend to make somebody happy but the two events might not be related. I may intend to make somebody happy through giving them a present. They turn out to be happy because they have received a proposal of marriage and could not really care about the present I gave. So, somebody telling me they were happy is not a good measure of the moral worth of the gift. In addition, returning to some of the issues outlined above, another person may tell me they are happy but as a result of actions that do not appear to be particularly ethical. Say for example I told you that you were the greatest, warmest and loveliest person I ever met and you told me this made you very happy. This on the surface may seem to be a perfectly ethical action. The problem is if it is a lie and I made the statement knowing it to be untrue. My aim may have been to make you happy but I did so by telling a lie. Of course, some deceptions are about trying to maintain the well-being of another person but others end up hurting people. If I told you that you were the greatest, warmest and loveliest person I ever met and this made you happy but I did it to gain favours from you. This example highlights problems where I try to make you happy in order to make myself happy, discussed previously. My statement and my actions may make you genuinely happy and by this judgement the action should be seen as ethical and yet if the focus of an action is not the intent to make the other person happy but to make myself happy through my pleasure, then often this can leave us feeling uneasy about the ethical nature of the action.

This is other determination of our action, the person telling me whether what I have done makes them happy or not. Ultimately, we can never finally know what makes another happy. The opposite of other determination is self-determination of the other's happiness, where I determine for the other whether what I do should make them happy or not. This, though, is even more problematic and could lead to some extreme positions where people are told what they receive should make them happy and if they are not that is their problem. Identification is entirely removed and the self is allowed carte blanche to do what it pleases and call this ethical. This is immoral and unacceptable. Yet, it is not an uncommon position. Let us take some examples. Firstly, a devout religionist who believes the only way you can be happy is if you have accepted the presence of God into your life. According to the religionist, the ethical action is to try to convert you to accept God, as this is the only way you will save your soul and ultimately be happy. Equally, I could be a committed communist, who believes that the only way we can all be happy is if we are all equal. Therefore, because you have more than some others, I will take what is yours and redistribute it. Let us take another example. Say, a moral philosopher who has come up with a theory by which everybody can be good. The moral philosopher acts according to this theory towards you, yet you find this makes you unhappy. Thus, we cannot rely on the other to tell us what makes them happy but we certainly shouldn't just rely on our own opinion either and foist our theories upon others. We must enter into a dialogue with other. To do this, though, we must have a starting position, some idea of what good will look like. Some account must be taken of the person's wishes and they should only be overridden if there is an alternative ethical justification to do so. Mostly, this will be around the sort of happiness the other is bargaining for. Even if we cannot allow that the other fully determines what I do to make them happy, there must be some account of this.

In such a dialogue it must be understood that we cannot make another happy. We can only have that intent; it is up to the other to choose to be happy or not. This, though, should never be a carte blanche allowance that I can determine the other's happiness; I must be constantly adjusting what I do on the basis of what I am told by you. The focus is still to make the other happy through providing them as much good as possible, not on providing an excuse for the self. The moral worth of any action, though, lies in the intent and not on the outcome. This is easier to have personal control over and to be responsible for. In the above example, the giving of the present could still be moral not because of the happiness of the other person but because I intended to make the other person happy with my gift. It would also mean the other actions could be seen as immoral because the focus is not on making the other person happy but to make them happy in order to manipulate them or the overall situation. There are various issues with intent, though. One issue is that it is easy to fabricate. People may say they intended to do all sorts of things and we have no means of checking whether this is true. When actions are examined, people often have incentives to lie about their intent after an event. This means we can never know what another's intent is; we can only know our own, provided we are honest with ourselves and have adequate insight and conscience. In addition, good motives can make a mess of things if we are inept and don't know what we are doing. We have an obligation to take reasonably informed evidence-based decisions.

Intent means our happiness giving is hidden to others, as ours is hidden to them. Having agreed culturally available proxies and scripts on how to behave may help smooth the process of showing our intent. Generally, there will be a culturally available set of signs and symbols that show an individual is concerned about another's welfare. Scripts can act as a form of proxy for happiness. By performing certain culturally approved scripts it is sometimes assumed that these will automatically transmit happiness. There will often be some code for greeting, for example the handshake, a bow or a peck on the cheek. One common code is any kind of gift. We may offer a drink, for example, or a declaration of appreciation. These cultural scripts are often carefully choreographed and if we fail to follow the custom we risk causing offence and embarrassment, for example if I offer my hand in greeting to somebody but they refuse to reciprocate the offering. Giving money is often seen as a proxy for giving happiness. Sometimes these scripts can be enacted on a very large scale. Governments often measure their success not by reported happiness but by the success or otherwise of the economy and how well people are being paid. These proxies, whether performed individually or on a large scale, are often about showing that we mean no harm rather than making people happy per se. There is of course a relationship between doing no harm and people being happy. Generally, if I do harm to you, you will not be happy. The opposite, however, is not always the case. As such it is probably easier to avoid doing harm than to make others happy. Another way to see these scripts is as a form of politeness. Politeness, though, is open to misinterpretation but it may oil the wheels of society and make it more comfortable. One person's politeness is another person's fakery and lack of honesty. For scripts and proxies are culturally relative and ultimately any series of acts are open to interpretation. What most people want is not a script being followed but somebody who is genuinely warm and interested in them.

An important common starting point for an ethical dialogue is known as the golden rule. The golden rule is essentially a contract and states if I want good things from you I will have to give good to you first. It takes the self as a reference point and then imagines from this that you would want the same and then seeks ways to provide this. It thus relies upon the skills of identification. Yet, it is a contract of which I have control of only one side, namely what I do. It also acknowledges what I do impacts on what others will do. There are various versions of the golden rule and they occur in many different cultures at different times. Some version of it is found in all major religions. The commandments of Jesus Christ, such as love your neighbour as yourself or do unto others as you would want to be done by, are versions of the golden rule. In order to be able to do you good or refrain from harm I must recognise your specialness first and recognise at an emotional level if this hurts me it is also likely to hurt you. I must also recognise that if I like something then you also may want this for yourself. As such this could represent an idea of ethics as a mutual respect of specialness. All versions of the golden rule will be about the happiness of the other, but some versions will be more direct than others. The golden rule, though, does not go as far as complete selflessness. Selflessness is about self-denial, whereas the golden rule is a contract with the intention of achieving parity of exchange. As previously stated, the problem with complete selflessness is that it takes as the standard for ethical behaviour the needs and wants of others and these can be potentially limitless. In contrast, the golden rule takes as its standard the self. I will do for the other person what I myself would want. Alternatively, I will refrain from doing what I also wouldn't want done. As such the golden rule means you would not go beyond a certain standard that you would expect for yourself. The self provides certain limits which complete selflessness does not provide and as such can be a buttress against exploitation. It also avoids the other extreme of total selfishness where I have no concern about you and see you as a utility.

The golden rule can be seen as an opening offer in an ongoing negotiation, which it is hoped will leave both parties happy. There are alternative negotiation starting positions which sit between complete selflessness and the barricaded versions of the self where other is always seen as bad. The latter negotiating position means that whatever I do to you, whether good or bad, the other will always be unhappy, and thus we are doomed to fail. This could mean we give up on this person, remove their specialness, attribute a bad reputation and avoid them. Sometimes, though, we need to ask why somebody has taken up such a barricaded position in order to persuade them to take down their defences. It can also be difficult sometimes to see the difference between the barricaded self and alternate negotiating positions. The other can assume we are bad unless we are able to prove we are good. This is a stance where the other will wait for me to act, will judge the act and then give back what they think they are given. The trouble with this as an opening offer is that it means we can be waiting a long time if the other person is also employing the same gambit, or worse we can get into hostilities. Yet, the golden rule can overcome this negotiating position, although we must accept it can leave us vulnerable if the other sees us as a threat and wants to do us harm. The self, though, as a starting point can prove a fallible guide to what the other may want. What I want for the self may not be what others want for themselves. This is potentially a problematic foundation for judging other people's wants and needs. If the golden rule becomes give to the other what I myself would want, or avoid doing to other what I would want others to avoid doing for the self, we could end up with problems. If I feel I need a luxurious lifestyle for myself, the golden rule would demand that I also want this for others. If I have constrained wants, the golden rule means I may have low expectations for those around me as well. It is possible, however, to adjust the golden rule.

The golden rule can be divided between positive and negative versions. A positive version would be do unto others as you yourself would want to be done by. A negative version would be do not do anything to others that you would not want for yourself. The positive versions aim at having positive results for the other person, whereas the negative versions aim at not doing any harm. Not doing any harm is a prerequisite for positive results but does not necessarily bring the positive state we seek to imbue in other. Yet, not doing harm is easier and can be done to more people. The golden rule can also be varied as to the nature of its target. It can either be targeted at the emotional or mental state of other or concerned with acts and deeds towards the other. It probably is more commonly framed around acts or deeds, either doing something positive or avoiding a negative act. These are not directly targeting the other's happiness per se but, using the self as a guide, we will do acts that we ourselves would want to bring about our own happiness. The positive act formulation tends to be obvious as to what should be done to behave ethically but has the problem that it overdemands exact reciprocation of deeds. Thus, I should act towards you as I would wish you to act towards me. This could include if I wish to enter a romantic relationship with you, but you have no interest. Most ethics would demand I should respect this but, according to this version of the golden rule, I should act in the way I wish you to act towards me. Thus, positive act versions of the golden rule tend to be too mirroring of the self. Negative act versions, such as do not do to others what you yourself would not want, tend to provide minimum standards of behaviour which we would expect. This would mean I would not kill you, steal from you or commit adultery with your partner. As such it is probably easier to use this formulation to cover larger numbers of people. Yet, there may be conceivable instances where I should harm you. Say, for example, you are a criminal and I am a judge and I ought to hand out a prison sentence for the crime you have committed. Yet, going by the golden rule, I would not want to serve a prison sentence, thus I should not give this to you either. Again, using acts or deeds to formulate the golden rule can demand too much reciprocation and doesn't take account of circumstances.

Alternatively, we can formulate the golden rule around the alteration of an emotional or mental state of other. Again, this can either be framed positively or negatively, either by inducing something positive or refraining from inducing something negative. So, the commandment of Jesus Christ to love your neighbour as yourself, would fall in this category. It has been argued, though, that love is a problematic emotional state to adopt. Since it has been argued that the happiness of the other with specialness is the very definition of ethics, we could also come up with versions of the golden rule directly using happiness. If we transposed happiness into the example of love, we would get something like: intend others should be happy as you yourself are happy. This example takes account of the idea that we cannot make another happy but that we should intend to make another happy. The issue with this version of the golden rule is that for it to work it is entirely dependent upon the self being happy. Thus, it seems to imply that we should ensure the self is happy before attempting to alter the emotional state of other. This has some logic to it as it would be difficult to make somebody else happy if I myself am obviously unhappy. Yet, it also means that, unless we are happy, we would be unable to act ethically at all. The version of the happiness golden rule, though, can be altered to become something like intend to make others happy as you yourself would want others to want your happiness. This imagines happiness as being part of a mutual exchange, although the measure the self can control is the intent to make others happy.

The advantage of such a formulation of the golden rule using an emotional or mental state is that it gives more leeway as to how we should act. The emotional state requires we do something to indicate what our intent is but it does not say how we should do this. If we are aiming for somebody else to be happy, we can do this according to what I know about them, not do the same things that make me happy. Yet, as has been said, we cannot make anybody happy; we can only make this more likely. Although happiness may be quite a good target to use in formulating the golden rule, the previously identified problems remain. Making the other happy in certain ways and for particular reasons may not be ethical. We could thus adjust the golden rule again with these caveats in mind. The golden rule could become something like: intend to make others happy so long as this does not undermine them, their reality or the happiness of others around them as you would expect others to intend the same for you. Yet, if our aim is the achievement of an emotional state, it requires us to make our intentions visible by some means. Unless we do, they remain intentions, are hidden and could be seen as ethically useless. They require the performance of deeds and acts. It is why the golden rule is often formulated in terms of actions rather than emotional states. The intent may be to achieve another's happiness but the other will not know that unless we can demonstrate it with actions. Actions make our negotiating position transparent. If we want a universal guide as to what our actions should be to make them ethical, then basing the golden rule on happiness is going to be problematic. Yet, ethical action can be highly individualised. What is right for one person may not be right for another. This makes situations more ethically complex. Plus, I also cannot tell whether I have finally succeeded. I can just intuit from the available evidence or not. Thus, going back to the example of the judge and the prisoner, I can see that the prisoner has been getting their happiness at the expense of others and their own future; I must act to correct this so hopefully they can realise that there are alternative ways of achieving happiness. Thus, I can conclude that in sentencing the prisoner I am hoping they will come to realise their mistakes and correct them, plus I am protecting the happiness of others. It can thus be concluded it matters how the golden rule is formulated and that it should be formulated in such a way that it accepts individual circumstances and variations and doesn't seek to convert the other into an exact copy of the self.

It is also possible to formulate the golden rule according to the keeping of another's specialness. We keep another's specialness living within us. Not to the extent that we become them and want to live their lives, but enough to keep hold of their story and undergird their existence positively. If this is the case, it leads on to the reciprocal conclusion that others keep our specialness living within them. This opens up the possibility that to live well is to have our image kept well by others. For others to keep our own specialness well we must keep the specialness we have of others well. Specialness is not reputation. By reputation we mean the positive or negative evaluation of the other according to their utility to me. Keeping specialness doesn't necessarily mean keeping a universally positive view of you. I may judge actions and what you do positively or negatively but I will undergird this with positivity and undertake to educate you. If some of your actions we regard as bad because they deviate from reality, or they harm others or harm the future self, I have a right to view these negatively. It does mean, though, I will endeavour to understand you and to help you to become a better person. We detect the specialness of other through generosity of spirit, and to see others with potential, not just as an agent. This reading of the golden rule suggests a little bit of other can exist within the self and that some of the self is given out into the other to keep. We can only control how we keep another's specialness. How others hold our specialness or whether they convert it to reputation is beyond us. It is ultimately something that is beyond our line of control.

There is another aspect to the golden rule to discuss. It can be seen as an ongoing ethical standpoint, which we should then try to maintain no matter what is thrown at us. Alternatively, it can be seen as an opening bid in a negotiation, where we need to subsequently make adjustments depending on what comes back from the other person, whether it is positive or negative. If we look at acts and deeds, we could do unto others as we ourselves would be done by and find that what comes back is outright hostility and threats. We can then either adopt a different position that gives back what has been given to us, or we can maintain the position in the golden rule. I can either respond to defend myself, get out of the situation, and possibly then complain about it to anybody who will listen, or carry on with my opening gambit in the hope the other will realise I mean no threat. The latter reading is suggesting some Christian positions. It possibly wouldn't be the most common. Axelrod (1990) outlined a computer experiment that was run whereby different computer programs running different negotiating strategies interacted to see which had the best outcome. The most successful of these programs was one called tit-for-tat. It was a relatively simple negotiating strategy in that it assumed the other program would cooperate initially; however, if the other program did not cooperate it then gave back, tit-for-tat. Cooperation has better outcomes, but it is fragile and can be undermined. If we find somebody who doesn't then this can be extremely damaging and we need to defend ourselves. Thus, act versions of the golden rule that do not change become vulnerable. Ones based on emotional or mental states, though, offer more flexibility of response. The aim will remain to keep the specialness of the other and to make them happy, but if the other cannot be made happy by the initial actions we pursue, or pursuing their happiness may damage the happiness of others or their longer-term future, we can then pursue alternative strategies without the need to undermine the initial golden rule statement.

THE PROBLEM OF NUMBERS AND THE FORMATION OF GROUPS

We may be able to emotionally engage and behave ethically towards the person standing in front of us, or with colleagues, close relatives and friends. We may be able to do the same for our pets and even build up relationships with plants. Yet, when we have to relate to billions of beings on this planet, things get potentially difficult. Empathy and the golden rule may get us ethically so far. However, there are vast numbers of people who exist but we don't know. All will potentially be capable of having specialness attributed to them. There is evidence of personality and the ability to morally choose; thus, we owe an ethical debt. We won't come across but a small fraction of those in our day to day. We cannot possibly build a relationship with all of them, even if we wanted to. Very often, we can manage ethically quite well without concern. Specialness is something we only have to attribute when we come across it and, as long as our lives are socially limited, we can behave ethically to those around us. Yet, there will always be times when we cannot socially limit our world. There will always be new situations, new people to meet, opinions to have. We will need to move out of the bubble we know and take account of the world around us. Perhaps we manage a large company, are a politician or just care about what is going on in the world. We could end up taking decisions that have huge ramifications for people we never meet day to day. Such decisions, say whether to build a large dam for a hydro-electric project, to build a hospital, to cut benefits to the poorest or a declaration of war, are likely to be applauded by some but derided by others. Even if we don't have to take such decisions, we may want to have an opinion whether we think they are right or wrong. Although having the ability to empathise and identify always helps us ethically, arguably, the ability to do good to large numbers of people we can never hope to meet could be seen as a more significant ethical target. The more we are able to do good to more people, potentially, the more significant the ethical impact. We could be the most ethical person in our day-to-day interactions, whilst the world goes to hell in a handcart. It takes time to know one person in order to do the acts that may or may not make them happy. This is time-consuming and problematic if we are running a large corporation, country or charity.

When it comes to dealing with very large numbers, we can adapt our ethics and rely on imaginative shorthand. One way we can manage large numbers is by deliberately limiting the amount of specialness we attribute. The specialness we ascribe is often limited by circumstance, to those we meet frequently day to day. This will be a limited number and is fine if we are taking decisions or having opinions that just affect those people. Yet, the minute we are taking decisions or having opinions that concern many others, we then need to expand our attributions of specialness. This makes ethical decisions more time-consuming and problematic. So, one way round this is not to expand our conception of specialness. We can do this by placing individuals into groups. Groups are formed all the time with people and allow us as individuals to get much more done than we ever could alone. Such groups do not necessarily constrain specialness. Indeed, being in a group where we are well known and is functioning well can enhance the specialness of all its members. This is not what is being referred to here. Grouping for ethical reasons refers to the self being seen not as distinct but only as a member of the group to which it is allocated for the purposes of deciding upon ethical actions. Lots of individuals then become one group which we can then interact with. One way we can do this is to maintain the attribution of specialness to those who are close to us, but then those we don't know or are socially distant we place into groups. If we are making big decisions, it is difficult to even have sight of individuals, who will be just little specks on the horizon. Thus, those within the decision-taking clique will be maintained as individuals with specialness. Those we are taking decisions about will be lumped into groups. Alternatively, if we outside the decision-taking circle have opinions that differ to those in power, we can reduce the specialness of those taking decisions. They can be placed into a self-interested group. Those who are trying to change the decisions being taken are attributed specialness. These examples concern status groupings, but could equally be groupings around locality or interest, for instance. Specialness is maintained in near sight but groups are placed at a distance, often because of status or what is seen as important to the self.

Alternatively, rather than dealing with individuals with specialness at all, we can lump all personalities together into groups, including the self. The self is merged into a group we identify with and we lose our individuality into that of the group. In this case, specialness recedes and what becomes important is the team any person is seen as playing for. Each person then needs to be immediately classified into a team and this will be the main way they are defined. They then can be further classified according to their likeness or dislikeness in relation to the team the self is seen as playing for. Reputation was differentiated from specialness by defining a person according to their utility and whether this is positive or negative. Defining people through their group will mean seeing them solely through reputation according to team membership. Those that are deemed to be in the same team as the self will be given a positive reputation; those that are in teams different or opposing the team the self is in will be given a negative reputation. Unless you are seen as playing poorly for the team. Yet, even within groups it can be difficult to keep specialness at bay. Having decided which people to trust through the group they belong to, this can become a filtering mechanism by which specialness could then be allowed in a limited way, so long as this doesn't interfere with the overall schema.

There are also other ways in which we could construct ethical groups in relation to specialness. In addition to specialness being close and groups far away or groups being the main way we construct our ethical world, we could also place the self within a group but see specialness as far away. An example of this would be where the self sees itself as part of a hard and oppressive group where we are made to conform to ideals we don't agree with and can't escape. It then becomes possible to dream of being an individual with specialness outside the group, achieving our individuality and freedom, our specialness. We also see those outside the group, as having achieved specialness. Alternatively, we could imagine being inside a group positively and want to persuade somebody that it is right for them to join our group. Let us take the example of being a religionist, who has achieved salvation by being a member of a religious community. We want others to also achieve salvation but it should be entirely of their own free will. We should not put any pressure onto them to choose. All we can do is offer the vision of the group and leave it up to them to decide for themselves. Whichever choice they make will not alter how we regard them; they are a child of God. In order to do this, we need to get to know them really well, to know their likes and preferences. To take their specialness seriously. For the sake of completeness, the final theoretical option would be to regard all ethical group formation as negative. That any subtraction of specialness, whatever the advantages in other ways, is too high an ethical price to deal with large numbers of personalities.

Assuming we decide that group construction is the ethical way forward to deal with large numbers, it then depends on our perspective as to how groups are seen. If we are looking at groups from the outside at a distance, often what we will be doing is grouping people around particular shared traits. Trait formation can also be used as a means of getting to know somebody and attributing them specialness. On its own, trait formation is not a bad thing. What happens in group formation, though, is that we use the identified traits, not to weave into a story about the person along with other traits we come across but to take these traits out of context and to use them to compare and contrast with other people. This also fixes the traits within the person which means they then cannot change or evolve over time. The person themselves may or may not give much importance to these traits that we are using. It means rather than seeing the person in front of me as a unique individual with a personal life story I may see them as being defined by a particular role, say the work they do as a police officer, doctor or pilot. As previously discussed, a role is a socially packaged skill, which allows us to limit specialness as in the case of respect. Alternatively, people can be seen as having a particular status, whether they are rich or poor, are educated, have a health condition or stigma, and are talented or intelligent. I may see other as being defined by a particular ethnicity or nationality, say somebody from France or Latin America, or being defined by age, a younger or older person. People can be divided due to colour of eyes, astrological sign or shoe size, for example. Just because there are culturally common ways of defining group boundaries does not mean these are particularly correct or helpful. If a trait of introversion is accorded to somebody, or of speaking a particular dialect, or of preferring a style of clothes, all of these are really mechanisms for linking them to other people who also share that trait. Having put people in groups by ascribing them particular traits, we can then begin to ascribe all people in the group with other associated traits they may or may not share, often with the same positive or negative hue. A group of introverts may then all be seen as shy, socially awkward and depressive. Some of these linkages may have some scientific validity; others may be based on overgeneralisation. Group formation places together all those with a particular reputation deemed significant.

Having categorised a given population, we can then work out which groups are worthy of ethical effort and we most want to appease and those we can safely ignore. We do this by mapping positive and negative views onto these traits. I may have a positive view of doctors, for example, or a negative view of politicians, the rich or benefit cheats. I may view the elderly as a repository of wisdom or as a group who have served their time, are now of little productive use and can be ignored. This easily leads to stereotyping. We may for example see people from France as having certain characteristics or see teachers as being of a certain type or mothers as having certain personality traits. The reason stereotyping has got such a bad reputation is that these linkages of traits are frequently inaccurate and overgeneralised. Just because somebody is from Germany doesn't mean they are well organised and hard-working or that because somebody is a man that they are a social incompetent who likes sport and fast cars. It can be used for amusement but it can also be used to denigrate and undermine. When stereotyping is based on physical appearance or connected with how we value a person it can be particularly pernicious. Some traits are easier to change than others and if we have a negatively perceived trait we could then try to socially disguise this. It is possible to fake things such as my political or religious beliefs or my qualifications. Other traits are more difficult to hide. I can choose to have an interest in bird watching but generally changing ethnicity, gender or age is difficult or impossible. Yet it is these visible traits that can be the most unfair to form groups around. There is also a self-fulfilling element in stereotyping. This is important as some traits are more socially valued than others and if we are deemed to possess less socially valued traits this can undermine confidence if we let it. By grouping people together, although it may seem effective shorthand for dealing with large numbers, it will always be at the cost of truncating people's specialness and individuality. We are sometimes forced into positions where we need to take decisions that will upset people one way or the other but we must always keep in mind our skills of empathy and identification. Although we may conceive of groups, this must never be the defining means by which we meet people. We must always try to get their story and get to know them as individuals. Anything less than this is to depersonalise.

Such is the experience of groups from afar. As described, this can make being in a group seem to be always a negative experience. Even if we are thought of as being in a positively evaluated group, it will stunt who we are into a positively evaluated trait, which we are then forced to live up to. Yet, for the most part people often enjoy seeing themselves as being part of a group. The experience of being in a group up close, though, is often very different to seeing a group from far away. Throughout history there have been far more practical reasons for humans to work in groups rather than remaining individuals. Groups are a good means of getting far more done than we could accomplish alone. In addition, groups can offer protection and reassurance in a potentially hostile and unpredictable world. Such groupings are not defined by single traits but by people being part of a community or organisation using multiple traits often trying to achieve defined goals. This goal could be anything from having fun together, survival and education through to complex commercial enterprises trying to sell goods and services. Such groups will encompass many different people doing different things. For example, a relatively simple commercial organisation will need people filling many and different roles, including managers, technicians, sales people, administrators and the like. Each of these people will have different competencies and traits. All they may have in common is belonging to a particular company. The key thing such groups have, whether it is a tribe, a business, a political party or a religious organisation, is structure. That structure may be formal, governed by a defined group such as a board with a post that heads it up and rules, regulations, policies and procedures. In such formal groupings, if there is a violation of those procedures there will also be disciplinary measures. There will also be means of making and transmitting decisions. This is true whether I am a citizen of a state, in an army, have a job in a company or part of a campaign group or political party. The structure, though, could also be a lot more informal, where people work out for themselves ways of working that get the job done, where there may be no formal leader as such but where that role may be taken on by a person suited to the task. Often groupings will be a mixture of the formal and the informal and will only vary to the degree. The aim of such groups is to form people into being part of the organisation such as they no longer think and behave like individuals but are part of the bigger team. The issue with these groups defined by structure is that they often want to submerge the individual within it so from the organisational point of view they are more easily controlled and from an external point of view they become easier to relate to within a set role.

Having groups is a necessary occurrence in any well-functioning society. Ethically, the issue comes when an individual begins to identify emotionally with any group, that it fulfils most of that person's social needs and they see themselves as ethically identical to the group, so much so that they would find it hard to leave the group without harm being done to the self. To emotionally engage to this extent, we must attach a 'super-personality' to the group as a whole. The key to relating to a 'super-personality', as with an individual, is through feeling. Yet, the means by which we were identifying with others and according them specialness are not possible in relating to a 'super-personality'. We can only empathise with an individual; we cannot do this for a group as a whole. Yet it is undeniably possible to feel things for groups. There are whole ideologies based upon feelings of group loyalty such as nationalism and communism in which love of country and love of your class are prioritised over all else. To explore this love of group further let us take the example of nationalism and let us imagine a person who is a profound patriot. This patriot may well be preoccupied by love of country and continually think about it. The patriot may term his or her country 'motherland or fatherland' to give it more personality and make it easier to relate to. The patriot may see his or her own identity as being a part of the story of the nation and see the nation as an extension of themselves. The patriot may have lots of symbols such as flags and pictures celebrating important personalities in the history of the country. These may help the feelings of a patriot endure over time and endure any privations. As such, nationalism or any other group ideology can be a remarkable motivator to acts of selflessness and surrender. Yet, we cannot imagine what it would be like to be a country because a country is not another individual. We can, however, identify with individuals who are part of any group and have significance for the group as a whole. The patriot therefore may have a profound respect of a founding national hero or similar figure.

In group identification, instead of our ethics being based on empathy with an individual who is given specialness, our self boundaries are expanded around a collectivity which is given the labels 'we' and 'us'. This grouping is often strengthened by creating an opposed group labelled 'them'. It is this sense of an expanded self that gives real potency to our emotions in group identification. An expanded self boundary means not only do we feel emotion for our self but for all the other selves in the collectivity. This results in intensified positive and negative emotions. It also attaches to any goals the group as a whole may be striving for, so we will feel heightened positive feelings at any successes, but also increased lows at any perceived failures. That which the group owns collectively can become subject to heightened emotional attachment. It was pointed out when valuing objects, we can do so on the basis of being part of a group. Things can be valued not because they are mine or good but because a group shares possession of an object, a way of doing things, a language, a shared history and the like. Previously, it was identified that in love we could imagine another person as an extension of self. Such an idea of group is taking the idea of love and expanding it to cover whole swathes of people as extensions of self. Therefore, we are no longer doing good to another independent being when we act well towards another group member. According to such group ideologies, if I do good to another person in the group, I am doing the same as if I am doing good for the self. This is no longer a love of the other but a love of an expanded self; we have merged the self within a greater group. We then no longer have individual controls over our own boundaries but participate in maintaining a group boundary and identity: a boundary that surrounds 'us'. It becomes important to weave the larger story of triumph of the group and to see others as contributing to this. The thought that you are part of something greater and will go on after your own personal demise can be a great comfort. Being isolated can lead to feelings of great distress and anxiety. The 'super-personality' has significance for both our relationship to other but also the way we potentially construct the self. It becomes relatively easy, particularly if the self feels negatively about itself to take on the wider identity of a group to which it can feel positively towards. To find a 'super-personality' is an easy way of doing this. Our identity becomes enfolded into the group we feel we belong to and the 'super-personality' we construct.

In love, there are two dangers: that we try to take over the other, or we become submerged to the will of other. Both are present in such ethical groupings, defined by a 'super-personality'. Likeness and dislikeness is the crucial dualism when examining identification with groups. Relationships based on likeness rest on the imaginative fantasy on escape from isolation. The escape here is a flight into something larger than the self. The trouble is we can never finally escape from isolation in any meaningful way. We can never become more than the self. Once a group is considered 'us', numerous issues begin to arise that are potentially problematic. For one thing, if the group as a whole is seen as an extension of the self, we could demand control in the same way as one applies to the self. Not everybody in the group will act as extensions of the self. Not everybody can exert power and influence within a group either. We then can either get involved in power struggles or surrender the self to the greater will of the group. The emotional commitment demanded by some groups can mean they only function by exerting considerable punitive sanctions on those who are deemed to have violated internal rules and norms. Such a violation is seen as a person being wayward who has disrespected group identity. Much of the conflict within groups is over what are seen as the powerful positions to make decisions. This sets up rivalries and those not seen as playing for the team can be treated very badly. People become valued not because of any specialness they may have but because of what they may be deemed to contribute to the overall group project. This will turn everybody in the group into a reputation that is kept by those in the higher echelons, who could pour judgement upon those below at any moment. As stated, in such circumstances dreaming of not being in the group can then be an attractive option.

If the group can be a bad place to be for individuals who are considered members, it can be worse for those who are not considered part of the group at all. It is often worth differentiating between those who are mere outsiders and therefore of no or little consideration and those who are rivals. Many systems of ethics urge compassion and aid be given to the stranger. The outsider is not always considered a threat and may be a way that individuals in the group can demonstrate to each other their virtues. This does not make the outsider any less of an outsider. It is fairly easy, however, for the stranger to be turned into an enemy. The effect of loyalty to the 'super-personality' of the group is to divide everyone into insiders, those like me, and outsiders, those who are not like me. When we strongly identify ourselves with a group, as part of a nation, as part of a tribe or a company, anybody that is seen as a threat to the aims of the group can then become regarded as an enemy and a target for the group as a whole. This is where a strong positive negative dualism is projected onto likeness and dislikeness. Some of the most horrific acts of brutality have resulted from people being cast as enemies by virtue of having perceived characteristic differences. We then value the group as positive and the enemy as negative. Small examples can then be magnified to demonstrate the negativity of the enemy group. For example, much of Nazi ideology was based on the idea of a world Jewish conspiracy where Jews were cast as insurgents trying to take over the world. Under communism, those who had a talent and wanted to promote it were cast as enemies of the people. Such scapegoating is a widespread human phenomenon and regrettably tends to reinforce feelings of group belonging. We can only conclude therefore that this occurs as a common exercise of human imagination. Being inside a group and emotionally identifying with it means that those outside the group can barely be seen along with any specialness that should be accorded. Alternatively, specialness can be removed altogether and the person can be seen as an enemy.

Therefore, it can seem that the emotional and moral problems of imagining people into ethical groups can outweigh any advantages of being able to deal with large numbers of people and the feelings of group belonging as well. Specialness must always be reserved for individuals and cannot be amalgamated into groups either when looking at others or when considering the self and its identity. We must though interact with others and belong to groups periodically. Without this we could not get much done. Yet the self must never be subsumed within that of the wider group. One way to determine the level of group control is to see how easy it is to leave. If we are free to leave and can express opinions freely as long as they are respectful of others then that group is relatively open. It is when the group imposes its 'super-personality' upon us or we see people as part of a group and not as individuals that issues begin to arise. Yet, the issue of numbers remains. If the use of ethical groups to manage numbers is not considered an option, then we must consider alternatives. There must be a basis for making ethical decisions when we cannot base them upon direct empathy.

KANTIAN ETHICS AND THE LAW

One important strand of ethical understanding has been Kantian ethics, named after the philosopher Immanuel Kant. The foundation of Kantian ethics is the categorical imperative. This adopts some of the same basic formulations as the golden rule outlined previously. Kant saw it though not as a version of the golden rule but as an improvement upon it. He saw the golden rule as relative, deriving ethics from the interaction between self and other, and sought to escape this relativity. Kant sought to argue that there were certain a priori rules such as the categorical imperative that would be true for everybody at all times. There are different versions of the categorical imperative but basically it states: treat everybody in accordance with universal rules which you would want everybody to be treated by. Although the formula is essentially the same as the golden rule, it represents an attempt to universalise it from the person standing in front of me to everybody who is owed an ethical debt. The standard is still the self – it is what I would want the universal rules to be – but the end point becomes the wish for generalisable rules we would all want to live by. This has certain advantages. Of particular significance, it is an attempt at dealing with the problem of numbers. It does this by treating the person in front of us the same as we would anybody else. Thus, the shorthand we are using is to not bother to find out what the other wants or needs. Instead, we are conceiving of universal rules everybody in any community would want to live by and acting accordingly, irrespective of who you are. Thus, Kantian ethics places emphasis on acting according to duty and from correct motive. Correct motivation is a reference to the emphasis upon intent rather than consequences. This has previously been discussed. The self can only have control of intent not consequences. Thus, in Kantian ethics it matters that we intend to live by universal rules, not that we achieve this. We should intend to do our duty.

It also addresses some of the moral pitfalls with happiness that were outlined previously. It does so by removing the happiness of the other person entirely as any kind of ethical aim. Thus, I would not do something to make the person in front of me happy; I would do something because I believe it is the correct thing to do and it should apply to everybody equally. Thus, Kantian ethics rejects totally the link between the happiness of other and the good of other. Yet, if we are not concerned with the happiness of the other person but are concerned about doing good, questions are raised about happiness as the emotional detector of good. It could be that happiness and good are unrelated. This is absurd. Happiness will always detect somebody's feeling of good, even if this isn't considered particularly ethical. Alternatively, it would suggest if we were not concerned about making the other person happy, we must be concerned about making somebody happy in order for what we are doing to be called good. This could either be the self or alternately a wider body of people around us. If we see the self as somebody who needs to do the right thing in order to feel good, then doing one's duty will bring happiness to the self. Thus, one place happiness will be is with the self. It could further be suggested that a possible description of the good society is one where there occurs universal rules that are acknowledged and obeyed by everybody. So, another place where happiness could be is in the wider ordering of the population as a whole. This, though, could veer close into group formation in order to make Kantian ethics work, unless the rules apply absolutely universally to all equally. Such a vision of an ideal society could be seen as other people's version of hell, where all individual difference is expunged!

It could also be argued, though, that Kantian ethics never escapes the relativity it seeks to. We can never escape being the self and we can never get to a universal good, although we can develop certain algorithms that can be helpful in dealing with others and having an opening offer is always helpful in any ethical negotiation. Kantian ethics though comes close to the example given previously of the moral philosopher who has come up with a schema for deciding what is good and does this regardless of the expressed wants and wishes of the other. The problems begin because my wants for universal laws may be very different from your wants and wishes. This is exactly the same problem as with the golden rule. I may want a universal law that means I smile at everybody when I meet them; you may regard this as inane and pointless; nevertheless, I will smile at you, even as you are in mourning for your late father. I will smile at everybody whatever the context. I am doing so because I believe this should be a law that applies to everybody no matter what the context. This may be a trivial example, but it does expose some difficulties. I imagine the sort of society that would make me happy and project this onto everybody I then meet. In then pretending I am in the perfect society, even though you are not, I then call this my duty. Duty implies a follower of rules or convention that can appear less human and less caring than a motivation from seeing others in pain and wanting to correct the situation. Happiness is very much present but it is my happiness that results from following my duty. This is not a problem, if my happiness stems from the attempt at making the other happy, without an agenda of getting my pleasure, but this is not the case with Kantian ethics. Instead, it is about acting as if I am in a perfect society which should ultimately make everybody happy and then acting accordingly, and remaining at this point whatever the responses that come back.

Thus, the pursuit of universal laws has generally not been left up to individuals to determine for themselves but is determined on behalf of individuals by a wider system. Laws are usually seen as necessary. It is possible to see law as minimum standards, which set necessary parameters by which any large, healthy society needs to function and people need to uphold. By being written down they should be clear to all what they are and they should apply to all. In the discussions on the golden rule, a differentiation was made between positive and negative formulations. Negative formulations gave certain minimum standards which were then easier to apply across large numbers of people. It is possible to see the formulation of law in the same light. The basis of law can be seen as the minimum standards which human beings need to live thriving lives. Laws are often about prohibiting things such as running a red traffic light or thumping somebody else when you get angry but they can be positive commands such as a duty to maintain food hygiene in a restaurant or fire escape routes clear. Even here, though, there is a purpose of maintaining minimum standards of safety. They maintain rules that make things safer for everybody. They enable happiness to be more likely but they don't of themselves bring about happiness. Rules and laws, though, are undoubtedly a way with which ethics can deal with large numbers of people, relatively fairly.

Instead of being left up to individuals to negotiate, the drafting of laws is generally seen as the responsibility for legislatures to undertake on behalf of broader groups. In terms of laws this is usually the nation state, or a delegated trans-national or local body, but quasi law-making bodies can include anything that drafts and ratifies policies and procedures. Thus, the laws are never truly universal but apply only to a group which resides in a particular territory or within the particular jurisdiction of whatever law-making body is applicable, thus allying the idea of law as something performed only by a group to which we are a member, often by accident of birth or circumstance rather than any active choice. The power of drafting and enacting laws is so powerful that it has often been seen as necessary to provide extensive checks and balances against its abuse. Ideally, laws are mechanisms where written guidance is given to large numbers about how to behave so that a better society can be had by all. Yet, laws because of their very nature can be used maliciously to exert power over people, backed up by powerful sanctions that can blight lives when used injudiciously. Laws are often worked out by contested legislatures that are subject to periodic democratic elections. These legislatures enact lengthy documents that then need interpretation through independent judicial mechanisms. Thus, can be seen the separation of powers between the executive, the legislature and the judiciary in many nation states. The legal process and the drafting of general rules can be seen as a working out of Kantian ethics practically. The drafting of laws can be seen to retain an aspect of universality that was so central in Kantian ethics. Universality here, though, means that a law must apply to x and to y equally. This is a fundamental tenet of law. The law, though, will generally only apply within the jurisdiction of the making body, and thus won't apply to everybody. Laws can also be seen as the rules of any given group, reinforcing the belonging to the group and defining it and its power. The problems of groups, which have a super-personality to define them, have been discussed, and the law can then be seen as the primary means of defending the group with the super-personality, rather than the fairest means of managing ethics for large numbers of people. It then matters not what the law contains so much as who is making the law for whom.

Law can also become lengthy and complex quickly. Say, I think it a good idea that people have one day off a week for their rest and leisure. So, I enact through Parliament a simple law that states that everybody gets Sunday off each week. Then, I go out to enjoy my Sunday, have an accident and find there are no ambulances to take me to hospital because everybody has the day off. I thus decide, assuming I recover, to make an amendment to the law to say that certain essential workers are exempted from the duty to take Sunday off. I then need to define who those workers are and that they get another day off in recompense. This represents how the law works. A universal principle is drawn up that we think will be good for people. We then find exceptions where this isn't so good through applying the principle to everyday situations. We then need to revise the law so that it then becomes more complex to account for these situations. The issues with the law then are that they apply to a particular group or jurisdiction and they can get very complex. Law and rules can rapidly become unwieldy. To manage the bulk of human behaviour through imagining rules for everything is highly problematic. We have to take all the possible scenarios we can imagine and then provide some form of guidance upon this, often based on particular principles. This will often get so lengthy that, when we come across a rare situation, we probably wouldn't be able to locate the appropriate guidance anyway.

This also suggests that being ethical is synonymous with following the law, and all I would have to do to be ethical is to follow this. The reason for having so many checks and balances is that the law can be used for purposes of protecting and giving advantage to some people against others. Say we live in a particular jurisdiction. This jurisdiction covers two very different groups of people but they share a common law-making body. Both groups of people have tended to create super-personalities for their groups and consider each other to be rival groups. One group has just slightly more people than the other and the law-making body is made up via democratic elections. People vote for candidates of the same grouping they feel associated with. The larger grouping always has more delegates elected in the law-making body. The laws passed are those that favour the larger group. Thus, as much as laws can be seen as necessary, they can just as easily be unjust and implemented to protect corrupt regimes. In these circumstances, it is easily possible to imagine that not following the law can become ethical, if we go back to our original understanding of ethics, about happiness. If the law, rather than a means of dealing fairly with large numbers of people and protecting their happiness, has instead become about giving pleasure to some at the expense of others it is possible to imagine scenarios when breaking the law would be the ethical thing to do. Thus, the law, which was supposed to be an ethical extension, can if not controlled become the very opposite of ethics.

This leads onto the idea of universal human rights. Human rights are an attempt to distil down the law to certain underlying principles which all laws should derive from. As such, human rights should act as a guarantor against unjust laws. Besides, we might not be able to carry around every written instruction and guidance on every possible lived scenario, but we can carry around basic principles that we can then appeal to against corruptly administered law. The defenders of human rights see them as applying to all jurisdictions, and thus being universal. Human rights could thus be seen as an attempt to re-establish some of the Kantian principles of universality and considered the minimum that would be necessary for all human beings to require to lead happy and fulfilled lives and should be upheld at all times and in all places. Yet, there could be considerable disagreement as to what should constitute even these minimum standards. Most human rights drafts include the idea of the right to life. So much everybody would agree is essential: if we are to be able to experience happiness, we must be alive. Even here, though, this is not absolute, for there are times when it would be right to take somebody else's life, as when they are committing murder and there is no other way to stop them. Some would include the idea of freedom or liberty, which is often cast as the right to not have the state interfere unduly in your life and with your decisions, including the right to privacy, the right to a fair trial and not to suffer torture and degrading treatment. This is balanced against more positive needs such as the right to have a decent income, healthcare, housing, or a sustainable environment. To fulfil the latter, though, would potentially require a large state with appropriate funding, which is seen by some as impinging of the former rights. Some though would see freedom from state interference as meaningless if one is suffering the blight of poverty. Thus, agreement with universal principles becomes contested around what is important for an individual to be happy.

Even if there is scope to agree, and perhaps we agree to list all these as human rights, there is then plenty of scope for human rights to conflict with each other. Much of the study of ethics can then become the study of scenarios that are thrown up as to what to do when particular key ethical principles conflict. It can become the study of situations where the human rights of one individual who has violated the rights of others are then denied them in some way. It also can become the study of the precedence of rights, for instance thinking when right to privacy conflicts with the freedom to know. The right to say something conflicts with the hurt this can cause to others. A system of human rights, or legal founding principles, can be helpful as one of the means of checks and balances, along with democratic checks and separation of powers on the excesses of the law. Yet, if people are in quite fortunate positions in life, the rights of most concern will be those of freedom. Those in less fortunate positions are more likely to be concerned with rights to fairness. Either way, these rights could be quite minimal and the means of being ethical would not be violating those rights. Yet, what potentially results if the law becomes the main means of regulating relations is the replacement of getting specialness intuited through emotional empathy with reducing others to the possessors of rights.

Let us return to the original scenario. We are faced with a random individual in front of us. According to Kantian ethics we should not be so concerned with finding out about the person, but instead we should do our duty towards them. Although there is another aspect of Kantian ethics which sees the other as always an end in themselves, rather than as a means, which could push us towards the more open-ended giving of the self indicated in love and sympathy. Let us park this thought though and do our duty. Rather than identifying, we will be looking to certain established universal principles, such as those contained in human rights, to see if there are any issues that are highlighted. Thus, rather than specialness, we see the other person as reduced to a bearer of rights. As long as we see no obvious rights being violated or in jeopardy, the other person will be of no concern and we can safely pass by, leaving the other person in peace. Thus, the issue of numbers has been dealt with through reducing the other person to being a rights bearer. If the other person were to want to attract our attention, they would have to persuade us their rights were somehow in jeopardy. The default position though would be to ignore unless otherwise persuaded. People can then feel the only way they can be heard and have ethical existence is to assert those rights in some way. When they feel those rights have been violated, they can then resort to the bureaucracy that is the law and the trauma that is involved in going through the process of trialling any competing claims. The law should ideally be a last resort, sitting in the background if everything else fails. Unless, we have risen high up in the law-making group, we ourselves will not make laws or enact human rights we will just observe their principles. We will do so through still using a version of the golden rule: I will respect your human rights as I would want you to respect my human rights. This guarantees certain minimum standards but little more. It also is an attempt to be fair, giving attention only where needed. Much as we would do if specialness was defined by compassion, with many of the same issues. Having minimal standards unfortunately has proved necessary but seems also to end in a truncated ethics where the person we are meeting is hardly seen.

UTILITARIAN ETHICS AND THE VOTE

If Kantian ethics and the law are potentially problematic means of dealing with numbers, there is a rival school of ethics that must also be considered: utilitarianism. This posits that the concern of ethics should be the happiness of the greatest number of people. The original aim of ethical action was the happiness of other and this is maintained in utilitarianism. Yet, if we have a person standing in front of us, we are not solely concerned with their happiness. Instead, we should be concerned with the happiness of the greatest number of the population around us of which the person is a part. The idea provides a guide as to where we should put our ethical energies, namely into those acts that give happiness to the most people. Utilitarianism points us to an idea that in examining the ethical we need to see happiness as bigger than exists between two people. That we are part of something larger and our ability to see what is good will in part depend on what is around us. The end becomes everybody's happiness. We cannot make the person in front of us happy, if this is going to have a detrimental effect upon large numbers of others. Yet the opposite becomes true: if there is a choice between making a large number of people happy at the expense of a smaller number of people, then the former should be chosen over the latter.

In classical utilitarianism good is achieved when the greatest number of people are actually made happy. Not that we intended to make the greatest number of people happy. Thus, focus is on the results of any action and not our intention. What we intend to do is of no ethical concern. It is what actually happens that matters. The problems, though, of relying upon consequences to determine ethics have already been outlined. Not least that we cannot make another person themselves happy; we can only intend to make this more likely. If it is impossible to make the individual in front of us happy, how much more so with a whole population? Happiness depends on how people perceive what is good for them and this can be fickle. People's emotional state may be quite nuanced and complex. To resolve this issue, so far we have been relying on our intent, over which we have control. Yet, for all that intent is something that is easier to control than results, it is also vague, fuzzy and easy to fake. This may be not so much of an issue regarding our intent, as long as we maintain reasonable insight and conscience. Yet, if we cannot judge another's happiness easily, we certainly cannot get to their intent. If that is the case, ethics becomes something of a private affair of the self, where we manage our own intent and leave others to manage theirs. When dealing with large-scale numbers this could be seen as difficult. Even if we are just managing our intent, it is useful to have some information by which to judge our success or not.

As we cannot directly reach another's happiness, rather than resorting to intent, we can turn to proxies for happiness that are more easily seen. One proxy that can be used is a simple time-tested way to find out if large numbers are happy with something or not. It is to ask them, through forcing a yes or no response, through the use of the ballot. A simple majority becomes what is sought for a decision. Thus, instead of drafting a framework of rules to deal with large numbers of people, we resort to one of the checks and balances used to control those rules, namely the democratic vote, if not always literally at least in metaphorical conception. We could imagine the scenario. Say the decision is whether or not a hydro-electric project should go ahead. This will supply cheap, sustainable energy to large numbers of people. Yet, it will come at a cost of flooding an area so some people will lose their homes. It will also have a devastating environmental impact on the immediate area of the flooding. If we determine whether this should go ahead through the means of the ballot, there would be a vote and whoever gets the most votes would determine the fate of the project. Yet, some people will be extremely adversely affected by this but we would expect the vote would go on the numbers who would think the project would benefit them. Yet, what we are often finding out is not whether something made somebody happy, but whether they think it will make them happy in the future. Going back to the decision whether to build the hydro-electric scheme, hypothetically, we could ask people how happy they are before the scheme is built. We could build the scheme and then a year down the line see whether people's self reports have improved, gone down or stayed the same. If they had stayed the same or gone down, we could then knock down the entire scheme as it didn't make people any happier and it has blighted the lives of some very seriously. Yet, we could find that people's happiness or otherwise has nothing to do with the hydro-electric project but because there has now been a global recession which has caused a massive downturn in living standards across the community. To go even further, we could select two communities which are almost identical in every way, where we could potentially build hydro-electric projects, one where we build the project and one where we don't. Again, we take a measure of happiness before the project is built and then again afterwards. We then measure the happiness in each community. If we find the happiness hasn't improved in the community with the hydro-electric project against the one without the project, again in theory we should demolish the project.

None of this is very practical and so if we were to apply the principles of utilitarianism to the hydro-electric project we would have to stick with having a vote to decide whether it is built across the one community that it affects. Knocking it down would patently be a waste of time, expense and resources and, besides, much of the damage would already have been done once it had been built. Yet, we don't really know our future happiness. In the scenario of having a vote, the situation isn't very often of people being given impartial information and then making up their minds. What often results are campaigns to emotionally persuade any given electorate that a particular viewpoint would make them happier. These often offer partial information or even deliberate misrepresentation. Those with the well-funded means and an organisation to do this are often at considerable advantage. We go back to the metaphor of having a performer and an audience. In this case the electorate are the audience but what they are judging are particular scenarios and what would make them happiest, presented to them by different campaign groups. Instead of doing good by offering a plebiscite about any given issue and then doing whatever the majority decide, what usually will happen is that doing good amounts to the emotional manipulation of others to vote in a particular way so we can maintain power and status.

Yet, even the act of holding plebiscites for all major decisions is pretty uncommon, except in relatively small countries such as Switzerland. It is time-consuming, costly and bureaucratic and can lead to contradictory results. Instead, the vote is frequently constrained to electing delegates or representatives for a period of time through general elections, where, rather than single issues, people elect a grouping called a party which proposes a group of policies, some of which you may agree with and some you may not, all of which are future-directed. The election then becomes not about a single issue we need to form a future judgement about but a whole range of issues, and these are then compared with the proposals from other parties and a judgement then formed as to which of these programmes will most likely lead to me being happiest. Once elected, these representatives decide what will happen on behalf of a given population until the time the next election comes around. After the election, representatives may keep an eye on polls and the like but will often rely on judging their performance through other proxies for happiness. The vote is one proxy that could be used in utilitarianism but there are other possible proxies we could use. For instance, if we are selling goods, we could count the number that are sold to see if people are happy with the object or service. If we are a government, we could also see how wealthy people are and map this over time. Whatever is used, it needs to make happiness measurable. Once it is measurable, we no longer have to rely on the vagueness of intent. What we have are numbers and we just need to work out whether they add up. We need a majority of a given population if we take a general poll. If we are selling goods or services, all we need to do is make a profit. We can then look at an action, examine the result and determine whether this worked or not. Yet, all the proxies will only work to the extent that they capture people's happiness. Like the vote, if we are buying a good or service, we are buying because we think this will make us happy. It is future-directed and what we are often faced with is campaigns by sellers to emotionally persuade us how happy the good or service will make us. We measure people's wealth, because this measures people's capacity to buy things which they think will make them happy. Although it is easy to measure, the capacity of increasing wealth to equate to people's happiness has become increasingly questioned. Particularly given that the increasing pleasures of consumption that result from wealth are leading to a rapid depletion of the Earth's resources and environment.

Let us now return to the scenario of facing a random person. It no longer matters what this person does or says or whether I can make them happy or not. What I am concerned with is whether I can make the majority of people happy. I will probably not be in a position to take a poll and I may not be in a buyer or seller transaction. I could give money, but doing this for everybody I meet would be impractical and leave me poor. Thus, very often I will take other shortcuts. I will do what I think most people would want, perhaps because that is what most of my friends would want the same. I will instead use a variation of the golden rule, do to others what I think the majority of people would think is good in any circumstance. The way we often get to what we think the majority will think is good is through the people around us at any time. Utilitarianism then can become an exercise in the very group formation and pleasing an identified audience we were trying to avoid in dealing with the problem of numbers. We create an imaginary group of people around us, use this as a reference for the majority and do what we think they would want. This has dangers of not only getting what the majority think wrong but having our actions determined by a kind of groupthink. There are also further dangers with utilitarianism in relations to groups. Going back to the previous example in making the law, if one group with a super-personality is larger than another group with a super-personality within any given jurisdiction, then the larger group will always be able to decide on the things they think will make them happy against the smaller grouping. Thus, I will always appease the majority at the expense of the minority. Happiness is undifferentiated in the idea of utilitarianism. Thus, it doesn't matter what sort of happiness I think will please me. So, I may want happiness because it gives me pleasure, which may undermine the future community, making decisions short term. I may take a decision because I am frightened of the other community and want to be protected from them as much as possible. I may believe all sorts of myths concocted to make me feel more secure about how good the government is and how bad anybody is who criticises them, particularly the threat from the other community. Thus, in order to make the majority feel good I have to undermine the other community who are seen as a threat. The majority will always determine the good in utilitarianism even if this can lead to what other systems of ethics would see as unethical. Utilitarianism could be used to support lying and cheating as long as this leads to majority happiness. If what made a majority population happy was seeing a minority group unhappy this could be supported. Happiness of the majority would be happiness whether that happiness was based on something profound, something negative or something frivolous.

Utilitarianism overstates how much we can bring about the happiness of others. Happiness is slippery and complex and can be caused by all sorts of means which cannot be accounted for by proxies. In our attempt to make happiness measurable, we risk constraining what makes people happy to wealth or to a vote and on its projection into the future. It fails to take account of the richness of human relationships and how giving can be more important in happiness than taking. Happiness is constrained to what is measurable, but what will bring that future happiness could be anything. This allows people to admit anything they choose as happiness, including all the problematic versions outlined previously. It makes the ethical going along with whatever we think the majority thinks will make them happy. Yet, the alternative to having to imagine what may make the majority happy is to imagine either what would make the self happy, the immediate other happy or the minority happy. Of these, though, it is only the self we can control the happiness of. The others we cannot control we can only do what we think is good, in the hope that this has a better chance of making the other happy. In the example of the single person, it is easier to get to know them better, it is easier to do good. With larger numbers of people, if we are in a position to, it becomes necessary to choose the proxies we are working with. Yet, there are surely times when if people are deriving happiness from running others down that we need to make sure our proxies do not discriminate, are as universal as possible and fair. Otherwise we end up ignoring our own self and the person in front of us, and decide by guessing what the prejudices are of those around us and acceding to them. This is not either to say that voting and democracy is a waste of time. Yet, it is perhaps better to see it rather than as a determination of what people will think will make them happy, but as a check on the past competence of those who have made the law and whether they have done a good enough job. We are, thus, still left with the person in front of us and the self, but left in the knowledge we cannot just consider their happiness but need to account for the wider happiness of others. The two main means of doing this, through universal laws or through the vote, are imperfect. Instead, perhaps we come back to revising the golden rule: in making the other happy, ensure you consider their specialness as fully as you can and seek their happiness as far as you can, as long as this does not undermine them, wider reality or the needs of the wider community. We should always strive to make as many people as possible happy on the same terms. If we have the opportunity to make more people happy we should as we would expect others to do the same for us. To be able to do this we need the self to be happy and to be able to share this in the best way possible.

Five

THE SELF AS CATEGORY AS THE END

GOOD IN THE SELF

So far, we have been exploring the other side of the self–other boundary. In the next couple of chapters, we will turn to the self. That the self, when not inverted, is the most prominent source of meaning and value makes it reasonable to consider it as an alternative end to happiness. Much like anything else the self can be conceived of as a trajectory or as a category or as a combination of both. In relation to the self, the problem with happiness is related to the future. If we take pleasure now, we can forgo future happiness and undermine our future self. It is this future self that will give us an alternate end and to get there we will need to cast the self as a trajectory. Yet, coming into this chapter we also needed to explore the self as the means of setting up what is good. It is only by being able to imagine the self well that we will be able to identify with other and it is only by determining what is good for the self that we can then determine what is good for other as well. This is the previously discussed golden rule. Confidence is the emotional means by which we detect good in the self. In founding the self with a robust confidence, we can withstand the vicissitudes of life and gaze out securely into paramount reality. How the self is set up to be confident then becomes of heightened significance. Thus, we need to explore the self both as a category and as a trajectory. The self will be explored as a category in this chapter. In the following chapter the possibility of seeing the self as a trajectory will be looked at. However, the self is probably more often seen as a combination of category and trajectory, as a category moving through time.

Let us start though by imagining the self as a category. A category is a concept which demarcates something as separate from its surroundings and links it to related things. When we apply a category to the self, we will situate it spatially. A boundary will be drawn around the self which demarcates it from the surrounding space. This is the self–other boundary we have often referred to. When we imagine this boundary as part of a category it will be a line that surrounds and envelops the self, distinguishing it from everything that is not self or other. Yet, the self is difficult to conceive of as a pure category devoid of time. It is always a category that must face out towards the future. As a necessity, we need to construct the short-term trajectory that is paramount reality. Thus, the self–other boundary apart from delineating place is also used to delineate time, even if it is the immediate present from the short-term future. If the primary way we are conceiving of the self is spatial, paramount reality can be seen as a kind of rotating searchlight beam emanating from the self, constantly surveying the horizon of other in different directions. This means that we cannot cover all of the self–other boundary but will pass our search beam across the boundary at different places.

In whichever way we construct the self, what we are concerned with is to have as reliable supply of good within the self as possible. It is through doing this we can experience confidence, a positive mood state, in relation to how we feel about the self. Confidence stems from seeing the self as good and allows us to face the future. As long as confidence doesn't stem from the need to do others down and feel superior, it also allows us to look at what may be good for others as well. Without it we are likely to be overwhelmed with anxiety and trepidation. Confidence gives robustness and resilience in adversity. In order to have confidence we must have trust in something. Without it, when faced with negative situations we are in danger of collapsing. Yet, confidence is more than the feeling of coping or getting by. It has elements of enlivening as well, which stems from the anticipation of an ability to manage and be successful. As such confidence is an amalgamation of resilience and enlivening. Confidence allows a forgetting of our limitations and fears. It is the very source of feeling good about the self. In searching what makes up the self, we are hoping to discover the secret of our confidence.

We have come across confidence before. Confidence was also discussed in the previous chapter when discussing compassion. It was asserted there that confidence could be problematic for compassion as it often stems from status. One common way people get to feel good about themselves is to compare how they are doing with others and to feel they are somehow superior to them. As a result people could therefore become suspicious of motives related to confidence. Yet, we need confidence and to feel good about ourselves but this need not be at the expense of others. As will be seen, what is trusted in order to bring about good in the self and therefore confidence, can be many and varied. This then has an impact on the confidence we have, our relations to others and how resilient it is. Some things we trust in can be more helpful than others. In the chapter on truth, confidence in the truth was introduced as a feeling that was able to provide a foundation for the self. What this means is having a reliable framework by which we can regularly negotiate day-to-day life without coming to any major harm. A minimum to feel confident is that, when we put around the searchlight that is paramount reality, it is reliable in detecting what we need it for. If we feel this isn't functioning well and cannot reliably detect good from bad and cannot protect us, we will not be able to feel confident. Yet, this on its own will be insufficient to feel confident. Confidence results from having good within the self, not just the ability to reliably detect good and bad in our environment, although this is clearly helpful.

There are ostensibly two places we can place our confidence. One place it can be is in other, that somebody or something from other will somehow protect the self. The feeling of confidence is related to faith. Faith is a religious term and a form of confidence in which the something we trust is God and rely on God to provide us with good. This can provide a world view that allows the self to cope in hostile environments; that there is a big guy with a master plan who will fight for us when the chips are down. Faith, though, could be used more broadly to mean any trust in an external force from other, over which the self has little power. The most the self can do is have faith things will work out. This, though, depends on the veracity of this belief and can be undone if we find nobody is fighting our corner. The self cedes control of its confidence to external circumstances. The alternative is to found confidence with the self and its abilities to cope on its own, with self-confidence. Self-confidence can be defined as a trust in the abilities of the self to be able to cope and manage in differing situations. This is strongly related to the belief that the self can act and make a difference, a belief in self-efficacy. It is possible, though, to see the replacing of the divine with the self, however spiritually manifested as self-worship: a form of total selfishness and self-preoccupation to be contrasted with the selflessness of the last chapter. This need not be the case but it places huge emphasis upon how we derive our confidence. In addition, if we are unable to cope and manage, any self-confidence can evaporate as easily as any faith, but we can then only blame the self.

We can feel confident when there is sufficient good in the self and we don't feel this good is threatened or possible to undermine. If our confidence becomes insecure and we feel we may lose the good we have, we risk becoming preoccupied. We have previously discussed preoccupations. It is something that stays in the self when we have turned away from paramount reality. Preoccupations are often held in the self through anxiety or worry, as something we don't want and can't get rid of, or do want but can't get or fear we may lose. As well as detecting what is good and bad in other it is possible to see emotions as detecting what is already in the self that shouldn't really be there and needs to be expelled, or what is good but we may risk losing. In relation to confidence, if we determine our good comes from other and we risk not getting an adequate supply or, alternatively, we have good within the self but feel we may lose it, in these circumstances this can cause preoccupations. Preoccupations can loom prominently in the mind and become a source of bad in itself rather than a source of good. If we define the self by what is constantly within our mind and we keep returning to, it could be our preoccupations that define us. To begin, though, we need to understand the nature of confidence and its relationship to happiness. Happiness is usually conceived of as an emotion, whereas confidence as stated can be seen as a mood and this difference needs to be explored further.

CONFIDENCE AS MOOD

Confidence is a mood state and the starting point is thus to explore the meaning of mood and differentiate it from emotion. Mood as a term has a variety of ways it can be compared to emotion; for example, mood is often considered less intense than emotion. Compare the euphoria at winning a trophy as opposed to the laid-back joy of a good mood. The variation of mood can be seen as something that comes and goes like the weather but an emotion is our reaction to something that is happening now. Emotion is often defined as being of short duration, lasting only as long as the situation that caused it. Mood by contrast is usually seen as longer lasting and may not have an immediate focus or cause. For example, happiness is caused by something good happening to me but I can also be just in a positive frame of mind because I am just in that kind of mood. Happiness most often is regarded as an emotion and for the most part is our detector of good crossing the self–other boundary. So, if we are just in a positive frame of mind, we are not detecting good entering the self, so we must look to other explanations and to why we feel good.

The term mood then covers a number of experiences and can be understood in different ways. One possible understanding of mood is as a form of 'background music'. This could reference two concurrent feeling states, one in the foreground called emotion and a second one in the background called mood. If this were possible it means contradictory feelings could exist at the same time, so, for example, anger and joy. It is difficult, however, to imagine two such states existing like this concurrently. It is however possible to imagine rapidly cycling between these feelings. This encapsulates the feeling of mixed emotion. Rather, though, than being a reference to mood and emotion, this often refers to emotions caused by objects with both good and bad elements. This may be the same object such as the experience of addiction described previously in the section on love or we have both good and bad experiences going on at the same time. For example, we may be going through a messy divorce but that something good happens such as my best friend phones up. This, though, is not experiencing opposite emotions at the same time. It is about having different emotional responses to different occurrences.

Yet it is still worth persisting with the idea of mood as background music. Thayer (2001) associates mood with our naturally occurring biorhythms, which emphasis,es the importance of time cycles in mood. The human body has many biorhythms.

One of the most obvious is the sleep cycle. Most people will find that energy levels and abilities will fluctuate during the day. You may find that you have more energy in the morning, say an hour or two after the effects of sleep have worn off, or you may find you have greater energy levels in the evening. Many people will have a low point for energy levels in the afternoon sometime after lunch. Such energy levels are an important aspect of our mood. If we feel confident and alert, we are likely to respond to challenges differently from if we are sluggish and tired. This is suggestive of a background feature of our general receptivity which then provides a frame for various emotional reactions. It is background that is likely to influence our foreground perception and perhaps destabilise our confidence when entering paramount reality. One way of seeing mood then is about general receptivity due to natural fluctuations in energy levels and overall well-being which operate in the background. It therefore makes sense to be aware of these fluctuations and to mark them in some way. Yet here we are specifically concerned with confidence. It is probably worth understanding our daily rhythms but on its own this is not likely to be a pointer to what makes us confident. We learn to live with our biorhythms, not control them to bring about good.

Another possibility is to see emotion as something that is happening in the here and now which gives it immediacy and therefore has more prominence in the psyche. It is caused by perceiving something good or bad crossing or potentially crossing our self–other boundary. Mood by contrast is still a feeling but is something conjured from our memories or imagination and therefore is seen as originating on the self side of the boundary. We can usually tell the difference between an emotion and a mood. Mood becomes a regurgitation of things that already exist within the self. We potentially have control over memory but it has a habit of throwing up things, particularly when nothing much else is indicated. Memory can be deceived and tends to degrade over time into something fuzzy. Our imaginations can connect things together with the same emotional hue to bring about rough whimsical feelings. Yet, if something significant were to cross the self–other boundary our emotional attention will often be rapidly drawn away from these daydreams. Yet, there are times when we can find ourselves reliving the same experience over and over; we feel we can't get rid of it and it becomes an ever present memory and a constant regurgitation.

This is mood as an elongation. Here, emotion can be understood as a reflex response but mood as the aftershocks that follow on, an emotional 'echo' sustained by our imaginations. Elongation is what happens when we become preoccupied, which we have previously discussed. Here mood becomes the elongation of a normal reflex emotional reaction. In general, it is easier for bad to be remembered than what is good. For example, I may get a shock from the death of somebody close to me but the process of grief that follows is part of the aftershock of mood and becomes emotionally preoccupied. It is possible to imagine such emotional aftershocks going on for years or lifetimes after an initial cause and they can include positive and negative emotion. Thus it is possible to imagine a person who never gets over the death of a loved one, particularly say where the death has been particularly shocking or traumatic. Similarly, anger can be prolonged through revenge fantasies, leading to blood feuds over many generations. This means that it is possible to imagine mood traversing whole groups of people. Such negative moods, if they become the basis of the self, will drive out confidence and leave the self in a precarious state. Usually, then negative emotional labels are easier to recall than positive ones. Something with a negative emotional label can seem to stick firmly and we can reimagine the event over and over, bringing to mind the same emotion. In contrast, we can remember something positive, but it becomes fuzzy and vague over time; it habituates. We may remember what made us feel positive but the emotional label is faintly felt. The only way to get that feeling again is to actually repeat the experience in paramount reality.

Yet, we can seek that a positive mood state is elongated in a similar way to negative emotions. Applying the elongation model of mood to confidence means bringing something good into the self and then trying to elongate it, to keep it in the self. Any elongation, by definition, creates a trajectory, a line into the past of the self as a memory. Thus, if we create the category of the self based upon an elongated confidence, we are doing so with a time-based trajectory. The elongation of good suggests that the original happiness we felt when that good first came into the self can be elongated by storing it as a memory and then returning to it in the imagination to experience that feeling at will. Such an elongation of positive mood would then drive out the other preoccupations we are having. This suggests in turn that in order to feel confident in this way we should avoid elongating negative emotion, which could be the very definition of inversion but elongate the good for as long as possible. To be feasible we would need to be able to overcome habituation, which normally happens in relation to good. One possible example of a positive emotion being elongated is love. I may feel a reflex response of attraction to somebody but the experience of love that follows on from that can be seen as a mood. Although love is held by many to be a positive emotional experience, we have previously questioned this positivity. Love leaves us vulnerable, relying on attaching the self to other. If something then acts to undermine what we are attached to then this can become painful. In addition, the reason as to why love elongates can be seen as negative. The basis of the elongation of love is preoccupation, which is based on the fear of loss of our beloved or not properly integrating the other. It also potentially takes us away from being able to deal with paramount reality and living in the moment. Another alternative positive scenario is when we experience relief. Here, I may move from a very bad situation such as a diagnosis of cancer, being a drug addict or having no money, which is then overcome. Thus, the overcoming of a perceived negative circumstance prolongs the positive feeling of relief and consequent appreciation of life. Extended relief is brought about through experiencing intense negativity and again this probably isn't the best way to elongate positivity. In an elongation of mood what is elongated is not the emotion directly but that the emotion becomes attached to something that we then for some reason don't readily become habituated.

The only way habituation normally doesn't happen in relation to positive emotion is because we are preoccupied through either the fear of losing what is good or through seeing good we feel we need and not being able to bring it into the self. Such preoccupations are experienced as worry and are emotionally negative. Instead, what could appear desirable would be a way of overcoming the habituation of good that did not involve these processes. If this were feasible, what we would be left with is deriving confidence from something within our imaginary past. Good would be in the past and we could recreate that pleasant memory as if it were now a reminiscence. One way we can attempt to delay habituation of good things is through thankfulness. Thankfulness is not used here in the same way as appreciation. Appreciation refers to something we recognise as good but make no attempt to bring this into the self and control. We appreciate it at the time we interact with it and see it as good but then move on as a nomad. To use appreciation effectively we must be able to see as much in other as good as possible. This is different to thankfulness. Thankfulness is where we do bring good into the self and, through bringing the object idea to mind, try to reinforce how good it is and then delay its habituation. To elongate the emotion over time. To delay habituation using thankfulness, we use the count your blessings approach to life. Rather than always be searching for the next new good, we become thankful for the good we already possess. Such thankfulness appears a positive way of dealing with habituation and slowing down the habituation of what is good. Yet, what such thankfulness relies upon is the same techniques as outlined previously, imagining life before we had the good or what it would be like without the good. We are being grateful by using the fear of loss. Thus, the thankfulness is actually based upon the same imaginative techniques of pain. It therefore is negative and a clinging to the past. Besides, this, though, sounds more like an escape from the here and now, rather than allowing us confidently to face the future.

We could, though, look at this elongation in a different way. Rather than as a one-off event or object to keep hold of and escape to, instead we see the past as part of self-formation, deriving confidence from what we have successfully done. By creating a positive story for the self this can then drive out negative elongations and preoccupations. To do this we create a story that strings together our accomplishments. We often feel an accomplishment is what has worked well for the self before and we have been applauded for. That applause will often be in comparison with peers we feel in competition with. In such cases, the source of our confidence is based upon doing better than others. We often predict the future on the basis of the past and believe what has worked for us in the past will work again in the future. Our accomplishments can then be projected into the future as what we are next trying to achieve. This is the self as an elongated linear trajectory, the progression. This is opposed to the truncated trajectory that exists in paramount reality where we just focus on the next few steps ahead. Such ideas are introduced here as a common way by which we feel confident but as they involve the self as trajectory it is properly the subject of the next chapter. Yet, by creating a story, if things don't bolster the narrative we have, it will be seen as bad and consequently we risk inversion. Alternatively, we need to constantly rewrite our story but over time that devalues any narrative we once had. A life story as our means of confidence can lead to a tale which becomes little more than self propaganda. As stated, confidence should enable the self to feel enlivened, such that it can enter paramount reality positively but it should also provide resilience to be able to protect the self from the bad that it will necessarily have to manage when it is there. In order to feel confident the self must found itself upon something, but the conventional life story, projected to others in the form of identity, can easily be undermined and this can prompt a search for other ways to feel confident.

We could bypass the issues of elongation and habituation if we ensure a ready supply of good. It then doesn't much matter that good will degrade if new good is available. It is possible to see positive mood not as a direct elongation of positive emotion but as a trigger point in memory. We create a store of things we feel we like, that have created happiness in the past in our memory. Yet, we cannot directly go back to these memories to get happiness. This could be seen as a bad thing anyway as it would create a sanctuary where we would avoid paramount reality and remove us from living in the moment. To base confidence upon our own supply of good in this way would mean we would never have any incentive to face paramount reality. We would instead isolate ourselves in a reverie of self-stimulated good. Instead, by having the faint echoes of happiness labels, we are incentivised to return into paramount reality to relive these experiences again and again. This isn't a problem provided there is a ready supply of good that we seek in order to fill up our bags of happiness. This in turn makes it more difficult to become preoccupied by bad. The good can be things we have or own or things we have done or know. For this to be successful, though, we would need to be able to identify something of which there is a reliable supply. If not we risk having wants, needs and goals inside the self which pull us towards other but with no means of assuaging them. We risk becoming dependent upon this supply of good in other for our confidence and need to do everything in order to protect the supply. If we lose the supply for any reason we are then left feeling bad and risk inversion. There is also an additional risk. We can still habituate to receiving the same new thing repeatedly. We can find that, although something brought us happiness in the past, we can do the same thing but if we do it too much or too often we can become as habituated to it as anything else.

There is another meaning to mood, though, as a disposition, a basic state of feeling. It has already been discussed that it is unlikely we can feel two opposite feelings at the same time. Yet, it is still possible to conceive of a basic underlying background feeling that is experienced when all other emotion and mood is stripped away. A mood state the self returns to and rests in when there is no other emotion is indicated and there is nothing else going on. It is possible we could have a basic feeling that is positive and that all we have to do is strip away all the concerns, the fears, the bad memories to reach it. It would have to be a very mild and barely discernible feeling that would only be detectable in mental silence. Otherwise the feeling would interfere with the other emotions we use to detect good and bad. It would be nice if we could momentarily strip all away, including our memories and sit awhile in faint joy. That this experience would be open to us at any time we could silence our mind from its constant chatter. We could, though, just as easily find when we do this that we are left with ennui, dread or boredom. The issue with such a basic feeling is that, whatever we find, there will be nothing we can do about it. This is our basic feeling that we have that arises spontaneously within us. It was probably placed there by our genetic inheritance or our upbringing. If it is not subject to anything we can change, we can use it if it is positive but, if it is negative, all we can do is disguise it and cover it up with more positive emotions. Such an interpretation of disposition is unhelpful due to the lack of control we have over it.

There is, though, another way we can reach a disposition, which is more open to self control. This is disposition as our basic assumptions about the self and the world. The disposition results from the feeling we have towards the world, and the place of the self within it. Confidence can then be brought about by having a positive view of self in paramount reality. Of particular concern are our assumptions about good and bad. We need a means by which we can reliably detect good and bad in other and predict where it is and when it will arrive. We also, though, require a method of having as much good in the self as possible and keeping away bad. This subject was also broached in the previous discussions on value good and how we can conceive of the self–other boundary and the good–bad boundary. These are our assumptions about paramount reality and will be our starting point when we enter this reality. The preferred scenario is to maximise good in both other and self. Although confidence comes when we feel good about the self, if this comes at the expense of other, we can feel good about who we are but extremely bad when we enter paramount reality, leading either to the barricaded self or the expanding self. This leads to high emotional instability and possible inversion. If we can feel as good as possible both about the self and the paramount reality we are facing and our ability to handle it, we will feel confident.

CREATING THE SPATIAL SELF FROM OBJECT PROPERTY

In considering our assumptions about how we can construct a spatial self, the obvious starting point is how we are spatially present. This is through the body we have. In considering truth, it was posited that self and other were creations of mind. This gave little consideration of body. Mind and self can loom so importantly in philosophy, it is as if we float about in the world as ghostly, disembodied entities. The body can be considered an afterthought, or even the seat of what is bad and evil. The source of our passions and temptations. If we have a barricaded self, self is good and other is bad. If we are led towards desire and the need for pleasures from other, this can be seen as coming from bodily appetites. The body, thus, can come close to being part of other as potentially polluted. In these ways the body can appear the opposite of self and mind, not really integral to who we are. So much so that, for instance, in some schools of Hinduism, the body is of no consequence and should be disposed of as quickly as possible after death, so the self can go on into its next life. The good self is often allied with what is divine and seen as soul and is eternal. Body occupies a liminal space, which is physical, of the world and of other but is also self. It is how we occupy space and present ourselves to the world. More than this, it was suggested that the self–other was the boundary that ought to demarcate control. If we include the body within the self, then the body can often seem beyond control. The body is essential for us to interact with other and present ourselves but the body can be weak. When it goes wrong or is diseased it demonstrates the very fragility and illusion of that control. The body can do things we don't want it to do. This can demonstrate its separateness from the self and that it more properly sits within other. The alternative is to see body as integral to self. As all aspects of the same substance. Mind is how we experience our essential subjective experience; self is what we construct in order to exist within paramount reality; body is our essential vehicle within paramount reality and gives us the ability to interact and how we present the self to others. It is the embodiment of mind and self. As such, rather than being bad, it is important that body is seen as integrally good. If the body is our vehicle, it becomes essential we look after it and respect it. The body is both very strong, can enable us to do amazing things, but also very weak and fragile, is subject to decay and decrepitude. If we don't exercise it, feed it the wrong things and fail to rest it, to wash and tend it, it can fall into disrepair. Even if we do all those things, it will not go on forever. It is subject to disease, illness and mortality.

If we are looking at the self being constructed spatially, we can build it from the things around us, from object property. The first and primary property of the self could then appear to be the body. The body, though, is not property as it can be readily understood. Property is any good that can be tradable and be brought into the ambit of the self and which is amenable to control, for the time that it is being traded. It comes in two forms. Object property has physical presence detected through our senses. It is the stuff we can touch, handle and feel. Intangible property can't be given such a physical presence, although it can still be traded and brought into the self. We cannot, though, trade the body; the body is our self, our vehicle, it is intrinsic to who we are and at times doesn't appear readily controllable. Another aspect of control is the ability to dispose of something when we want to. That we can choose to transfer something out of the self when we no longer want or need it. We cannot do this with the body without also destroying the self. What we can do, though, is present our bodies in various ways that others can then relate to. Yet it is also impossible to ignore that for centuries we have been trying to commodify the body and turn it into property, to disregard its specialness. Others can use our body in ways that are useful to them. We can alter the body, decorate it, we can dress it up to impress to show off, to attract people to us or to repel them away. These alterations, including various transplantations and cosmetic surgery which can have profound alterations, don't alter the fact that the self, the mind and the body are intrinsically entwined. To do well for the mind and the self will mean doing right by the body, which means looking after it not to impress or gain favour from the other or to live well within them but to do right by the self and the mind.

Moving from the way we are spatially present, the body, other can be seen as the space existing all around us. From this we then have to carve out the self and give it existence from its surroundings. If the self is primarily spatial it will be formed out of everything around it, the objects we see, the places about us, the people we meet. To do this we need to demarcate our territory. We will need to decide what the self lays claim to and what we safely leave as other. Self then becomes a matter of assertion against other. In spatially situating the self, there is always a risk of the self sinking back into the space from which it has been carved. Extending control into other and determining what is mine become important themes in any spatially situated self. We want to have a store of good things that differentiate the self from other and enable us to survive. The self will become defined by those possessions, the stuff it accumulates. The self will bring things into its territory that are good and then maybe discard those things again when they are no longer of use. We have already said in category we construct two further boundaries. The firmament links the self to bigger concepts than it, thus, if we are constructing a spatial understanding of the self, one possibility is to link ourselves to something bigger than the self. Alternatively, the core boundary defines what the self is made up from. If we are concerned with what from other we are forming the self, this boundary will be our main concern. The core is the seemingly obvious place to start if we want to define the self and see what is essential to it. It is what makes up the self and makes us unique.

We can conceive of what makes up the core of the self as like a bag into which we try to put as much good as possible. The form of happiness called pleasure is the measure of the good going into the bag. The effects of pleasure, though, wear off over time through habituation. This is as if the bag we are putting our good things into has a hole in it. As much as we put good into the bag it will fall out again. If we are constantly putting good things into the self and have a seemingly endless supply, we can be unconcerned about what is in our bag at any time. We are solely concerned with the next thing we need to put into our bag. If, however, we are finding things to put into our bag are scarce, we may find the core of the self is not the positive source of value it should be. We can also end up putting into our bag bad things that we can't seem to get rid of so easily. Inversion has been previously discussed and is where the self is no longer a source of good and this then skews how we value other and what is around us. This happens because something seen as bad has been placed in the bag of the self and we can't easily remove it from our preoccupations. Constructing the self in this way will lead to the preoccupations that were described previously. We become preoccupied about what is coming into our bag, keeping hold of good and not losing it or getting bad and having to deal with it. The bag becomes our preoccupations and the self becomes defined by this.

Confidence will become the measure of good in our bag. We will feel confident so long as we have developed reliable mechanisms to allow a regular supply of good to go into our bag and we don't lose that good too quickly. As long as our supply of good exceeds our losses and we don't accumulate bad that displaces any good, we will feel confident. Confidence becomes an accounting mechanism of the good we have at any point. In doing this, the ideal things that will be put in our bag will be good, give us pleasure, do not degrade easily and remain good for as long as possible, giving us stable confidence. It has previously been said our universe of mind can be divided between self and other. In a spatially defined self, everything that makes up the self must at some point have come from other and been transformed into self. Other, though, can be further subdivided. The three categories of other will be demarcated as property, specialness or mysteries. Of these, the easiest to construct a spatially defined self out of is the aforementioned property. As stated, property is any transactional commodity that can be subject to the control of the self for the time it is being traded and is seen as good and can be divided into objects and intangibles. By definition, we can bring property from other, across the self–other boundary, as a possession and make it mine, part of the self. We cannot do this with specialness or mysteries, which will be discussed below.

Object property can be further divided between consumables and tangibles. Consumables are object property that by definition is transformed or destroyed in order to be used by the self. Examples include food and drink and energy sources. Any happiness that comes from these forms of property is likely to be short-lived. Food provides pleasure but it dissolves quickly in the mouth. There will also often be a satiation point. Beyond this point the benefits will no longer accrue and we will begin to feel increasingly uncomfortable. Yet, many consumables we cannot live without; they are a necessity. It was previously discussed that the preferred way of structuring the self–other boundary was to have the maximum good on the side of the self and the maximum good on the side of other. It was acknowledged, though, that there must always be some good to be had from other from which pleasure was derived. Such consumables are examples of such pleasurable necessities. Pleasure always leads to a sense of dissatisfaction within the self until we could then incorporate the good within the self. We then experience happiness until we reach the satiation point. Such pleasures are destroyed by the act of consumption. This means we never suffer from the illusion of control. Yet, they have inherent dangers that need managing. One danger is over-consumption. In order to derive good from the pleasurable experience, we require more and more of it. In the case of food, this can lead to obesity and health problems. There is also the opposite danger, though, of under-appreciation. Such consumable property is often desired solely for its utility and its goodness rarely seen. Consumable experiences can easily become habituated to even while they remain in other, invisible and taken for granted. They hardly enter the imaginational ambit of the self before being transformed into waste. Yet, such consumables sustain life and, without them, we will be in trouble. If we are to maintain our interest in such consumables, what we often need is a way to make them appear continuously new and interesting. Thus, we begin to notice them more. For example, we could sustain our interest in food by trying lots of different sorts, become knowledgeable about how they are made, appreciate the skill involved in putting together a dish and how it is constructed with flavours and textures. Above all, though, we want to show to others we are knowledgeable about food and build a reputation. In this way we don't habituate to the experience of the consumable good. We transform the consumption of property into a skill and a role. Yet, this transforms our confidence from being based on the supply of a good to a reputation we hold within a social group for holding a skill. This also risks over-consumption and transforming consumable property into something else. Alternatively, we can maintain that the preferred relation to such consumables is a position of moderation. They are necessary to sustain life but there are dangers of over-consumption or under-appreciation. Rather than transforming the property into something else in order to be a more memorable good that can stay with us, we should practise appreciation, not ever seeing it as part of the self but something that comes from other. It was this appreciation that we previously discussed as the good that remains with other, where we can savour what we have available.

If consumable objects need to be destroyed in order to make them part of the self, it may appear there are other forms of property object that do not. These will be termed tangible object property. It is possible to view tangible object property as a more solid means to build the self and get confidence. Yet, within the mind, all objects tend to behave in a similar way. All objects will degrade over time, even those we attribute as more profoundly part of the self. Physically, everything degrades over time with use. For example, if I buy a house, my living in it does not destroy it, but it will suffer wear and tear over time. Yet, it is not the loss of lustre that is perhaps the most emotionally problematic with regard to objects. In addition to the physical destruction or erosion of objects, tangibles will degrade emotionally over time, through the previously discussed habituation. As stated, when we first see an object we desire, it becomes for us the embodiment of good which exists outside the self. Excitement is our emotional detector of this experience. Yet, we will feel increasingly uneasy and dissatisfied unless we can successfully bring the object within the ambit of the self. Within modern capitalist society this is often done through payment to the legitimate seller. Any experience of happiness gained, however, often dissipates quickly as it habituates. We do up our homes not only to make good the wear and tear upon them but to make them as new again and can then feel again the initial pangs of excitement when we first got the home. Even though we may not feel the initial happiness this does not mean we are not attached to an object. Thus, building any confidence from tangible objects means we constantly need to renew them. We need a constant supply of what is good to replace that which we habituate to. Thus, although the timescales may be different along with what happens physically, the emotional effects of habituation are the same for both consumable and tangible object property. Yet, the danger with tangible object property is we can become attached to it as part of who we are. We no longer feel happiness at the object but, should we lose the object or it becomes threatened, we feel pain. It thus becomes an emotional liability and possibly a source of preoccupation. This means there will be a constant risk of loss and feeling grief.

Tangible object property also tends to extend control beyond the self–other boundary. The boundary descriptors of controlled and uncontrolled were previously introduced. When discussed previously, it was concluded that control is a useful definer of the self but should not be used to value. Part of the definition of property is that the self will need to be able to control any objects it wants to accumulate into its bag. Once in the bag, the self will try to keep tangible object property there for as long as possible. Control then becomes an important theme around tangible object property. Tangible object property becomes any good that the self can control for itself. The good becomes what we can control in our environs and the bad is what we can't. Tangible object property, by definition, must be considered a good otherwise it would not want to bring it into the self in the first place. Such a construction of the self would mean confidence results from the control of such property. As stated, we can either try to locate such property that elongates in the self or find a ready supply of property. As object property is good, controlled and uncontrolled will come to define what is good through such property. Thus, there is the risk that ,if we define the self in this way, what is good becomes what is controlled through being property. What is bad is anything that is not controlled through being property of the self. Thus, controlled and uncontrolled become allied with value, which as discussed previously is problematic. The self will become defined by the space that is physically controlled as its property. The self–other boundary will be the means by which that space will be defined. So, when in paramount reality we primarily become concerned as to what we control, and control is what is good. Any potential loss of control becomes a threat to the self and a source of preoccupation. That loss of control is threatened because we no longer control property or because we cannot gain control of things from other. Thus, confidence will derive from the feeling of control that we have over tangible object property. Yet, if confidence comes from control, due to the effects of habituation we will always need to ensure a constant supply of property in order to remain confident. Thus, by defining the self through property, the boundary descriptors controlled and uncontrolled will gain in prominence and will be allied to value. So long as we are primarily concerned with getting more control, we will constantly feel dissatisfied with the control we already have. This will force our gaze into other as we look for more things to get and cause us preoccupation. The self will never be in the position of total control that it seeks, causing unease within the self, letting in bad. Other will occupy an ambivalent place. It will predominantly be seen as a place lacking in control for the self but also the place where more control can be derived. As the self possesses what is good, yet that good is always degrading and under threat, we constantly require to identify more good. To engage with the other, in order to get more good from it.

Yet, tangible object property forces an even stronger relationship than just control. It is possible to see control as something that just exists in the here and now. In the case of consumable object property this doesn't matter much. It is destroyed in the act of consumption, therefore we lose control as soon as we gain it. Tangible object property, however, gives the illusion that it continues as a usable good long after this point. This is the entire point of getting it in the first place. We can store it up and come back to it. If I buy a house, I expect this will be my house and that I can continue to live in it long after the initial purchase. Yet, if control is something that exists in the here and now, whilst I am away from my house, if somebody else moves in then they control it. The only way to get my house back, when here and now control is the sole determining factor of boundaries, would be to use force. If ownership of tangible property were determined through control in the here and now, might becomes right. It would therefore seem that with ideas of control, particularly when applied to tangible property, we arrive at a brutish and unattractive social order. In this situation, however, there are limits placed upon the self as only a certain amount of tangible objects can be controlled or held at any point in time, that which we can carry with us. We become a nomad living in the here and now. Thus, a differentiation needs to be made of controlled and uncontrolled in the here and now and when it applies across time.

To get to a point where the house can continue to be part of me we must have some concept of ownership over time which is mutually acknowledged and the ability to then trade that ownership. This requires a concept which will be termed 'mine' and 'not mine'. Mine or not mine is still about control of possessions and property but that control of property is not just about the here and now. Linguistically, in English 'mine' signifies far more than an object as property of the self. 'My' and 'mine' designate that all sorts of things are part of the self rather than being part of other. Anything that we can stick the word my in front of is a claim that the item is part of me. My eye means something different compared to my book or my home or my wife. Not all these things can be brought into the self by means of a simple trade. The object may be understood to be in that space as the result of years of learning, as having been born with it or as a result of forming an attachment bond. By attaching 'my' to something does not necessarily mean it is my property as described but it does mean it has significance as part of the self. I am marking it as a part of myself even though it doesn't always indicate property ownership. For example, the term 'my road' does not usually indicate I own it. The road may be owned by the council but it is my road not because I own it but because I live on it. There is an alternative marker I could use and that is signified by the word 'ours'. 'Ours' signifies a sharing of possession. More correctly in terms of ownership, the road should be termed 'our road'. In contrast to my, mine and our, there is a variety of linguistic terms in English to designate that an object is in the possession of other. Your and yours, thy or thine, his, hers, its or theirs can all be used in a variety of different contexts. The English language then gives us clues as to how our boundaries may be structured. Yet for all of this the term 'mine' is used in this more restricted sense here to mean the ability of the self to hold possession of an object over time. Mine in this context suggests that control means more than the immediate ability to use something or how something is destroyed. Having a sense of mine and not mine means we can extend control over time and we can begin to accumulate and store up extensions of self. Control becomes the ability to put into safe storage; that when we need something we know its location and can access it readily.

As long as there are communally guaranteed rules that we mutually respect each other's possessions then it becomes possible to leave possessions somewhere and trust that when I return they will still be mine. Confidence becomes dependent on the belief that the social guarantees of ownership can be enforced. Problems ensue, however, if people have mismatching boundary markers. If I have a sense of mine and come up to somebody who only has a sense of controlled and uncontrolled in the here and now, then if I leave something such as a house the person may feel a sense of entitlement to be able to occupy my house. If a sense of mine is thus to be guaranteed there will need to be regulations and sanctions in place to protect what is mine. In addition, once we have an idea of mine there will also have to be some idea of how mine can be passed from one person to another with a means of mutual agreement to transfer ownership. The idea of mine therefore necessitates both the idea of law and trade. Once the ability to control through more permanent possession has been introduced this allows for a larger and more permanent bag as our core of the self, keeping things over time. By having an idea of mine, we will extend the existence of the self over time, even if this is something we didn't intend. We form an elongated linear sense of the self extending back over history and memory through the object property we have accumulated. With the idea of mine, it also becomes possible to expand the self in space as well. If a house can be secure if we leave it, we could have two houses or more. We are no longer just where we are and what we possess at a point in time; we can put things in different locations and are able to come back to them. The self can move around in space, traversing to differently located self spaces.

Although the idea of mine means we can have multiple sites for the self and elongates it backwards in time, it is illusory because the problem of both physical and emotional erosion still remains. Thus, our core will be permanently shifting and having to renew itself. We will become attached to more and more things, all of which we could lose and will cause us pain. This may oil the wheels of consumer capitalism but means many houses in affluent countries are full of items that are not really needed and at an unsustainable cost on the overall environment. Ownership of property suggests a way of configuring the self spatially around the theme of control as a means of achieving confidence and getting good. Yet, what we have turned control into is something that will ultimately always escape us and means our confidence is precarious. If we then lose control, which is inevitable, this can then threaten the self. Control per se is not a bad thing, indeed without it we could not survive. The issue is trying to extend control into areas where it does not belong, primarily transforming other into object property, which can be controlled, transacted and put into storage where it is bound to habituate and recede from memory. This is not to deny that the world is not a better place for having laws and trade, but our confidence and the good of the self should not be dependent upon this.

Object property though is a necessity to survive. There is, though, a way of conceiving of property in relation to constructing the self which does not revolve around personal control. This is communal property, where an object is shared in its use and is never the exclusive single possession of anybody. Communal property behaves in a different way to private tangible property. The self cannot incorporate it into its bag and have the illusion of control. Instead, property must always be regarded as a loan, which must be given back at some point. We become custodians of the good for the time we have it and then we need to hand it on, so others can share it. When considering the value good, the best position was that the self was mostly good and so was other. Such an attitude towards property maximises this, as we no longer desire the good for the self and will try to keep hold of it. The main issue, though, with communal property is its scarcity. Thus, if we have a communally owned house, who decides who should live in it? The house would not be able to accommodate everybody and we thus have to ration numbers or length of stay, in which we potentially turn the house into a hotel. One way to ration communal property is through belonging to a group. If we are a member of the particular group which owns the property, we become entitled to use the property on a shared basis with everybody in the group. It would be the group that would then decide who lives in the house and for how long and what conditions are attached to any stay. In which case, the level of control that the self has over the house has diminished and must accede to the wishes of the group. It may not just be houses that could be the communal possession of the group. For example, if you belong to a particular religious group it is possible that certain objects acquire a shared revered status. If these sacred objects were to be ransacked and destroyed it would not be an individual who feels the pain but a whole group of people. Such group-owned objects can bind people together but also intensify any negative emotional experience. Objections have already been raised to groups as a means of identifying specialness due to this intensification and the exclusions entailed. In this example, communal property takes on an intensified meaning for the self as a result of the symbolic value it has for the group. Thus, the membership of any group destroys any emotional moderation that communally owned property has. It is, though, not necessary to have communally owned property through any group. We can regard all tangible property as a loan and not seek to found a core of the self upon it. We are custodians of everything we have. Although we may acquire it in the same way as if we are purchasing something, we do not regard it as property for the self. We will at some point have to give it back and we often never know when this point will be. We should just appreciate it whilst we have it. Thus, the two forms of object property, consumables and tangibles are both best left primarily as part of other, that the self merely borrows or destroys to survive, in order to give back. We are thus left with little in our bag, travelling light.

INTANGIBLE PROPERTY – IDEAS, EVENTS AND SKILLS

Property, though, may not just be conceived as physical objects. Intangible property is anything that we do not ascribe specialness to and can be transacted but does not have the appearance of a physical object. There will be three classes of intangible property– ideas, events and skills – considered here. In relation to property as ideas, everything is constructed out of categories and trajectories, so, from one viewpoint, all property is ideas, whether it is an apple or a house, an event or a skill. It exists as a sense impression in our mind. We have previously said that we construct other and self from within mind. If we remove the construction of self and other, we are left with being mind and everything will be a sense impression. Sense impressions though are not tradable. By definition, they are our subjective experience which must stay with us. Yet, when we enter paramount reality, we split self from other, we then need to be able to discern physical objects. We learn over time to construct a map of a world that has the quality of appearing as external to us and we attach immediacy through feelings to physical objects. Then we interact with and manipulate this world but our actions and choices are constrained by it. If we are unable to build up a reasonably functional model of other, we put ourselves at extreme danger. Paramount reality, though, can have such a hold, that being able to conceive of things as just mental impressions can be extremely difficult. We can, from the moment we wake up to when we go to sleep, seem to be engaging with paramount reality. If we aren't doing so directly, the mental flow of preoccupations and elongations will frequently keep us within its imaginative thrall. In paramount reality, ideas exist as the background model that make sense of what is happening. This was discussed in the chapter on truth. We may scarcely be aware of the ideas that enable us to predict how our interactions with other may transpire. If we are looking at confidence as a disposition, if we see the self and the world as basically good, then we will have access to confidence. Thus, ideas are crucial for confidence and we need to be able to reflect upon any models we may be using. Becoming aware of the beliefs and models we are using allows us to adapt and change our actions when in paramount reality and to have confidence.

These categories and algorithms can be highly specific such as how to find food, interact with strangers or change a light bulb. Yet, we are unlikely to see many of these useful ideas as crucial to the self. If I have an idea of how to change a light bulb, try it out and it fails, I might then look again at the algorithm. Yet, we can have familiar everyday algorithms that give us comfort. This may include sitting in a favourite armchair at a particular time or having a favourite food we want to eat. Perhaps it is style of communication, a catch phrase, or a hobby we do. These algorithms taken together can become habitual. The self can become the pattern of the algorithms we use frequently. If we cannot for some reason enact our familiar comforting algorithms, this can cause distress. They create a sanctuary in our memory we can return to. These algorithms, though, tend to be personal to us, we can suggest them to other people, but we don't necessarily want to trade them. They will have arrived as a good once upon a time into the self. We may well have long forgotten when, but we want others to take account of our habitual style and understand us. What we tend to want to trade are those larger sets of algorithms, that try to make sense of life as a whole. They stipulate how wider society should be constructed or how the self is situated. Much of the content of this book is examining the construction of these meta-algorithms.

They help define who we are and give instructions on how to construct a model of paramount reality. In doing so they determine what is good and bad for the self and how we should conceive of other. They include important philosophical, religious and political ideas, termed ideologies. These ideas are sticky, and readily adhere to form a core of the self. We will receive them through learning from others and they will spark some recognition within us: that they are good and make us happy. We may work in some ideas for ourselves. The new connections we make will also make us happy. We will then store this system of ideas within our memory. These meta-algorithms or ideologies will then become like the glasses through which we can see the world and make sense of it, to be brought to bear on our interpretations when we see the relevance. To discard an ideology can be much more of an enterprise than re-evaluating how to change a light bulb. It would mean re-evaluating our way of being in the world.

Thus, for all that ideologies are freely available and easy to adopt, they can adhere to the self very easily and be difficult to remove. It is possible to see these ideas as more easily making up who we are than object property. Meta-algorithms and ideologies come in all shapes and sizes. They allow us to firmly construct paramount reality and position the self–other boundary. In doing so, we are attempting to steer a middle course, avoiding delusional certainty and complete unknowing. Meta-algorithms and ideologies may construct other negatively and see this as a place to escape from. The former can be dangerous, as we need to engage with paramount reality. Otherwise, we can end up with either a barricaded self or an inverted self, or possibly both. Alternatively, other can be seen as a place we need to understand and manage as best we can. If ideologies do view paramount reality positively they can be simple. For example, where the purpose of the self is seen to be able to identify as much good as possible and bring it into the self. Sometimes, they may be complex. Ideologies can take a viewpoint on everything, such as how the self can best interact and define other. They may describe how others interact and are ordered on very large scales.

Meta-algorithms and ideologies are a necessity in order to create a consistent paramount reality. If we don't at least have a sketch of an ideology, then paramount reality risks becoming an alien place that we can't understand or structure. In doing so, though, there is a danger that ideology becomes the main firmament concept of the self. Objects, however they are conceived, relate primarily to the core boundary. They describe who we are and what goes into our bag. Intangible objects, though, particularly ideas, can not only relate to our core, but also give instructions as to how we should relate to other. They can turn the firmament boundary, which otherwise looks towards mind, into looking towards something else. In the case of meta-algorithms, or ideologies, this will depend upon the ideology. The self–other boundary, when seen spatially, is like a circle around the self and requires constant policing in order to moderate emotion. If the firmament also looks towards other, this will extend the positioning of other to surrounding the self from above as well. This potentially makes the boundary very long. Further, if the self becomes defined by the ideas that it possesses to explain the world, the self can become its ideology. Rather than being glasses through which we can see the world, the glasses themselves become who we are. That can obscure the previously defined firmament concept, mind from view. We get stuck in the model we create for the self and can no longer see mind. To experience mind directly means breaking down concepts into sense impressions and disconnecting them from their original emotional hue. Instead of mind surrounding self or other we become enveloped in whatever ideology we have become.

Yet, ideologies need not become self nor need they obscure mind from view. Some ideologies are provisional and open, such as that connected with a scientific outlook on life. They accept that knowledge is highly unstable and is constantly evolving depending on evidence. If this is accepted, paramount reality needs to be open and adaptable as a model we construct for ourselves. Other ideologies do not accept this and seek to impose rigid explanations upon paramount reality. Paramount reality becomes something given and that we need to accept, because others of greater authority have determined this for us. If this model isn't working for us it is not because the model is wrong but that we are not using it correctly. The former ideologies are highly adaptable but the latter ideologies are hard and rigid. By building barriers to other we can hope to protect the good of the self and its confidence, but in doing so we often undermine the good in other.

We can keep ideas as private to the self. Ideologies could be seen as solely a means of defining paramount reality. We take in helpful ideas and discard unhelpful ones and leave it at that. Yet, many ideologies call for more than this. We may seek to inculcate our beliefs in others. We may do so to help others engage with paramount reality or rescue them from the bad of other. This results in education and learning. If people share the same model of paramount reality, this can make it easier to negotiate and understand. Ideologies are property to the extent as a system of thought; they are seen as good, can be incorporated within the self and can be exchanged from one person to another. Transaction of ideologies is made through discussion and argument and can be transmitted to the susceptible through black arts of persuasion, propaganda and advertising. The self in category exists spatially. If the self defines itself in relation to objects, this will create the self spatially. Ideas as property, though, do not necessarily situate the self spatially. It very much depends on the nature of the ideology as to how the self is then conceived. If the self is conceived as primarily being made up as object property, then this will lead to a spatial concept of the self. The self can also be situated in social space. If we are concerned to spread any ideology we have socially, how that social space is conceived becomes imperative. This will be discussed in greater detail below but social space provides an opportunity to spread ideas we may have.

Giving away our ideas is potentially opportunity another means for the self to feel happy. As stated, we can regard ideas as part of the self. Others accepting our ideas can give rise to feeling good about the self as it indicates that others are accepting of who we are. Thus, we are enabled to have another supply of good for the self. The acceptability of ideas will then much depend on the reputation of the self and how we are situated in social space. What we will often be concerned with will be sharing our accepted ideology as widely amongst others as possible. As long as we are then concerned with who accepts our ideas, this will lead to group formation, those that accept our way of seeing the world and those that don't. How those groups are then treated will very much depend on the ideology we have adopted but given the risks highlighted of dividing others into groups this could be problematic. The social distribution of any given ideology is important for another reason. To be meaningful, many ideologies need others to take up the ideas espoused and enact them. For ideologies can often only have meaning if they bring forward actions in the attempt to change paramount reality. It is often best to try to change paramount reality through group action with those whom I share my beliefs. Often, the only way of making ideologies meaningful is to persuade others of their validity so they can be communally acted out. This could be through the membership of a political party or participating in group rituals. This will mean not only group formation but that the groups are formed with ideas at their core. Yet, we can never really be sure of the beliefs of those with whom an ideology has been transmitted. In addition, much conflict and war has been underscored by differences in ideology. Dearly held beliefs can attract controversy and the ire of those who do not accept their validity. In the worst-case scenarios where groups acquire a super-personality, any deviation from the group ideas can be dangerous for the self. Where uniformity of thought is required it may be necessary to try to keep ideas and beliefs private and hidden. It is, though, a difficult position for a person to have as their core a deeply held ideology they could not express.

Ideologies as property behave in radically different ways to object property. Whereas it is difficult to share object property, unless we take the use in turns, get a duplicate or somehow split it, ideas can be infinitely replicable and can be shared exponentially. This makes anything that is exchanged as ideas potentially highly equitable and sharable. It costs us nothing to adopt an idea. People may try to commodify ideas and turn them into objects so they can get a living through selling their ideas. If we can prove an idea originated with us, it may then be possible to patent or copyright it. This can turn the idea into a form of property that can be commodified, as in a book which is object property or an event as in a lecture. Yet, ideas in themselves can be freely exchanged. It means ideas are readily accessible to anybody who is able to understand and accept them. So, unlike constructing a core of the self from object property, which can be exclusive to those that can afford it, ideas are much more available. It also makes them easy to pass around. So, as well as accepting ideas, we can come up with ideas and then pass them to others. This turns an idea into something similar to a virus that can be passed easily between people. What affects whether they are caught is how they fit with other ideas that have been previously adopted and whether they make sense to the person. This can be influenced by those who are able to package ideas in an attractive, easily understood manner. As stated, though, once adopted, ideas, particularly ideologies, can be highly resilient and are relatively difficult to expunge if the self is determined to keep them. If I become my home this can be torn down but if I become a lover of peace this cannot so easily be erased.

For all that ideas behave differently to property they are still a potential good in exactly the same way as any object is a good. Thus, by getting an idea from other, we are potentially getting a good. As this good generally costs us little to acquire, it often makes ideas a much more ready supply of good than object property. As ideas are freely available they are potentially an inexhaustible supply of the good so long as we are open to them, they appear fresh, different and expand our horizons. Ideas gained from other can then be taken apart and combined by the self in all sorts of different, unique ways. It becomes possible also for the self to manufacture its own ideas, and thus its own good. Alternatively, we may try on an idea and find it doesn't work well for us. We may come across alternative ideas that we feel may explain things better and instead adopt them. This may also feel good. As stated, though, ideas can also be used to close off the self from other, to erect barriers to threats. To see other as bad and not a source of good. To be suspicious of ideas that do not fit our own views. In these circumstances, if our dearly held beliefs are then challenged we can feel this as an intense threat to the self. Thus, there is still a risk that these ideas can cause pain to the self as much as ideas can cause happiness. Ideas are also subject to habituation in the same way as any physical object. A new idea can appear good and exciting; we seek to understand it and we incorporate it into our outlook. We can find it helps us determine good from bad and that it works for us. We then file it in our memory, where it sits until it is useful for interpretation in the future. It will then stop feeling so good, unless we can gain or manufacture some new ideas that link to it. Either way, the ideas we ultimately adopt will tend to recede from immediate view and sit in the background of awareness over time. So, as a way of gaining good for the self, they will only work for a time before receding from view. This doesn't mean they have gone; their main use becomes making sense of paramount reality and the assumptions they bring to bear upon it.

By assuming that self and other are basically good is an important way to form confidence that is difficult to expunge. Thus, in order to have a functional concept of paramount reality, we need to have some meta-algorithmic ideas. These ideas can bring us happiness and confidence. Yet, they can also close us off to other, require the self to depend for its well-being on successful evangelism of those ideas and carve the world into those like me and those who are not like me. It very much depends on the nature of the meta-algorithms we adopt.

Another example of intangible property is events. Events are occasions of heightened emotional significance, both good and bad. This can cover all sorts of occurrences that are viewed either as extremely good or extremely bad for the self. Due to their heightened emotional significance, events can result in memory formation. This is because strong emotions become attached to the event. These act as labels in our mind and makes something easier to recall, leading to delayed habituation and preoccupation. It is easier to recall negative emotional labels than positive ones and thus usually delayed habituation and preoccupation will more likely result from negative events rather than positive ones. Although positive labels have some effect, they are not usually as emotionally significant as negative labels. Hence previous discussions on the issue. The attempt to then avoid such negative events in the future can result in learning and consequent adjustments of behaviour. One reason we experience heightened emotions is because we are being judged at a point in time. These are times of heightened social significance, where we find ourselves on stage as a performer with an audience judging us. This scenario has been discussed previously in relation to the emotion of respect. As long as we give an audience the power to judge us, these situations will become events. It is these events of social significance that can mean events become primarily about the organisation of our social space. This will be discussed in more detail below. Not all events, though, will be times of audience judgement and events are not necessarily spatially organised.

What makes something an event is because it has been stored along with significant emotion in memory. This can include those episodes of heightened social significance when we are judged by others but also anything where heightened emotions have been attached as labels. It may include life-changing things such as the birth or death of a relative or a significant way we choose to spend our time away from the mundane or routine. It can include birthdays, weddings, moves of jobs, break-ups, accidents, illness or injury, holidays, exams, reading about important ideas, a chance meeting, a rare occurrence. Only some of these things will necessarily involve an audience judgement. One way we can keep hold of positive events for longer is by stringing events together in the form of a narrative. Events become the building blocks by which we construct our life story, the self as an elongated linear narrative. Here, we can extend a life story over time, made up of these events as significant points in our life. In doing so, we can hope to offset negative events by keeping hold of more positive ones. They can include the beginning of something, or the development or progress towards a cherished goal and will tell the story of how the self has been successful. In part, we can do this in order to delay the processes of habituation of positive occurrences. It then becomes easier to keep positive events alive within the memory. Thus, although many negative events are easier to remember, they will often be edited out of such an elongated linear trajectory or become part of the story of how the self successfully overcame adversity. If we include too many negative events in our story and it becomes one of tragedy and hard luck, the self will be turned negative. Although traversing a negative event can give resilience, it can also threaten the self. Confidence, how we get and keep good in the self, can then come to depend upon how we manage to construct such an elongated linear narrative. Such a means of storage of events is related to a self, constructed temporally and not spatially. This view of events will be looked at in greater detail in the next chapter.

Yet, we can store events spatially. If we have constructed the self primarily as a category, we can store memories around our landscape and space. Thus, the space we inhabit also acts as the repository for our memories. So, rather than necessarily sequencing them in time through a story, the landscape becomes full of trigger points for events that may have happened to us. If memory of events is no longer sequenced into a story it will no longer necessarily be time-related. The place we went to school will be next to the place we went for our first job. Where we had our first kiss will be near the place we were mugged. It no longer matters the sequence these happened in. Some of these trigger points may be positive and thus the landscape will be a place we can go about, to evoke positive feelings. Others may be negative. We interact with the landscape to find our memory. Some of those memories we may want to bring back and others we may want to forget and avoid. Yet, the landscape may be only one aspect of space that functions as this repository of memory. We may also find it from a smell, a music track or a photograph. Thus, the objects we accumulate can perform the same function as the landscape in allowing us contact to previous events, which may or may not also be linked into a story. We can build a home from the memories we have accumulated.

An event will always involve something from other, whether it is an illness, audience appreciation or a social gathering. Some events are about happenstance and we have little control over them and can merely control our reactions. Other events we choose to do. Yet, not everything that is classed as an event is property. In order for an event to be classed as property it must be seen as a good and be transactionable: incorporated into the self deliberately from other. This rules out all negative occurrences and anything that occurs freely and by happenstance, over which we have little deliberate control. If the event is beyond our control then it is not deliberate; it will involve another class of items which will be termed mysteries and these will be discussed below. When an event is property, what we are trying to do is buy memories. We have a lavish wedding to create an emotional impact so it can be stored in our memory as well as those who share the event, in the hope it can be indelibly stored. We go on exotic holidays to do the same. We may attend a lecture of a person whose ideas are important to us, or go to a concert of our favourite musician. We may go to a cup final of the team we support. All in an attempt to create positive labelled emotions to come back to. Such events are turned into transactions by restricting entry to those who have bought the necessary pass or have an invitation. Thus, we must buy a ticket for a concert, a seat in a seminar or a theatre. The whole event can be commodified through the purchase of a wedding package, throwing a big party or buying a funeral. Yet, such event property risks collapsing into something very similar to consumable property. Much like the apple, the performance, the lecture or the holiday are destroyed by their consumption as property. They are doomed to end and can be barely remembered in years to come. Events have been made easier to possess, store and trade through the use of electronic and digital technology. Music and videos can be stored and replayed. This turns one-off occasions into tangible objects. Yet, we will still habituate to the photos and music recordings; they can appear faint signposts of where we have been. The music track that once meant so much excitement now takes us to a barely remembered time. Faint echoes of a self long forgotten but still haunting us. However we store them in memory, whether as a story or as mementos kept in our landscape, events risk keeping us trapped in the past, not looking out to the future and engaged with paramount reality. The future becomes a space to collect precious memories which over time look jaded and irrelevant. Hence, we can regard the future as hostile. The issues with keeping events in sequence will be examined more fully in the next chapter, but spatial memories are only as good as the space around us. If we rely on space to keep our memories alive, then space acts as our library of who we are. If we then lose our space we lose our past, whether this is changes in our landscape or losing associated objects. This makes spatial storage vulnerable along with our confidence.

The final intangible to be examined here is skill, which are algorithms of practised actions. Skills have links with the other intangibles discussed so far. The performance in front of an audience that is the feature of many events is frequently underpinned by the demonstration of skill. Ideas and beliefs are a set of instructions for how to achieve a defined outcome; a skill is the practical working out of that belief. Skills are usually founded on ingrained talent but then have to be built up through years of practice, doing the same thing repeatedly. From the feedback we get, we then constantly refine the skill in order to improve or modify it. Feedback, therefore, is essential to developing any skill. The difficulty in obtaining and perfecting a skill can make it all the more worthwhile and may be something others greatly admire. Having an ability to play sport well, to speak many languages, to be a great inventor or writer are things that can be highly prized gifts. As much as they may be very rewarding, skills will, however, often be interspersed with long periods of drudgery. Yet, having built up a skill, it can easily degrade over time. Skills need to be practised in order to maintain them. Repetition is what maintains mental links, and the physical memories of where to place and use muscles.

In order to maintain motivation to maintain skills we often need goals or targets. It is where we are in relation to these targets or goals that provides the necessary feedback through which we improve the execution of any skill. Skills without the direction of goals or targets can become repetitive behaviour. One definition of ritual can be repetitive behaviour without an overall aim. Ritual is an act taken from a religious paradigm, where we are appeasing or entering the world of the gods. If we then dispense with gods and their world, ritual can become a meaningless idea and the very definition of pointless action. People can fill their life with such rituals in order to keep order in an otherwise unpredictable world. We keep doing the same thing over and over because it gives us reassurance. This reassurance in effect becomes the target or goal. Yet, it is an act of magical thinking. For doing anything over and over can give the illusion we have more control than we do. Instead we need to learn to live with the limited control we do have. This will give more resilience. Skills need more of a focus than just reassurance. Usually, in order to persist with building up skills there needs to be an outcome that captures the imagination and serves as a constant motivator. That outcome will often be the imagined applause of peers, significant others, or the roar of the crowd. We return to the metaphor of performer and audience that has been used so frequently previously. The skill is demonstrated in front of others and judged. If we have performed the skill well we will be rewarded by approval but if not we can be subjected to criticism and derision.

Subjecting a performance to the judgement of an audience turns the skill into a role. Like other intangibles examined, skill in itself is not necessarily spatial. Indeed, as something that has to be built up over time and practised in repetition, it is much more related to time which is repeated over and over, a trajectory oscillation. Yet, like all the other intangibles, skill can relate to space, depending on how it is conceived. By conceiving it as a role, skill inhabits social space. Not only do we imagine we receive the applause of the audience but we imagine the self transformed into a perfect possessor of the skills we are seeking to acquire and that this is socially acknowledged. We then can inhabit social space as having something seen as valuable to others, who judge us positively. Role can become who we are or can become. Role also becomes how skills become traded and thus turned into property. When providing a service we do not do so through our specialness. Specialness cannot by definition be traded. Role moves us away from seeing a whole person. Instead, the person becomes defined by their special skills. It then becomes those skills which become tradable. The emotional context is altered from one of empathy to one of respect. By turning skills into tradable commodities, audience appreciation can be shown by the financial payment that results from the performance. An audience demonstrates satisfaction by not only giving money, but also if that person is asked to perform the role again. Roles can be monetised through employment and membership of particular trade bodies which act to guarantee standards. Admission to these trade bodies is often through the completion of a course of education or apprenticeship. Having got these qualifications it then makes it easier to trade as somebody possessing a skill.

Role then becomes the way skills can be packaged in order to be traded and become property. The self can have two possible relationships with role. It can either employ somebody to perform a role, or the self can be the one performing the role. In the former, the relationship to other becomes one of property. Thus specialness is reduced and the other becomes somebody to be judged around their performance. It enables us to evaluate other, either positively or negatively. To do so moves us away from specialness, which should be the primary way we should relate to other. We are unlikely, though, to form the core of the self from such a perfunctory property relationship as we ourselves do not own the skill and therefore do not control it. The other possesses the skill. Alternatively, the self can be seen as performing a role. The role can become the self. In becoming a role, this can also threaten the self. It places the self at constant risk from audience judgement. Roles constantly need to be demonstrated. Repetition and practice, although they help, are no guarantee that we can maintain a role. Even with practice we can be judged against others to have performed poorly. Particularly if our skill depends on the demonstration of physical or mental prowess, as this will inevitably decline with age as our body declines. Although, as long as we can perform a role which provides adequate income, arguably this is enough, until someone removes our job.

Alternatively, we can try to develop skill without the goal of needing the approval of an audience or the need to become something in the future. The self always needs to develop skills. Without them we would be unable to function in paramount reality. We also need to be able to trade those skills, but we don't need to incorporate roles into the self as our core, and place the self at risk. We can acquire certain skills, they can help us for a time, but if we no longer find them useful we discard them and use other skills. They don't need to define who we are. This way the self doesn't put itself at stake through the fickle judgements of others or allow itself to become identical with a single role. Yet, to develop skills, we need feedback but do not need the imagined applause or approval of others for this. Instead, the self will have to be an accurate judge of its own performance. We still need to have something to aim for. In the next chapter a differentiation is made between targets and goals. Goals set something up in the future for the self to become. In this case a possessor of a particular skill. This creates dissatisfaction with the present in order to strive for a better future and suggests we can control that future by sheer effort. Not that we shouldn't work hard but it shouldn't be at the expense of the present. So, rather than the goal of a future self which has a role at its centre, displacing specialness, we replace this with a target to aim for. Something that won't put the self at stake if we don't achieve what we set out to. Skills often have something that is measurable about them, whether it is a time we run, the time we spend painting, or the number of loaves that we bake. We can often measure a skill not by the judgement of others but on how we have done previously, in the hope of improving or at least maintaining our achievements. In doing this we avoid skill becoming a role, but we still will need things from other and we still give to other. Yet, we maintain specialness throughout. We also need education and teaching in order to learn a skill and we can also provide education to others who are learning any skill. Besides, we never truly acquire a skill fully. Targets suggest we never get to the point of perfection and there will always be things we can improve on and learn. It is something we need to continually practise in order to maintain. Therefore, we cannot incorporate skill into the self as something achieved. Thus, skill doesn't become our core as such and it doesn't habituate. Skill becomes a directed habit of practised repeated actions. It does, though, place emphasis upon the target of the skill in order to maintain interest in it and our ability to maintain repetition.

THE SELF IN SOCIAL SPACE

Apart from constructing itself from property, the self can create space in another way. This section is about the socially situated self. Rather than conceiving itself in a physical territory, the self can also situate itself in social space, according to how it believes it is viewed by others. We can conceive of social space as made up of groups of others or as networks of others or both. Groups have been previously discussed and represent the merger of the self within a greater whole, which can then be given super-personalities. If we draw a circle round the self in relation to objects, in relation to groups we can draw circles within the space of other. Those within the circle are part of the group. Those outside the circle are not. The self can then place itself in relation to those boundaries. If the self is inside any group it loses control of its boundaries and surrenders itself to something greater. The main reaction expected of those within any group is subservience to the greater super-personality of which the self is now a part. This has been discussed previously, seen as problematic and won't be discussed further here. Social space though can also be seen as being made up of lines of connection. We create lines to people we know.

The better we know somebody the greater the flow along those lines. If the self enters a group with the view of actively participating it is best viewed as a network. This is a boundaried network as it exists within a group with a super-personality. Here we keep the idea of encompassing circles round groups but within the circle we also have an idea of lines of connection to others. The idea of a network, though, can also be used apart from the idea of the group. In this situation we keep the self–other boundary intact and don't merge the self into a group but keep connections to others. Social space then becomes defined by the social linkages we have and groups disappear. We become concerned as to how those networks function, who the self is linked to and how well, wherever those links are. This is a distributed network. Networks as a means of constructing social space will be the main concern of this section. If we are concerned with how the self fits into social space, whether we see this as consisting of a super-personality or lines of networks, we are concerned with the firmament. This is definitely not only by the self–other boundary but also by the firmament. The self will see itself as part of other, which is greater than it. As with self-constructed meta-algorithms, this creates a firmament concept that is not the mind. In constructing self in this way, self becomes a node in a much bigger social space, trying to maintain as many links as possible to what is around it. This can then effectively obscure mind from view, as the self continually inhabits this social space, even when not in paramount reality. Social space then becomes all-enveloping.

If we are concerned with maintaining networks, what often matters is reputation. Reputation is how the self is evaluated by others, whether positively or negatively. Specialness is always underscored positively. It represents the acknowledgement that the other has personality, has free choice and is beyond being property. Specialness is based on empathy, using skills of identification. Other may do things that are either good or bad. These actions can be evaluated, we should deal with them at the time, but should not affect the overall specialness of the other. Yet, if we include the other's evaluated actions in how we regard them, this will cause us to build up a reputation. Reputation is mainly concerned with deciding the question: is the other good or bad for the self? Thus, other is cleaved into two groups, those that are good for the self and those that are bad. On the side of good, we will extend the emotions of empathy further, into respect, compassion or love. On the side of bad, personhood will be withdrawn and the other can be treated as less than property. Assuming we create a reputation for other, we must then acknowledge that we also must have a reputation for the self. This will be held by others. The primary function of the network will be to transmit reputations. In constructing a network, little bits of the self have been distributed across it. The self will exist in distributed space. Our reputation that others keep will become a bit of the self abroad. The core of who we are will no longer be within the ambit of the self. Instead, the self will exist in how others regard us, through the compassion, love and respect they give or withhold from us. If others seem to demonstrate love compassion and respect we will feel good but if we feel this is withheld we will feel bad.

Thus, to feel good and confident, we will want others to hold our reputation well. Thus, we become concerned not with empathising with others but with how others are keeping our reputation. It matters how we are regarded. The risk is that reputation can be seen negatively by others. To have a reputation negatively regarded will potentially hurt the self. Indeed, the main reason we enter social space becomes to get the compassion, love and respect we deserve. This becomes our supply of confidence. If we don't then feel we are getting enough of this, we experience inversion of the self. Our starting point is having a deficiency of good. We then want good through having these emotions demonstrated to us. When they don't arrive as we would expect, it can then leave us feeling other is bad because they haven't delivered the emotions we wanted. We can though never really know what another thinks of us, how our reputation is being held. Yet, we can devise means to try to control this as much as possible. In order to get the adulation or help that we want, we need to control how we come across to others, we need to try to understand them and give them a good performance. We return once again to the metaphor of performer and audience. To do this we need to construct an identity. Identity is what we want others to see of the self so they can form a more favourable reputation. It is the mask we place upon the self–other boundary, a means to obtain the confidence to enter paramount reality. Self-identity is what is formed when we believe what makes up our mask is who we are, when the self becomes its own mask.

In constructing any identity let us start with how we present ourselves to others in social space, through our bodies. This is how we started the section on property as well. It was concluded that our bodies are not property. Our bodies, though, can be our canvas on which to construct our identity and project to others who we are. They are our calling card to the world. The first thing others see of us. Our bodies may be young, lithe and attractive; they may be wizened and haggard. There are bits of our bodies we are given and those we can easily adjust and alter. We can try and hide attributes of the body from view that we think will turn others away, or emphasise those points of the body that will create a positive impression. We wash, scrub and groom, perhaps apply balms, ointments and make-up. We choose clothes to match the impression we want to give. We style our hair. Perhaps, we get the odd tattoo here and there, or have plastic surgery. Through how we present the body we can say so much, perhaps to entice others or to push them away. We often try on many styles when we are younger and stick with one that feels right to us and then maybe not change it even if our body does. The body as a calling card, though, is one we can find difficult to control. It ages, succumbs to disease and never gets to the perfection of our imaginations.

Perhaps it is easier to construct our identity around objects. We can surround ourselves with things. Object property has previously been examined. One thing such property can do for us is signal who we are to others. Thus, it can signal our social standing and taste. Property can say something about who we are and can help form our reputation for others to hold and situate us socially. It can do so with the aim of altering the reputation others hold of us, bringing us closer into the ambit of those we want to attract. If we share a liking for a particular object this can then cement relationships. It can bring us into group formation with like-minded others. Objects that have significant cost can show our status or whether we are keeping up with fashion. This communication function of object property can often form our preoccupations. What we are preoccupied with, though, is not the object but the reputation it potentially leads to. It is not so much what we keep in the bag of the self but what we show to others is in our bag. Yet, what this is likely to induce is a preoccupation with our identity not any attachment to objects. This preoccupation is likely to be a negative one that will constantly be concerned with how our image is being held by the other. The ability of objects to control this image abroad may be limited. As social space is constantly shifting, it is likely we will need to constantly shift the objects we have to create new impressions. Although our concerns may delay habituation, the impressions we create are likely to habituate for others and so we constantly will need to change our identity to keep in the forefront of others' imagination.

Apart from how we are seen by others, we can also try to influence our reputation by what we do. Role, the social packaging of a skill into a performance for others, has already been previously discussed. This can become one of the main components of identity which can then be advertised to others. It describes our social use and the intangible property we can give to others. Role was first introduced when discussing respect and provides a means by which reputation can be judged. It allows positive and negative judgements in relation to a performance to be made by an audience. Role has at its core a skill or set of skills. The successful performance of those skills can be socially recognised and applauded, whether this is parent, teacher, superstar or hero. It is possible to see roles as an important means of forming both identity and self-identity and yet as a concept role leaves the self in a problematic place, for if the self and a role do become entwined, if we lose a role or if we are judged to be performing poorly, our whole self is put at stake. Basing self on the idea of role leaves the self looking very vulnerable. We can though leave a role and move on. This happens when we learn or develop new skills and then develop a new performance. This, though, becomes an issue if we cannot learn those new skills to a high enough degree. In attempting to perform a role, what we are wanting is the applause, respect or at least sympathy of an audience. The issues of relying on an audience though for our emotional sustenance have been already pointed out.

There is another way people hold reputation that we can try to influence. This is by characteristics. If role is a trajectory of what we do, characteristics are who we are and is a category. As a category, characteristics place people into groupings based on particular personality traits. Thus, characteristics, like roles, allow audience judgement. These whole groups will then be evaluated positively or negatively depending on the trait ascribed. Roles are a performance that can then be judged, characteristics are an abstraction of a person. They are formed from comparison with others and how they appear. So rather than looking at an individual and their unique story to arrive at specialness, characteristics are formed from comparing and contrasting snippets of that story with others. For example, a person may be labelled as shy, lazy, handsome, boring, truthful, gullible or gracious. Such labels are psychological shorthand, arrived at via a brief synopsis of others, on which we can then make predictions about behaviour in the future. They can form a screening process as to whether it is worth making the considerable personal investment of ourselves into this person. The forming of reputation is all about whether the person is good for me or not. Characteristics are evaluative in the same way as roles. Take a characteristic such as brave or one such as cowardly. They will probably have been arrived at as the result of a judgement about a particular performance, maybe heard about third hand. The person will then have that particular label affixed to them. These labels are evaluative. Most will view the former positively and the latter negatively. If we want others to hold a positive reputation of us, we must influence them to attribute positive characteristics to the self.

Role can be transferable, whereas characteristics are usually indelibly attached to the self. A role is not necessarily the person. I can cease to be a teacher, a criminal or a prostitute, although negative roles may begin to have characteristic traits and be difficult to shake off. This permanence combined with evaluation leads to a pernicious side of characteristic traits. They can lead to whole people being evaluated negatively due to ascribed traits having negative connotations. Lumped into groupings of outsiders that are disparaged. This is especially when they are applied to characteristics such as ethnicity, gender, sexual orientation, age, religion or disability. They can become the basis of discrimination and prejudice. A characteristic is also often used as a predictor rather than just a describer. If you are described as brave it is expected this is how you will behave in the future; if you are described as cowardly this is how it is expected you will behave in the future; characteristics cannot be bought and sold, given away or spread. They cannot be property in the way role can be property.

This does not mean that how we attribute characteristics cannot change, though. Somebody seen as brave may then do something cowardly. In such circumstances, it is often not the characteristics that are seen as changing. Characteristics are static. Instead, the explanation given is often that we didn't know enough about the person to attribute the right characteristics in the first place. Thus, the person seen as brave was really a coward underneath but was pretending to be brave all along.

That we can easily be given other characteristics makes them deeply problematic for the self and its confidence. If others hold characteristic labels that are positive for the self this leads to the self feeling good about itself and can give confidence. Some of these distilled labels when positively framed have formed virtues such as honesty, chastity, love, purity and wisdom. Yet there is a cost to the self to this. To be labelled positively is forever to be haunted by the fear of something happening that will throw new light onto who we really are. That others may learn who we really are, and that these labels do not represent us. That we may be seen as an impostor. We can find ourselves not living up to the ideals that we have been attributed. This can lead to splitting within the self where we try to appear one way in public but behave differently in private, thus creating a mask of identity. By contrast we can be labelled with negative characteristics and internalise these judgements within our own psychic reality becoming inverted. The self is constantly haunted if a negative event occurs that this will somehow be solidified into a judgement about the culpability of the self and a demonstration of an indelibly negative character flaw. This may be a judgement by others or it may be proof to the self itself of its own incompetence or ineptitude. The self may then adopt strategies to ensure that negative events do not become examples of characteristics attached to the self, causing inversion. Characteristics fix who we are in the minds of others and then reduce all future interactions to somebody contained within that category.

To overcome the threat of negative evaluation, the self creates its mask of identity. On that mask will be painted everything which can be used to evaluate the self. How we present the body, the objects we surround ourselves with that describe who we are, the roles we can persuade others we have in addition to any desirable characteristics. By having such an identity enables us to present our own version of who we are to others. It places a pre-packaged reputation on a plate for others. This fulfils a social function. It enables others not to have to work too hard to get to know us and hold a reputation. This strategy potentially works because often others do not want to work hard in social space. They are willing to take what is presented to them at face value until proven otherwise. Indeed, somebody not pursuing this strategy and not having a mask to wear may appear socially lost. We accept as inevitable that we will be evaluated by the other, we do our best to understand the likely categories we could be placed in and then seek to influence where we end up. Yet, this introduces a social game, where the other knows we are feeding them personal propaganda contained in an identity. The other then disbelieves what they are being told and seeks evidence of what lies behind the mask. In these circumstances it can then take huge effort to keep the mask on and believe what we say as others try to tear away our carefully crafted presentation of self.

If we live to impress an audience we have to wear a mask. Wearing a mask immediately suggests having a dichotomy between a true and false self. The mask represents the false self and when we take this off we potentially reveal the true self underneath. This happens because in impressing an audience we create parts of the self we want to show and others we want to hide. That which we want to hide is what we don't want others to see and we think will jeopardise our performance. We can come to believe if this is shown to an audience it would result in us being denied applause. The approval of others is that on which our confidence can become dependent. If we fail to get a demonstration of that approval, it means the self is no longer good and consequently our confidence is damaged. Given we wear the mask when on stage, it suggests we remove it when we are away from the audience, backstage, and not having to perform. One version of this scenario is that we perform to impress those whose applause matters to us. Those, such as our employers, our parents, our teachers, with status to reward us. Those with authority. We then try to protect our inverted or stigmatised self from being seen by those who matter. This then leaves a group of people with whom we can let our guard down with and can share the backstage, our peers, special trainers and fellow performers. They view all our rehearsals, and failures. They know our stigmas and our faults and we know theirs. Performance here doesn't matter and we are not seeking their approval. We share the pains of performance, we get their advice and they encourage us. We no longer have to wear a mask.

If our overriding concern is our reputation and its management, it is arguable that we would ever get off stage. Rather than having a public self which performs and a private self which we share with certain close, trusted others, we instead have different masks for different audiences. That we are as much performing when we are a friend as when we are in work. It is just that we are adopting different roles. When we are at work, we have certain social expectations we must perform to and when a friend we are also playing a role, where it is expected we should self-disclose, have a laugh and share a joke at our boss's expense. There are as many roles as characteristics; it is just they are different. We can then come to believe we must wear a mask at all times, even if we have to change them depending on circumstance, even if this takes huge emotional effort. The effort to maintain an identity can become so all-consuming that we end up believing our own propaganda. That we are the presentation of the body, the objects we have, the roles we perform and the characteristics we project. This is the creation of self-identity. The only place we are genuinely off stage is when alone and not having to accomplish anything. When we are alone we have no need to enter paramount reality either and thus no need to organise the self socially. We are away from social space. If we have constructed a self-identity, such spaces away from performance can then become very uncomfortable places. We exist to perform and, if we have no audience, what is the point?

This means we can continually seek to be on a stage, any stage at all. What matters is that we are giving a performance even with all the jeopardy that this brings. This could be with audiences we know don't appreciate what we do. Any reaction from an audience, even a negative one, can seem better than not having any audience. A mask of provocation and challenge can be worn just as much as one of seeking approval. We can think that it is better to have an audience with an identity and a mask than have no social existence. This may seem an odd assertion, if what we crave is the approval of others. When we seek a negative reaction we are either performing in front of an audience we have labelled negatively and are seeking to provoke or the self has become inverted and there is greater pain in the chasm of being off stage and having no existence, than in audience disapproval which we have come to expect anyway. With multiple performances, we are meeting lots of different people who may have lots of differing expectations of our performance. We don't want to be off stage for any length of time; if we take one mask off what we can do is simply put another one on. We can give one impression to one group of people and a different impression to another. What matters is that we perform, not the content of that performance or that we have diametrically different presentations in different circumstances. By taking one mask away and swapping it for another, we do not reveal a true self, we organise the self; in different ways. It is just we get used to wearing some masks more than others. Masks seem to offer protection, a means we can advertise to others, the tribes we belong to, the status we have, that we have something to offer others, that we want something from others. By having multiple masks means it is possible to have multiple identities and self-identities for the self.

If we are concerned about our reputation and gaining applause for different roles, it may be better to have different masks. This could theoretically give more opportunities to get good and be confident as a result, as it will possibly gain us access to more socially advantageous situations than having a single identity. This is particularly the case in a complex society where we have to traverse multiple different social scenarios. It also means greater resilience as if there are issues with one identity others could compensate. We could have multiple masks but some appear to fit better than others, and we could place some masks on top of others. We could have a mask we identify absolutely with which becomes our main self-identity but we have others which we put on at different times. Yet, we could also be in a situation of having multiple self-identities where we become different people in different scenarios but feel all these are who we are. Multiple identities will still be built up in the same way as having a single identity, so it may include what property we have and regard as important, the reputation we want to project, the life story we want to tell or the roles we have. For an example, let us suppose I have built my life around being the greatest footballer in the world. To become fulfilled in these circumstances I would have to be judged as the greatest footballer in the world by my peers. If, however, I want to be the greatest footballer in the world, the best father in the world, have a great house, lots of money, a great relationship, good leisure time, learn a foreign language, be generous to others in need, have great, fulfilling friendships, this complicates my idea of what being fulfilled is and suggests we will need to take on multiple roles and potentially have multiple masks in order to fulfil them.

By the self having numerous identities we can see a variety of effects when compared to having a single identity. One result is longer boundaries, which will potentially lead to feelings of well-being across many domains in life. Therefore by having multiple identities there is an expanded possibility of feeling good about the self. Yet, although this can sound attractive it can also begin to sound like harder work as well. With one identity we merely need to pay attention to one area of life. When there are multiple identities we must place our attention in several areas at once. If one identity fails this may be compensated for by other areas going well. One identity failing, though, may have an impact on other masks as well. If I lose my job, I will have less money, which means I can no longer afford to do my hobbies or pay my rent. This suggests multiple identities may expand the opportunities for confidence but may also expand the opportunities for a lack of confidence as well. If we are faced by the judgements of others in role performance by having multiple masks we also risk having multiple audiences to appease. The danger is that in wearing too many different masks we end up wearing them all badly and we perform none of our multiple identities well. In order to wear some masks well we may have to compromise on others. The idea of balance emerges because we have to compromise in achieving a certain standard in performance. Identities may not be compatible due to resources and time. I can try to be an artist, a footballer and a musician but I am unlikely to be able to do them all well. This is not because the identities contradict each other but because I am unlikely to be able to designate enough resources to both in order to do the required performances well. I therefore have to compromise on my identities and bring each of them into balance.

There are circumstances, however, where compromise is not possible. If I am perceived as an honest and respected member of the community who is also a thief and a swindler, these identities would undermine each other if discovered. It would not be a question of balance; I would actively have to ensure both roles are heavily demarcated and audiences who know about one do not find out about the other or are good at keeping secrets. Conflict often results because if somebody were to find out about one of our identities it would lead to having a negative view of who we are. The reaction of others is often imagined and represents the social opprobrium when taboos are violated. This can lead to a strong demarcation within the self as to which identities are shown to which audience, extending a demarcation into social space, where competing masks have to be shown in different circumstances. This can lead to many different selves, each appeasing different audiences. We may view these different selves equally positively but more often we see aspects of the self as negative. This in turn can lead to perceived negative masks being denied part of the real identity of the self. The self is split in an attempt to protect the self from mutually incompatible masks. Splitting is a common defence technique which the self uses to protect itself and have greater resilience but it usually has costs and is likely to lead to inner turmoil. The inevitable conflict gives rise to the Freudian idea that we are made up of warring components. Having multiple identities, though, may not be a lifestyle choice or an intellectual exercise in how to self conceptualise. It can seem to be an inevitable consequence of a complex society which places many competing demands upon the self. All societies tend to offer multiple roles, but more complex societies will tend to offer even more of everything which may appear radically disconnected from each other. The paramount realities we find ourselves in can appear to demand of us adopting different identities as we appease different audiences and organise around this.

The only way of not having a mask is by not seeking to control our reputation. Then we don't need a mask any more. We cannot control what others think of us, nor how they evaluate our reputation. Viewing our reputation as part of the self means seeking to control it and in so doing we risk over-extending the self and attempting to control other. Our locus of control is placed within the ambit of other beyond our self boundary. Yet, by not caring about our reputation, one possible consequence would be not caring what anybody thinks of us. This would mean not caring how we come across to the other, not having any censorship, saying what we think, not adjusting the self to the person in front of us. Then, when we upset the person because we have failed to empathise or identify we potentially become surprised or expect hostility. This is unethical and immoral. In addition we would have no means of organising the self either. An alternative organising principle is, rather than being concerned for our own reputation, instead we identify with other and try to do good by them. Not because we have a concern for how we feel as the self but because we feel happy when we do good for other. We keep the specialness of other and do not extend this beyond the self. We do not seek from others positive regard but are grateful if it comes our way. This is more genuine than anything brought about through a mask we have been wearing. The organising principle becomes the empathising and generosity we have towards the person in front of us. This could be risky but comes back to the golden rule introduced earlier. We can only really expect to have our specialness held well if we hold others' specialness well. Perhaps we should concentrate on this rather than trying to control what is beyond us. This means we still have social space but are more concerned with what we put into it rather than influencing what we can get out of it. This means developing our own internalised audience. In having our own audience, though, we still risk over-extending the firmament. It is absolutely necessary to have an internal reflexive voice inside our heads. When working well it will be able to judge our performances and our ethics as well and as consistently as any external audience. The issue is that it can become as much of a firmament concept as any other social existence. Thus, when we turn away from paramount reality, our own audience is the one that keeps chattering in our head. We must be able to turn off our audience when it is not needed.

THE SELF AND ITS MYSTERIES

'Mysteries' is a residual category defined by what it is not rather than what it is. Mysteries do not possess specialness but cannot be controlled and exchanged in the way that property is controlled. This, though, means we cannot form a core of the self from mysteries in the same way we could from property. We cannot put mysteries in our bag and accumulate them. Mysteries include much that has little significance and is ignored as property. These commonplaces will be discounted here as we are unlikely to form a self out of something we ignore and they are unlikely to provide confidence; the moment we notice them and regard them positively enough to want to build the self out of them they become property. This is not to say there aren't lots of people scouring our mundane existence trying to spot significance and bring this into the light. It is merely saying that whilst they remain hidden they cannot have significance. The category of mysteries also includes that which has potentially negative consequences for the self such as natural disasters or pandemic disease but that we cannot attribute direct responsibility for. A lot that is negative that happens to us we try to attribute responsibility to. This will be to a causer who by definition must have come from specialness. Arguably, we do this because we want to stop the cause so we can prevent it happening again, although emotionally the main driver is the need to put what we see as wrong, right. There are things though that are negative, where responsibility cannot be attributed and this forms part of mysteries. We are unlikely, however, to form the self from something that is negative unless we already have a negative view of the self and see it primarily as bad, adding to an already inverted self. It won't lead to the self feeling good and having confidence, unless what we are concerned with is the demonstration of mastery or bravery over a negative event; to demonstrate control over that which most people would find uncontrollable. Thus an undertaking to cross a desert wilderness, climb a mountain or explore an untamed river is often a wish to expand control into crevices where it hadn't been before. In a culture where apparent control has become so endemic, it can become easy to romanticise wildness, to see it as an escape from the mundane without experiencing what real wildness means where the self is potentially insignificant. In which case, though, we are primarily concerned with our reputation and not the mystery per se. Very often what we are also doing is attempting to tame what is wild and domesticate it so we can use it, so there can also be elements of turning a mystery into property. In this case mystery is seen as a threat that needs to be subjugated.

In addition, though, the category of mysteries includes everything that may be positive but is not easily commodified or controlled. It will include natural phenomena such as sunsets, a rainbow, the planet, the oceans and the sky. Often its very size or grandeur makes it impossible to own or control, yet it isn't a direct threat to the self either. As such, what is perhaps most significant about these mysteries is not so much the category in itself but an overall attitude it imbues towards other. These examples of mysteries are a bit like the communal goods mentioned earlier but without the necessity of having a group or community that owns them. They are unownable even by a group. The only way we can approach them, usually due to their massive size or awesome appearance, is as something we have on loan as an experience rather than anything we can control enough to bring into the self. They are a good that must by definition remain outside of the self. Earlier, it was suggested that the preferred way of being in the world was to see the self as mostly good and other as mostly good. Such positive mysteries lead us towards this viewpoint of paramount reality. They imbue an experience of appreciation for having witnessed them but we know they will always be at a distance. For the time we can experience such mysteries, it adds to who we are. It moves the self away from building itself around themes of extending control into other. Mysteries introduce a different way of making the core of the self leaving other untouched and returning it as is.

Yet, we can try to build mysteries into property through transforming them into an event. We try to clutch hold of the good time and bring it into the self as a memory: paying to see the mystery, maybe on a cruise to see the Northern Lights or travel to see a spectacular waterfall. Photos and videos are taken, maybe with ourselves in the picture. Yet, our attempts at keeping the mystery as an event will ultimately fade. We appreciate mysteries for a time and then they disappear. Mysteries suggest a way of being in space that is nomadic. Rather than the self being something we carve out of space and is then always threatening to overwhelm the self, or something where we have networks we throw out to others and then map the self as to how strong these lines are, mysteries suggest a different relationship to place. We become more concerned to map space as much as possible, to understand it and be as prepared as possible to move and respond, depending on where fate throws us. This way of being self though has become increasingly under threat. Humanity has managed to commodify more and more of the world of mysteries so that we have the appearance of control over far more than previously. Huge chunks of land and sea have been carved up for individual or national ownership, to be able to own and market the resources that come out of them. Things are bought and sold like never before. We can make far more than previous generations could ever have imagined. Even more opportunities have opened up for us to buy events or ideas. Yet, even property, which is founded on having control, has more of a mystery about it for reasons previously outlined. For, when it is examined more closely, apparent control evaporates. Property such as events, skills and ideas are always threatening to slip out of the control of the self, either as a faded memory or because ideas once put out into the public realm can be transformed and derided. Objects are either consumed or they degrade over time both physically and emotionally. Control for all that it seems to provide definition to the flow of things from other to the self appears inadequate. The control we often find we have is the one of decay and how things return to being other from the self. This suggests that the apparent subjugation of mysteries is more apparent than real. That far more of the things around us could be seen as mysteries rather than property.

The self–other boundary has already been introduced as the most important boundary we have. As has also been previously discussed, the self will often add definer terms on top of or in relation to this boundary. This can help to make sense of the self–other border. In addition, it is also necessary to value through placing a boundary to distinguish positive from negative. As previously discussed, if we believe it is important for the core of the self to be made up of property or reputation, control will be seen as significant; it will just vary as to what we believe it important to control. Control will then become allied to value, as we try to control property that makes up the self or the reputation others will have of us. Control, though, when it becomes allied with evaluative terms becomes problematic. Instead it could be argued that other defined terms are more significant when applied to the spatial self.

Other different definer terms, out of which the core of the self can be constructed other than the previously introduced controlled and uncontrolled or mine and not mine, have also previously been introduced. Other examples include pure and impure, belonging and not belonging, familiar and unfamiliar, and known and unknown.

Having boundary markers such as belonging and not belonging, familiar and unfamiliar and known and unknown means we potentially have a more passive relationship to the space we view. The self seeks to know the space it is in but not seek to carve itself out of it. Familiar and unfamiliar, in this context, means what we expect to be there and what is unexpected or unfamiliar, a deviation from the norm, or out of place. Familiar and unfamiliar and known and unknown suggest something similar. In order for something to be in place, familiar or known, it suggests we already have a well-formed model of the space of paramount reality. It also means that for the most part that model of paramount reality leads to accurate predictions of the world and how it works and that by and large we can avoid major pitfalls. Thus, we can usually spend minimal attention on it. It becomes part of our mundane existence and what we have habituated to. We can only have these assumptions if paramount reality is relatively benign and we have managed to form a reasonably effective model of it. Either way, the self is placed with what is known or expected; other is what is unfamiliar. If we have a reasonably effective model this means our self space will be relatively large and secure, but if we don't we can be reduced to a fearful being. This schema means, rather than control being the theme for establishing what is good and bad for the self, it revolves around themes of known and unknown. In order to incorporate something into the self, therefore, rather than having to control it we merely have to experience it and become familiar with it. Yet, we don't want a world which is entirely familiar; we want things that are unexpected and a challenge but at the same time we don't want this to overwhelm us and push us beyond our capacities. Therefore, as previously discussed, good and bad don't map neatly upon known and unknown; we need a balance of both. This is the relationship which mysteries can enforce upon us in relation to other. We cannot own and control a mystery; we can only experience it for a portion of time. It comes to us on loan, sometimes quite unexpectedly, and then disappears again. From the outset of the experience of mysteries we have no expectation of control. We are grateful for the experience but it is no surprise when it goes again. Yet this also is how everything is. Control in other may exist for a period of time, and then dissipates and becomes illusory. Therefore, it could thus be suggested that the lens of known and unknown or familiar and unfamiliar is how space should be viewed. Within each of the previous sections, whether it is space constructed through property or socially, there has been reference made to the body. The body didn't fit neatly into either. It is not properly our property nor is it properly a canvas to signify social messages, although it is often treated in these ways. It is instead our vehicle which carries the self, which needs care and nurturing. It is most properly considered as a mystery. It is something that should inspire awe and gratitude that is both part of who we are but also part of other. That enables us to have control and interact with other and yet can also be beyond our control and not respond as we would wish. It is above all something we should appreciate.

'NO SELF'

It could thus seem that space is something the self should minimally inhabit, hovering over and surveying, perhaps to the point of disappearing. In constructing the self, reputation over-extends the parameters of our control and property doesn't retain good and habituates. If it is so difficult to find good candidates to construct the spatial self out of, maybe a serious consideration is not constructing a self in space at all. What matters is having confidence and the ability to feel good. That need not come from existing spatially, either through control of property or inhabiting social space. It is this topic that will now be examined. Before we start, though, we have identified several terminologies which all mean something slightly different in relation to the self and we need to be clear what 'no self' means. Self, person, personality, mind and identity all have slightly different meanings as used here. The argument has already been made that we need to dispense with identity and self-identity. These are masks we wear when in social situations and presenting ourselves to others. They may lubricate social interactions but at significant cost in hardening and over-extending the self. We dispense with identity through not having an audience to appease. This only works, though, if we can effectively become our own audience. Although we don't want to appease others, as stated, we probably do need to take the advice of those we trust in forming our own audience to make sure our judgement is accurate. It could be argued that self and identity are the same. That the self is the masks we wear at any point in time and we only exist as a self when we are interacting with other in those masks. This suggests the construction of the self is not primarily around paramount reality, but around social interaction and how the self comes to be seen by others. This, though, will ultimately put the self out of reach of any control and will lead to it becoming very fragile. As an aside, when constructing specialness, masks are likely to be what we see of others and will be something we need to account for. We may see the mask and corroborate this against other evidence. This will be with the overall aim of being able to do as much good as possible for the other person. Any use of identity must bring the other alive and not deaden them through broad brushstrokes of characteristics or roles. Everything in the creation of specialness should be underpinned by empathy and identification. We need to use these techniques to create specialness because we can never access the full subjective experience of other, although we assume this exists. Doing this allows ethical behaviour and brings the other alive. More knowledge about other does not necessarily mean better known. We can get on well with somebody who we know little about, through empathy.

In considering the removal of the self, separate from identity, we need to examine what this might mean and why we might wish to undertake this exercise. The concept of 'no self' seems at odds with the premise of the chapter, which was to explore the self as candidate for the end. The self cannot be an end if it is suggested there should be 'no self' and thus we cannot feel good about it. Rather what is suggested potentially by this concept is the elimination of the self is what allows good. This in turn suggests the possibility that value is not always allied to having a self. The issue is then raised as to what is meant by the elimination of the self if it is not the elimination of social masks. One often perceived sure way of achieving the elimination of the self is suicide. This is the logical outcome of viewing the body as an integral carrier of the self. A body with a self will be termed a person. To the extent that the self is dependent upon an existing person and their body, the elimination of the person also destroys the self and would also destroy all subjective experience, the mind. Mind is our all-enveloping subjective experience which cannot be removed except through death or brain damage. Such a viewpoint links the concepts of self, person and mind. They all become dependent upon each other. Yet, person, mind and self are not necessarily identical. In many cultures it is possible to destroy the person in body but for the self to continue culturally and in the memory of the wider community. The self is often seen as spirit which has a presence beyond the physical body; when the body dies the spirit carries on. If the self could be differentiated it makes it possible that self could be eliminated and leave mind and body intact. Self exists as the opposite of other. We differentiate the world we inhabit into that which is me and that which is not me. To inhabit this world well we must be able to feel good about me.

To begin with, let us examine reasons why it might be useful to eliminate the self. One reason we may want to do this is because we see it as being in constant danger of being inverted. This is either because the self is seen as already bad and we feel we have no good within us, or alternatively that other is bad and we have no way of stopping this badness from entering the self, for example because all objects ultimately degrade or because reputation is beyond control. In either case, a way we could stop inversion is by eliminating the self completely. This is because by collapsing the self–other boundary, all good and bad also disappear. If we see other as the inevitable source of pollution and contamination of the self, it is perhaps better to remove the self entirely than live with the consequences. Such a viewpoint occurs when the valuing boundary of good and bad is placed directly on top of the self–other boundary. When good is placed on the side of self and bad on the side of other, although the self is good, it is inevitably threatened by anything that is other. A good way of describing this situation is through the previously introduced definer terms of pure and impure. The distinction between pure and impure is often used in religious ideas. Other is bad and is seen as contaminated. Contamination is often linked to disgust, an emotion related to the consumption of offensive items that leads to sickness and expulsion from the body. Being pure is about keeping out what is impure and contaminated from the self. This leads to a renunciation of everything from other be it property or reputation as evil and bad. It has previously been discussed that, in order to maintain purity, the self would have to ensure the decontamination of everything it needs. It could be viewed, though, that successful decontamination is impossible. When taken to these extremes this leads to seeing everything from other as potentially polluted and therefore we cannot accumulate anything to the self. The only way to protect ourselves from other is not to have a self and thus destroy bad.

The assumption may be that the self starts off as pure and good but by engaging with other it accumulates 'bad'. Since engagement with other is inevitable, the self will become polluted. This is highly problematic. The self will need to engage with other just to meet basic needs. Any interaction though with other risks contamination to the self and thus, unless decontamination can occur, inversion becomes inevitable. The self can become seen as the source for its own bad for wanting and needing things from other in the form of desire. The self can then be cast as the seat of desire from within the mind that causes its own bad and consequent restlessness and dissatisfaction. The very cause of the bad becomes the existence of the self. By removing the self, the mind can then recover equanimity; that self is constructed because of the existence of other and that bad originates from that distinction. It is then concluded that any way we construct the self will result in bad and only by removing the self entirely can we reach good. To crave the destruction of the self must therefore result from seeing it as pointless and illusory and a hindrance upon seeing things as they really are or as something bad within us that needs subduing. By removing self entirely, there will no longer be any risk of contamination. There will no longer be a self to contaminate.

Once we accept the self as the source of bad we can find other reasons to see the elimination of self as good. Having a self can be seen as meaning we are automatically self-regarding and self-preoccupied. We inevitably become selfish. Selfishness suggests we become concerned with our own good to the exclusion of the good of others. We can regard selfishness as how things need to be in order for the self to survive and prosper in a potentially hostile world, where other is always seen as bad. Consequently, we become so self-regarded that we grasp at all the goods around us, whether property or reputation, even though these will evaporate. The self becomes bad from needing to operate in a bad world. It could be seen that selfishness stems from a feeling that the self is superior to everybody else around. Yet, if the self is supremely good this in itself does not lead automatically to selfishness. It can lead instead to reclusiveness, as has been previously discussed. This is where a state of total self–sufficiency is attained. This is because, as mentioned, good and bad have been aligned with the self-other boundary. If the self is supremely good, other is seen as bad, and that bad is intrinsic to other, therefore the self needs to seal itself off from other. The worse other appears the more reclusive the self becomes in order to protect itself. In the condition of the 'no self' the assumption is that there is no way to seal the self off from other without destroying the self. This could mean the self will ultimately be overwhelmed by bad, even if it is good now. To be selfish requires the belief that the self is entitled to the good from other, whether it is supremely good or not. There is also a desire for recognition from others of that entitlement. This can stem from the belief in the superiority of the self, which is not then recognised by other who is bad. The only way to get that recognition is to assert the entitlements of the self against other. To embark on this path requires a belief in the efficacy of the self against other. Alternatively, selfishness can stem from the inversion of the self, in which the self has been done down in some way by others and has been inverted by the failure of others to recognise this. The fault for the inversion lies with others and the self needs to assert itself. From this comes a sense of entitlement as a proof of this recognition. The selfish mindset recognises some good potentially exists outside the self as the self could be made better by recognition and entitlement. Yet, that good only results from when the self achieves the recognition and entitlement, when other is transformed into part of the self. Often the act of bringing into the self more good is rationalised not as a demonstration of deficiency but as a demonstration to others of the greatness of the self. This form of selfishness is likely to lead to greater engagement with other in the wish to subdue it to the will of the self, rather than to a desire for 'no self'. For egotism to lead to a wish for a 'no self' there must at least be some level of insight that selfishness is not leading to the self being good and therefore content. To then become good we need to cut ourselves off from the bad in the world and the self that is caused by it.

A reason to eliminate the self results because the pursuit of self-establishment does not result in satisfaction. We find that nothing good is lasting and that we cannot find anything to build the self out of that is good, whether it is objects, ideas or reputations. Ultimately, everything that arrives from other is transitory and the self is constantly shifting and eroding. These things from other that we have constructed ourselves out of are bad. We feel dissatisfied with the self and the socially expected ways of feeling good don't seem to work. Again, we are inverted and what has come from other is bad. In the quest to define who we are, the answer we arrive at is nothing really satisfies for the reason that everything habituates or is beyond the self to really control. We therefore have nothing that warrants being incorporated into the core of the self. If we cannot conceptually form a core to the self we can therefore conclude the self shouldn't exist. It is a position which comes out of the problems inherent from other ideas about the self and truth in general. If we cannot say positively that the self should be then by a process of elimination the 'no self' is what is left. The idea of the 'no self' eliminates the self and the self–other boundary upon which it rests.

Having established the reasons why we might think being in a position of 'no self' is good, we next need to consider how we would go about getting to this state. This could be just putting on different glasses to see things. By collapsing the self–other boundary and regarding all impressions within the mind as the same, we can view things differently, not categorising things as self or other. Letting the emotional labels that come as a consequence of this division fall away. However, it may not be as simple as this. It may be something more drawn out and difficult. If we are intrinsically inclined to be a self, to move to a position of 'no self' could take years of practice and suggest that this is more of a skill we have to develop over time with a path or trajectory to follow. If the main issue with the self is seen as selfishness and egotism, one path to the 'no self' will become the elimination of ego. The path then becomes the battle to defeat the selfish ego and not grasp at what appears good in other. It means not placing too high a value upon the self, having a devalued self. A devalued self can be described with the word 'humble', a term which has positive connotations. Humility helps manage a problematic, overvalued self. The central ideas that support humility tend to take for granted the selfish negativity of the self and seek to constrain it to promote good. Devaluing in this scenario means moving the locus of concern away from the self. This in turn suggests if taken to a logical conclusion seeking to lose the centrality of value to the self ends up with the 'no self'. It is possible, though, to be humble and still have a self. It is just a self that doesn't seek its confidence and good through needing to dominate and take from other.

For all that the idea of the 'no self' offers several advantages, there are many problems with it. As a starting point, let us take the idea of removing the self in order to eliminate egotism and selfishness. When taken to extremes, this idea can result in extreme self-denial. Just having a self in this conception is bad. Thus the aim will constantly be to remove those inherent feelings of being a self. This is why ascetic ideas such as self-starvation, self-flagellation and self-denial in various forms can be regarded as virtuous when applied to the 'no self'. They can be viewed as ways of retraining the mind to discard the self–other distinction. The devalued self can be seen as a staging post on the pathway to the elimination of the self. This in turn suggests a sort of spiritual journey where decreasing value is placed on the self. There is, though, a logical inconsistency at the heart of the devalued self. Humility usually requires value to be placed on helping others. This is another way of retraining the self away from selfishness. Yet those very others are selves also seen as intrinsically bad. It could be seen that the main emphasis here is on doing good as a way of demonstrating that the self is good rather than on any aid offered, which will always be ineffective as other is bad. Yet, if the self is bad whatever it does, then it would be impossible for it to do good.

There is a further distinction in terms that needs to be made, between identity and personality in relation to the self. If identity is the mask of protection we wear when interacting with paramount reality, personality is our unique style that brings us alive. It is through personality that we attribute specialness. Personality is made up from the assumptions, much-used algorithms and style by which we enter and function in paramount reality. It is the sum of the repeated techniques we tend to employ and is adaptable to circumstance, the changeable essence of our aliveness. If we cannot adapt our ways of being we will end up with difficulties, as paramount reality is also constantly changing and evolving. To categorise and compare that style of personality ends up with limiting characteristics, where we are placed in a group with our masks of identity. Personality must always be seen as our badge of uniqueness. There must, though, always be a self to have either an identity or a personality and there must be a self–other boundary. To remove the self means collapsing the self–other boundary and therefore there can be no mask and no repeated ways of interacting with other either. If the self were to be removed it would automatically result in the loss of both identity and personality. The resulting loss of personality, our unique badge, might appear alien. It is something most of us feel within our bones, that I am an individual who is unique in the world. There is one word that seems to encapsulate the removal of personality, 'dehumanisation'. It is through giving personality that we attribute specialness to another. The 'no self' looked at from this perspective seems a perturbing idea. Dehumanisation encourages others to see the self as property: potentially traded and disposed of by anybody claiming rights over it. Without personality, the self can be seen as inverted and unworthy of good things. The 'no self' is an idea that is strongly allied with inversion, that the self is either intrinsically bad, or selfish, or will inevitably be made so because it interacts with other. It is as if we have to beat up the self in order to remove it. Even if it wasn't inverted before, we will need to make it so. It means that the self cannot be a source for good.

The elimination of the self requires that we collapse the distinction between self and other. Yet, the existence of this boundary makes possible the entry into paramount reality and the need to have values of good and bad. By removing the boundary, paramount reality can no longer exist. The good and bad that result from being in paramount reality will also collapse. This is because, by removing the self–other boundary, the boundary between good and bad also collapses, if valuing from extension. There is an alternative means of valuing though that has already been discussed which is the valuing from an idea of positive and negative. Valuing dualistically does not take its starting point from the self but finding what is good and bad in other. The self then takes up a position in relation to what is good. This form of valuing starts with what is outside the self. Therefore the boundary between good and bad is not identical with the self boundary. Yet, the self always takes a position in relation to the value field. If there is no self it turns any duality into a non-value-laden one. This means that the world can be chunked up into different categories but there is no self to situate in relation to those value categories, just an observer. Therefore good and bad will have no meaning and will not matter. There is an inherent contradiction here with what was asserted initially, that having no self becomes the way we arrive at good. We may feel an initial rush of happiness at the collapsing boundaries but it will habituate. Once we enter the state of 'no self', logically, we cannot feel anything. It would only be at the point of re-emergence back into a self that we could feel again.

Besides, we have already said we need to engage with paramount reality. 'No self' means there cannot be a barrier between self and other. If we cannot discern the difference between self and other it makes engagement with paramount reality dangerous. Where we have a boundary between self and other there must be a self. In addition, in order to eliminate something there must be something there in the first place. This suggests that the construction of 'self' is something we are predisposed to do and to recreate 'self' should we destroy it. This is perhaps not surprising if we always need a self–other boundary in order to enter into paramount reality. Consequently, we would need to be continuously watchful that we don't recreate the self every time and re-enter paramount reality. Any removal of self would have to be practised. If we have created an identity through attachments to how people judge us we would need to destroy this. If we have constructed the self from attachments to property, whether these are objects, ideas, skills or events, we would need to dispense with those. Likewise any concern for our reputation must be let go along with characteristics we would care to project or attachments to our life story which should remain unwritten. Yet, despite this we can keep grasping at these building blocks in order to rebuild the self from the rubble constantly created as we find we constantly need to engage with other.

It is possible, though, not to want to destroy the self because it is intrinsically selfish, or even that other is intrinsically bad. Instead we could place the boundary between good and bad at odds to the self–other boundary. We could even see the majority of the self as good and the majority of other as good. Yet, it is still inevitable that bad will befall the self. Unless we develop mechanisms to manage any bad, it can end up residing in the self as a lingering memory and threatening inversion. The 'no self' does offer a way of managing any bad that does befall us. By entering a temporary state of 'no self' we can strip emotion from anything we have accumulated to the self. We can then recreate the self afresh, without these encumbrances. Since any good from other doesn't last either, destroying any attachments would happen anyway. In a situation of 'no self' there is no good or bad. It is valuing that is the essential problem and this is what lets bad in, and allows us to feel negative emotions. It could be argued that these ideas originated when Adam ate the apple and obtained the knowledge of good and evil. Having this skill means that it becomes impossible for bad to reside in the self for any length of time. Yet, the mind would not seek to reside in this state permanently and we would come out with a recreated self.

THE CREATION OF THE 'RESETTING POINT'

In entering paramount reality, a self and the attendant self–other boundary is created. If we were to dismantle this permanently it would take a huge effort of will as well as being dangerous for the way we interact with other. Yet, we do not need to enter paramount reality continually. We could take breaks from it. Paramount reality is taxing upon the self and depleting of emotional resources. We could use a state like 'no self' to tackle negative emotions. At the beginning of this chapter, the idea of mood as a disposition was introduced. A disposition results from our basic assumptions about the self and other. By entering a state of 'no self' we can strip away negative emotion which attaches to experiences and elongates them into memories. Thus, we can structure a way of viewing mind, self and other that can become relatively impervious to bad. This can give confidence that we can face other, whether good or bad, and deal with it. Most fears and anxieties result not from facing bad, but from our perceived abilities to cope with that bad. Having a means of destroying bad can give us a dispositional confidence. This is a different understanding, though, of 'no self' than that outlined above. 'No self' is a state that is more or less permanently desired as the best way to exist. In this proposed situation, the elimination of the self will be a temporary state to help remove any bad experienced. To differentiate the two states, the temporary removal of the self from paramount reality will be called the 'resetting point'. It will be given this name as it potentially allows the self to reset itself. Here, we can potentially strip away the defences and negativity that are necessary when engaging with other and achieve a state unattached to any object.

The main emotional issues with the self often stem not from when we are engaged with paramount reality but when we are away from it, the elongation of emotion. Feeling emotion when there is no good or bad immediately indicated. We can do this by sustaining the self–other boundary and the existence of paramount reality when it isn't necessary. When away from paramount reality, we tend to review how our performances have gone or rehearse for future performances. We do this by engaging in what will be termed reflexive behaviour. Being reflexive and self-aware is human and has given us profound advantages. It is about being able to learn and adapt. It is also how we can provide judgement about the self in relation to a given performance, when we have dispensed with an audience. It enables the self to keep ethical perimeters. Yet, if we continually think about the self and its position relative to others and its reputation, we will have a churning of what has happened in the past in our imaginations: a continual replaying of events and speculations of what may happen in the future. We can be lead to spend our time in a reverie of self-comparison, self-pity and self-loathing: a way of solidifying the self through a core of bad luck and bad faith. We need to be self-aware and have insight, but inhabiting a self-consciousness continually is problematic. Mind becomes a self within the self, a way of constant monitoring of how the self is performing. We are then potentially creating exponential selves, each needed to monitor other selves. An internal policeman as draconian as any audience. We can often find ourselves engaged in an internal dialogue with our internal policeman. This is not to say, when in paramount reality, we don't need an internal audience, comprised of those who have given helpful guidance along the way. It is a voice that should neither give us constant criticism, but nor should it give constant adulatory applause either. This voice, though, should not be so present that we cannot remove it from time to time. This dialogue can then spill onto the stage as well. Collapsing paramount reality not only means the self-other boundary and value dissipates, but all the self–monitoring that often goes with it. To allow paramount reality to collapse when we are no longer on the stage seems emotionally advantageous. Thus, rather than destroying the self when in paramount reality, an enterprise that is likely to be forlorn, we should instead be concerned about the tendency to sustain the self when we leave paramount reality. Good and bad only exist when we underscore something with positive and negative value. We only need to do this when we are engaged within paramount reality. Once we leave this it no longer becomes necessary to value. If we can spend some time outside our paramount reality and let good and bad collapse, then potentially we remove what is negative.

The experience of the resetting point is a mental state that is analogous to mindfulness or meditation, where we allow the mind to sit in the moment and act as an observer of the thoughts that pass, to see the categories and trajectories and not things in themselves. This process means that emotion, whether good or bad, can be loosened away from the attached thought. We can see everything as just an aspect of mind. Once emotion has been loosened the thought can be cast into memory and is less likely to return unbidden. This, though, is easier said than done, as anybody who has tried meditation can often testify. Firmament concepts that link us to other will often block our clear view of mind, whether this is an ideology we have, the social masks we have been wearing, or the reflexive judgements we have about the self. Firmament becomes another boundary facing other, the marker of belonging and not belonging. It is another boundary that the self has to police, where both good and bad can enter and leave. In viewing the self as part of a wider social space, rather than just what is in front of us, other begins to hem the self in on all sides. If our view of mind becomes blocked it means we can find it impossible to see things as just aspects of mind. We are held captive within paramount reality even when we turn our gaze from it.

It was mentioned previously that we can use the mind as if a possession of self. The mind becomes ours, we own it, much as we can appear to own the body. Yet, when we looked at the body in more detail it appeared much more a mystery that appeared to straddle both the realms of self and other. Mind, by contrast, it has been argued is not a subset of the self but instead the self and other are both constructed from it. Mind is the ideal firmament concept which can get blocked. It is important that the resetting point can be maintained as a time to be in mind without the intrusions of self and paramount reality. Yet within mind there is always an attention point and often we seem consciously unable to control it. It is where our focus is at any point. Having formed the self and other, it is better that the focus is maintained upon paramount reality and the self is not broadened beyond that. That we focus on the here and now situation and the wider intrusions of the self to not interfere with our attention point. We do not find ourselves comparing the self to others, concerned how our reputation is being kept, or comparing the self to how it was in the past and seeking to retreat back there. When we enter the resetting point, though, and dissolve the self and other, it can seem though our attention point is constantly out of control. Rather than looking at the firmament of mind from a single vantage point gazing at its beauty, we can find attention zooming about hither and thither. It may bounce from one concern to another, from one memory to another, from one emotional label to another. Part of the experience of being in mind and the resetting point is not only letting the self and other dissolve, and the emotional labels drop away; it is to practise keeping attention on a point, so mind can become still.

Assuming, though, we can switch off for a moment and imaginatively dispense with paramount reality. This, though, will loosen all emotional labels, good and bad. As bad emotion is more likely to stick and good emotion would habituate anyway; this isn't too concerning. It means all emotion is less likely to elongate. However, it is a practice and a skill. We can still be overwhelmed by bad. It could seem that having the ability to enter the resetting point would enable us to enter any bad situation at will. Yet, the ability to sit in the mind without ascribing value or ordering sense impressions is something potentially difficult and takes time to learn. Paramount reality has a habit of continually intruding. The resetting point also cannot be a place of escape, more comfortable than paramount reality. Paramount reality is the site where we should experience good in the now. The resetting point is what enables the self to be reformed anew to be able to face that reality. To do this, we must have a continual cycle of creating and destroying the self as we enter and leave paramount reality. Yet, this suggests that, in order to destroy and recreate the self, something else needs to do the destroying. This suggests a need for a limited self-consciousness within mind to be aware when we are entering and leaving paramount reality. To observe the destruction of the self but its reformation too. We need sufficient self-awareness to be able to switch itself off for a time and then start up again, when the self needs recreating.

In recreating the self, we need to be able to reflect on the models of paramount reality we have constructed and correct them when they are not working. Resetting becomes part of a process by which this is done. Having destroyed the self–other boundary we then have to rebuild it again. In order to re-enter paramount reality we must move from the resetting point and reach what will be termed the set point. We must do so in a state of confidence, feeling good about the self and that it can handle and manage whatever we meet. This confidence must stem from the ability to manage the bad that comes to us. Thus we can build our confidence through this closed loop trajectory of creating and dismantling the self. Of breaking down things into sense impressions, into trajectories and categories and of building them back up again. Entering the resetting point loosens all emotion. It is this loop that allows the self to ensure confidence and displace negative preoccupations. There is no such thing as having too much confidence, being over-confident. We can, though, have misplaced confidence, where we trust in the wrong things to bring about the feeling of good, such as through controlling property or concern with reputation. It is enough to know that we can manage bad, we do not need to grasp at good which cannot last, we need to appreciate it and leave it where it is by and large.

Six

THE SELF AS TRAJECTORY AS THE END

LOOPS AND LINEAR TRAJECTORIES

In the last chapter, the preferred way of relating to the self was established: that the self is dismantled and rebuilt in a cycle. The spatial construction of the self was concluded not to be helpful. Instead, it is better to have a spatial map which we move through. Having ruled out constructing the self as primarily a spatial category with a core, this leaves constructing self as a trajectory. Meaning that away from the resetting point, we experience the self moving through time. There are two primary forms of trajectory we need to consider. One trajectory is linear, moving like an arrow, where nothing repeats itself. There will be a foundation point where the trajectory starts and an end point where it finishes. Once the self is experiencing paramount reality it will be in a linear trajectory of some description. A second sort of trajectory is circular, moving between two or more boundary markers over and over, as where the self is moving between paramount reality and the resetting point. Another example of this can be found in the biorhythms of sleeping and waking. A trajectory loop can be made up of any number of boundary markers, so long as at some point it returns to where it started. Foundation and end can still exist in a trajectory loop, but they are less obvious. This book began by looking for the end point of the self. To have an end, the self must have a sense of time passing, which means it must be in a trajectory. The self must also be seen as capable of causality, of making a difference to other and changing outcomes. It has been suggested that, for part of the time, the self will not exist. In the resetting point the self will not be capable of experiencing any emotion including happiness. There will be no end whilst in this state. For the other part of the time, the self will be in trajectory. So the self will be capable of experiencing happiness and have the possibility of an end. This trajectory could be linear with a defined foundation and end. Alternatively, it could be a trajectory loop, made up of recurring boundary markers. If we are experiencing those boundary markers recurring whatever we do then there will be no defined end as such. If, however, we are a self and our aim is to maintain a trajectory loop and there is a risk we could fall out of it, our end becomes maintaining the next boundary marker to be repeated, until we reach it, when everything inverts and it becomes a foundation and the next boundary marker becomes the end.

The minimum trajectory the self must experience is paramount reality. Away from the resetting point, the self could exist solely as paramount reality. If the self just exists as paramount reality, it will have a defined foundation and an end when in this state. Here, the self–other boundary faces forward in time. Self can be portrayed as static with other moving towards us from the future. Alternatively, we can see other as a static which the self moves towards or we can see both as moving towards each other simultaneously. It doesn't much matter. It means that, contrasted with the self in space, the self–other boundary is much narrower and is only looking forward in time. As previously mentioned, though, we can extend the conception of the self from just the narrow trajectory of paramount reality. We can use our ever-powerful imagination to create both an elongated past and a time horizon way into the future. There are several reasons for doing this. In the last chapter the construction of identity was discussed and seen as problematic. If, however, we are drawn to constructing an identity, to have a story to tell is extremely advantageous. Yet, pinning our confidence to such a story will mean that we must progress it or risk the self becoming inverted. In addition though to constructing identity, an elongated trajectory has other advantages. It can also give hope. If confidence is necessary to enter paramount reality it is hope that will keep us there and give our engagement a point. The future is privileged over the past as we can only head towards it. We can either do so with expectation and gusto or by digging our heels in and trying to delay it as much as possible. It is hope that gives us relish in inevitably going forward. If we do not have the linear narrative we need to derive our hope from somewhere else. In addition to hope, an elongated trajectory can also give us a sense of our past, a link to our history that can aid memory formation. It shows us how we developed, the skills we have acquired and how we have reached the present.

In constructing an elongated trajectory, we move from the foundation from being situated now, in paramount reality, and instead we shift it backwards. Potentially we shift it way back, to our birth and possibly beyond that. We also potentially move the end point to way in the future, possibly to the point of our death or beyond. Between these two points, we will run the line of a story. This will contain edited highlights of our life, how we understand ourselves now, how we got to this point, and where we think we need to get to. In doing so we usually identify the important stops upon the way, the little births of something new that changed us but also the little deaths where we lost something profound and meaningful. Thus, birth and death are the two great enlivening experiences when life is examined as an extended trajectory. Not only do they frame the trajectory as a whole, but they also provide a metaphor for the boundary markers we come across along the way. Birth involves the starting of something potentially good, whereas death represents the loss of something and having to rebuild. If we are entering paramount reality, then we will always be in a position of birth looking forward. Moving to a position of an extended trajectory, however, will mean we become aware of many more little births and deaths as we progress through our narrative.

Such boundary markers can be unique to a particular life but others link us in a common experience, whether this is of birth, adolescence, maturity or ageing. Often, though, our life story will be made up of well-remembered emotional boundary traversals which are weaved into a trajectory. Events were introduced previously and are situations of heightened social significance that leave an emotional memory. It is events that make a life story unique. Some are obviously significant life changes such as marriage, the experience of major illness or promotion into a new job. Such changes, however, could also be found in the apparently mundane such as the reading of an important book or having a conversation. Some changes may be slow and almost imperceptible, only becoming apparent upon reflection and yet others are so dramatic that we are changed from that very moment. Boundary traversals may be commemorated through the use of anniversaries such as birthdays. Sometimes, after a traversal, we end up with the event being with us each day as a stain on whoever we are. Maybe that line seems to be something that happens by chance, as we are thrown this way and that and at other times the line seems more like an arrow heading for a defined goal.

There are two potential sites of the elongated linear self. One place is an extended paramount reality. This means having an elongated sense of self. In entering paramount reality, our interactions will be informed by any story we have been writing and it will become our identity. Having an identity has been previously discussed. It also means that our attention is taken away from the here and now moment into the continuing narrative. When we then spend time away from paramount reality, in the resetting point, at most we could suspend the story we are telling. For when we re-enter paramount reality we are not entering a situation afresh but we are entering back into the previously written story. Otherwise, this would mean we destroy the story only to pick it up again later, which doesn't make sense. We could not dismantle it otherwise we couldn't readily return to it when needed. Thus, the resetting point would become at most a place for rest or diversion. Perhaps, it is where we could escape to for a time or explore other narratives but never entirely destroy the story of the self. Adopting this suggestion would mean we would have to radically revise the view put forward about both paramount reality and the resetting point. The alternative is to site the elongated linear narrative within the resetting point. It is possible to be in the moment in paramount reality but build an elongated linear narrative whilst away from the fray. In this case, the narrative ceases to be an identity as long as we do not readily share it. It becomes something we write as a record to make sense of what has happened, rather like a private diary. Yet, keeping the narrative away from paramount reality would seem to be difficult. It means when we are away from that reality we would spend our time going over in our heads the story we have written and adding to it. The danger of this is it becomes the site of rumination. To avoid rumination we must disidentify with the narrative we have been writing. We must let go of the very story it has been writing: something we acknowledge and then let go. If we cannot do this then any rumination will intensify any feelings we have and likely elongate emotions into moods. It then becomes possible that the elongated linear narrative spills over into paramount reality from the resetting point and becomes present in both. At this point we are likely to so identify with our story that it becomes not only it become our identity but our self-identity as well. Thus, the danger in holding an elongated narrative is that it infects both paramount reality and the resetting point.

As well as where we site the elongated linear trajectory, it is also possible to vary the type of narrative we are keeping. There are different sorts of extended linear trajectories, each made up of boundary markers or events. One is an account of how we got from one boundary marker to another with no judgement as to which point is better than the other. It will be made up of births and deaths but with little or no emotional significance placed on these. This is a simple linear trajectory. We are most likely to adopt this story if we don't want to become too emotionally invested and want to learn from it. It is likely to be a narrative formed out of our past as it will be a simple recounting of our story up to our present. It is a record we can learn from, much like any other, but we do not form the self from it. Another form of elongated linear trajectory adds emotional significance along the story. We can add positive emotional significance at any point along the elongated linear trajectory in our past, our present or our future. The way we will do this will be to identify the little births and deaths and add significance to them. To do this we will place our core or firmament in time. The self will become a full category in those moments. Rather than being our essential self now, the core will be a point on our journey when we were or will be our authentic self. Likewise, rather than finding the firmament of the self when in category, it becomes a point in time when we were something bigger than the self. By applying either being in core of firmament to a trajectory adds emotional significance to the story we are telling ourselves. This will be termed a dynamic trajectory and it enables us to form a self. Where we add significance though will have different effects. If we add positive emotional significance solely in our past we end up with what is termed a regression. The elongated linear trajectory reaches its pinnacle sometime in the past and we are now in a position of decline. There will have been some great event or achievement that happened which the self becomes attached to and attempts to keep hold of. Such important positive events can be a means by which the self gets confidence and can feel good about itself. Yet, the confidence the self derives is vulnerable to habituation and the passage of time. If these good events then stop and we find we can't get them back, we can end up living in our past trying to relive past glories. This can result in an inverted self where the self loses its confidence. The self has become so attached to the past that the best days are viewed as gone and the future offers little hope.

It is also possible to place heightened positive emotion in the present at the expense of both the future and the past. In this case the present time is the best it can be but both the future and the past are seen as bad. Being in the present much of the time has been advocated in this book so far but in this case there is the addition of the elongated linear narrative. In this scenario although the positions are related, the results are very different. We are in the present in order to run away from the past and the future. If the past is bad we won't care about it or believe it can teach us anything. Our memories will be painful and will have such emotional power; all we can do is try to block them from view. The past is a place we want to escape from. Yet by having the elongated narrative at all we are hanging onto this past as part of who we feel ourselves to be. The negative feelings it imbues will have been elongated into moods. We will be trying to stay in the present moment as a means of avoidance. In addition, we will be indifferent to what happens in the future. Instead of the present being the start of a progression, the future extension of the self will be seen as bleak and as a repetition of the past. In these circumstances it would be very easy to see how the self could become inverted. The only way the self could be viewed as good would be by supreme confidence. That confidence is likely to derive from bravado and wit, bordering on the delusional, which would be very vulnerable. It will become a philosophy of living for the moment grabbing as much happiness as we can for the fear little more will come our way.

It is probably more sustainable if we have constructed a dynamic trajectory as a progression. This is where the elongated linear trajectory shows improvement over time. There are several forms of progression. One form is where we believe now is the best point we can be and that the future cannot offer any improvement. The progression is built solely in the past and is about what we have improved over time up to the present moment. This is the truncated progression and positive emotional investment is placed in the immediate past and the here and now. We will want to show how we reached the summit of our achievements through constructing a line of events. What gives events significance is the part they have played in the progression of the self either because the event added something to the self such as winning a prize or achieving a particular social status or because it showed how the self overcame some adversity. Where the self has either become authentic or has grown. These events give emotional meaning and gravitas. Since the self is viewed as being at its peak now, the future, though, is seen as risky and may precipitate a fall. What we want from the future will be a continuation of the present and the immediate past. We have created a positive memory of the past which it is hoped can be recreated and passed on in the future. Such a progression is not necessarily against the future, yet we will fear it. If we adopt such a position we will want to create a future that recycles the past and to hand this on. This truncated progression will not be especially good at inspiring hope.

Another form of progression is where positive emotional significance is added in the future. One way this can be done is with a gradual build-up, inclusive of the past. Such a progression, like the truncated progression, is constructed to show the self as developing and improving over time, that we are a better self now than we were but with the addition that the progression is continued into the future. This is the elongated progression. Our relationship to the past is to show improvement over time up to the present. The relationship to the future, though, is different and is significant in the elongated progression. Now is not the best the self can be. The self will hope to improve itself in the future. The overall aim of the elongated progression is to show how the self is in a continual state of improvement. Alternatively, the positive emotional significance is placed solely in the future, so the past and the present are regarded as bad. In this form of progression, the self has become inverted and the focus is on the future as the site of redemption. This acute progression is only concerned with the future and wants to change the self and let go of the past. Both these forms of progression are particularly good at giving hope, but also because the self was in a less good position before it can excuse mistakes or negative occurrences. We don't fear the future. Yet, they are likely to need heavy editorial control. If we need to have a positive future for this trajectory to make sense, death is particularly problematic. Death threatens to obliterate everything and ensure all our achievements are meaningless. It represents the ultimate loss of control of the self. Thus if we face these future orientated trajectories we will usually try somehow to obscure the fate of death from view.

Both birth and death are usually accompanied by some very powerful emotions that can be profound and disturbing and are problematic if we are constructing progressions. By curtailing elongated linear trajectories, to less than the full lifetime, we can avoid these feelings. Despite this truncation, birth and death provide two emotional poles around which we will find ourselves strung out between and will still have to deal with. We often do this by attempting to draw a veil over them and denying their emotional significance. Therefore, we truncate our life to sometime after birth when we have formed an acceptable individuality. Instead, if we are constructing a progression, we need to concentrate on how the self has either brought about its own improvement, or plans to do so in the future. We want to show how we have managed to get to the point in the present which is an improvement on the past. Therefore the aspects of life where we haven't had control or have come to rely on others, need to be excluded. What is wanted in a progression is the construction of a story that makes sense of the purpose of our life. This means construction around a theme, often around a role or an achievement or a desire for a role or achievement. What we want the past to do is show signs of how we have managed to get where we are today. This could be from our proud lineage, or how we discovered our unique talent or the people we honour who taught us and changed our life. In the future, in the case of the elongated progression, it will be to a point far enough into the future to cope with our hopes, but not too far to veer off into decrepitude and death. Alternatively we can elongate life to beyond both birth and death. This, though, requires the construction of supernatural existences for which there is little evidence. If we manage to bypass this, it makes possible the construction of a trajectory loop where we can return to live a new life again and again on a conveyor belt of existence.

If the self has become inverted there are other possible trajectories that we can use. A common one is the story of hard luck and is primarily used to cope with, manage and ultimately excuse the inversion of the self. Rather than being a progression or an observational record, it will seek to show how an essentially good self has been undermined by some event or events that are beyond its control. The self is cast as the hero who tries to do the right thing but despite all efforts is thwarted by circumstance. It has all the literary hallmarks of a tragedy. This builds around a mood of self-pity, an uncomfortable feeling brought about by unfavourable comparisons with others. That those others have done better through luck or duplicity and not through being better than the self. The predicament of the self is seen as having been brought about in some way by those others. There is thus a sense of injustice and the negative feelings are elongated and excused. Yet, elongated negative feelings, whatever caused them, are never good for the self and exacerbate any inversion. The only way the self can see to rectify the situation is to get back at the other who is seen as having caused the problem. There is then a clinging onto the grudge-filled feelings as the other is cast as bad and hostile. The only way forward for the self is to then remove this bad and evil and this becomes the means to feel good about itself. The common route to having a hard luck narrative is through adopting the story of progression but then finding that this can't be maintained. We have a sense of what life ought to feel like and then find things don't live up to this.

We have previously discussed the construction of an extended linear trajectory as problematic. It risks becoming a hardened identity that extends the self boundary over lengthy terrain and in doing so lengthens our self–other boundary that then needs defending. We are locked into a narrative that we are in the process of writing. From something that faces narrowly forwards, it becomes something that covers our past and potentially our extended future too. Rather than just facing towards the future with a narrow boundary which is relatively easy to police, we instead face in all directions simultaneously, surrounded by other. If anything comes to challenge that linear narrative, this will be experienced as problematic and therefore as bad. This extends our capacity to feel negative emotion. A progression is particularly vulnerable to inversion compared to some of the other stories. A simple story can go off in any tangent without essentially damaging the thrust of what happened before, even if our hopes may be dashed. The regression is a story that is told, so unless this is challenged it cannot be undone by future events. A progression must be in a continual state of improvement to maintain meaning. It then becomes necessary to defend the sense of progress come what may, which can end up in self propaganda or as a story of hard luck. Progression trajectories can become a privilege of a select few: the socially successful that have opportunities. The young may be indulged their stories as they are still shaping them. They have so many possible trajectories they could take and thus a sense of progression can be a helpful way of structuring the self. To those that have made their stories, though, only those that can be shaped to be interesting generally have the right to retell them. It becomes increasingly problematic as we get older particularly when the ultimate end, death, comes more into view to see life as a progression. We must then learn to forget we ever tried telling a story. Yet, although having an identity through an extended self-trajectory increases emotional vulnerability, as mentioned, it can perform other functions.

THE CONSTRUCTION OF MEMORY, REPETITION AND THE SET POINT

The progression is something we are perhaps predisposed to create even if we are aware of its dangers and shortcomings. If we felt it necessary to destroy our progression we would have to be forever watchful that we didn't rebuild it, much like the self. This is perhaps not surprising; having a linear story can seem integral to what being a self is. It may constrain us, but we may feel we need such a device around which we can hang our memories and our skills. Having a story, then, is a common way we can manage memory formation. For most of the time we need to live in the here and now with a short-term time horizon. Yet, we need an arsenal of effective learnt algorithms to do this effectively. We should not live in the past but we need to learn from it. Yet, we cannot possibly remember everything that makes up our history. The construction of a story with events that provide explanatory staging posts is one way to aid recall. If we don't use a linear story, what are the alternatives? A linear narrative also seems to provide an explanation of skill formation. We form skills by learning small tasks and then joining them together in a sequence. Each of these small tasks can be cast as a boundary we need to pass through. Sometimes we need to pass through boundaries in a particular order. This recasts boundary markers as rites of passage: something directional and sequential. It is a model used when teaching children and explains development. Here, it is possible to see that not only do we have to pass through a particular gateway before reaching the next one but there is a particular time limit to do so. The gateway can then close forever and we become stuck at a particular developmental phase. If we have a prescribed model of progression, failing to make it through a gateway can leave us feeling stuck. A progression also implies that once through a gateway it becomes difficult to slip back. This, though, may not be the case. Yet, the dangers of such a sequence should also be apparent in that failure to traverse a particular rite will leave the self forever stained with failure. If we are to abandon a linear narrative of self we need to be able to understand skill differently. It is vital we maintain the idea of skill but what we don't want to do is harden this into the idea of role, where our happiness and progression are placed in the hands of an arbitrary audience.

If we were to write a story then it will need a beginning. Let us start with the inevitable beginning of the extended trajectory if we could go back far enough, which is our birth. For all that birth is an obvious place to start our narrative, an event that cannot be remembered can be difficult to believe as significant for the self. This is particularly the case if our main concern is to create a progression. In a progression, we are concerned with how the self has developed and found its purpose and meaning and how it wants to develop in the future. One option is to site the birth of the self later than the birth of the body to the creation of consciousness and awareness. My early experiences may help form the self but it is only when I can choose for myself and make my own decisions that I myself am born. This often is a boundary into adulthood. Yet this is a far more ephemeral marker. The problem is that consciousness is changing, growing and declining all the time, often with little personal awareness. It then becomes impossible to give an exact definitive point. It is, though, possible to have more than one birth and for that matter more than one death. The story of our life is constantly changing with things being born and ending repeatedly. They only become significant sometimes upon reflection with the use of imagination. Even so, a culture may require a marker into adulthood that is more obvious. This may include the marker of sexual maturity, an event marked in many cultures. The institution of marriage can also be seen by some as a pathway into adulthood responsibilities.

We may, however, be less concerned with what a culture or group of people consider should be significant as events and instead be concerned with what has shaped the individual story of the self. This may include the place we were brought up, where we moved to, the friends we had, the formative experiences we had in school, the subjects we studied, whether we felt accepted or rejected. It may also include the time we moved away from home for the first time, the first relationships we had, the first job we had or a personal achievement. It could also include the ideas we come across that help us make sense of the world. All of these are formative of who we later become and could be considered as much a birth of the self than some of the culturally ordained events. The advantage in doing this for a progression is the placing the beginning of the self to potentially a time we can remember. It places the past far more under our control at a point where we are not so dependent upon other. Yet this can also be the site of regret or excuses if we wish to construct a hard luck story. We can be looking from our story as to reasons why we have been propelled to success so we can repeat this, but if we fail to reach those heights we can also be looking for excuses as to why.

Yet, it is also feasible that instead of bringing the birth of the self nearer to the current time that we could push it further back. We could do this supernaturally, by seeing the self or spirit as something that existed before we had a body. The self then comes to inhabit the body for a time. Self is cast as a soul which is not dependent on a mind and body for its existence but can have existence independent of both. Soul is often seen as something out of time and eternal. Such ideas can help us emotionally manage the trauma of death, which will be discussed below, but can also be used to extend the linear trajectory to before birth as well. This would make possible ideas such as reincarnation. In reincarnation, we don't abolish the linear trajectory, in each life we still have a unique trajectory, although there may be recurring themes, but it is placed within a larger trajectory loop. This is the opposite of say having an elongated linear trajectory; which has trajectory loops within it, which is also possible. Say we have a sense of life as a linear progression but draw comfort from having the same routines each day or each year. Perhaps the routines can be seen as a form of resetting point, escape from the ever-changing nature of the elongated trajectory we are in. It is also possible to see life as primarily made up of routines and recurrences and lose sight of its linear nature. Progression could then appear an escape from the monotony of recurrences. Yet, it is possible to have the idea of the self as pre-existing our birth without resorting to such supernatural comforts. One way of doing this is to situate the self as part of a wider culture or group which we are part of and attribute to the group a wider personality. In doing so we can adopt a linear narrative of the grouping we feel part of. The self will have a story but it will be part of a greater linear narrative. It is a story that existed from before our birth and one that will exist after we die. We must try to add to that narrative in a constructive way to hand on to future generations. Rather than being the linear narrative of the self it becomes the story of the group and adds to the sense of a super-personality. Yet the dangers of being part of a group have been elucidated before. It is though possible to draw on many strands of history together without constructing a super-personality associated with a group.

The only way we can have a past is through memory. One of the main reasons suggested for having an extended linear narrative is the help it gives in the construction of memory. By having a linear narrative we construct for the self a mental filing system which extends back over time. The first thing, though, is to question whether or not having a memory is a positive attribute at all. We have said that emotions help us focus on the moment and that is where our attention needs to be. By having a memory, events from our past could intrude at any point and act as a distraction to the moment. Memory is how we hold onto things that ought to be let go and delays habituation, where things gradually disappear into a familiar fog. Hence, memory is the way we keep hold of things and stop living in the moment. We therefore by this reasoning should try to stop remembering. If this were the case, we would have to laud diseases such as dementia where our memories erode. Yet, having a memory is patently a good thing. We need to remember in order to keep things that work for us. Instead, we need to concern ourselves with what we let go of and what we retain. Memory is not something that happens magically, like some tape recording. The mind is not a library where everything that happens to us gets placed in a repository and all we have to do if we need it again is rewind the tape. Vast swathes of our past disappear to us, we may have a vague fog of familiarity such as the name of a school we attended and how we got there, perhaps a few names of those who we were classmates with but, as for which lessons we attended, the timetables that were so familiar, the colour of the doors we went through, which desk we sat at, maybe not. It is possible that prompts such as an old photograph may bring these back or maybe we could just confabulate to fill in the gaps. Much of the haze that is our memory is remembered because it remains useful to us now. If it has not been useful at best it is planted in some distant recess. Some people seem to have generally better memories than others and the sorts of things we remember and see as significant can be very varied.

Memory is generally divided into working memory and longer-term memory. We need to keep hold of things that will be useful for us in the here and now such as algorithms or how to do particular skills. We also need to remember the specialness we are keeping so we can re-engage and empathise with those with whom we are familiar. The mind, though, cannot remember everything, so we need to be able to remember what is useful to us when we enter paramount reality. Can we assume that the mind is a giant vault, and things that are not immediately useful we have to discard into the vault, much like the metaphor of the bag we were employing earlier to describe how we might conceive what makes up the self. This is where we accumulate as much into the bag as possible but at some point the bag becomes full and we must remove items; the constant process of deciding what is important for now and what we can safely lose. Discarding implies a deliberate removal but memory doesn't work like this; what goes to the vault is what we don't use. It is questionable as to whether everything in the vault is retrievable or whether over time it becomes lost forever. Yet, we do not always know what is about to come round the next corner when in paramount reality and which of our experiences we may need again. For that which we cannot get hold of immediately, we need a means of retrieval from the recesses of our mind. If we are to have a memory that is in some way accessible we need to construct a means of tracking things that go into our vault and getting them back again should we need them.

One means of doing so is to organise the self around the extended linear narrative. The line of the self is extended backwards in time into the vault of the mind. This suggests, though, that memories in the vault are no longer automatically part of the self. Since memories cannot really be classed as other unless there is the self, the only place they could be, if the previously introduced classification is correct, is within mind. We have said that if we enter the resetting point and lose the self–other boundary everything becomes mind. This would mean that a large part of mind is memory: the constructions of categories and trajectories we have accumulated over time along with the constant forming of new connections. So memory no longer belongs to the self once we have processed it and it passes into the vault of mind. By extending itself backwards in the form of a narrative, the self is keeping hold of some of the memories as part of itself. The construction of self backwards, though, by default also extends other backwards as well, for where there is self there is also other. Consequently, memories will become classed as either self or other as long as we keep hold of them through having an elongated narrative. It will become the narrative of what the other did to self or what the self did to other. By building memory through extending the self it becomes constructed through important events: those times when we expanded the self or felt it as essential. Yet, if we do this we may have to have a lot of events. Everything we want to remember will have to be placed in the context of the linear narrative, whether it is when we got married, had children or learnt how to calculate the sum of the angles of a triangle. Time, though, perhaps isn't always the best or most helpful way of linking things together. This kind of narrative is good for remembering events but perhaps splits up things that ought to be remembered together. It may give purpose and shape to who we are and can direct us but means things that are linked together are separated because we learnt them at different points in our life. This is in addition to the issues already raised in relation to the extended linear narrative.

If we fail to construct an extended linear narrative for the self, the self will primarily exist in the here and now, and will consist largely of working memory. Longer-term memory then will entirely exist within the vault of mind. The self, though, will still need access to those memories and a means of retrieval. An obvious alternative means of categorising is thematic. Rather than constructing a line backwards and filing the most recent stuff nearest to us, we can instead group everything together that is related. There are various ways that memory could be organised thematically. Earlier on, the idea of spatial memory was introduced, where things are filed according to the space they occurred in rather than in order to form a story. It means that the space we inhabit becomes our vault for memory. The issue is that, if the space changes, then our memory storage will be undermined. This is also the case if that space is defined by an area, or marked by objects and trinkets of significance. Yet, this is one example of thematic memory storage. Another way we could do this is around emotional themes. Thus, rather than telling a story, events that have significance are labelled with an emotional hue. Emotion indicates importance. If we want to remember things of importance, this can be signified by attaching an emotion to an event. Events can then be grouped together under the banner of a particular emotion. This is another viable alternative schema to the elongated linear narrative. Thus things that have made us angry are placed together, things that have made us sad are grouped and things that have made us happy or excited are placed together. We have said the ideal is to strip away emotion from events and not elongate them into moods. If memories are grouped around emotional themes, we then need to maintain the emotion in order to maintain the memory. In doing so we are inevitably extending the emotion. Even if we plant the emotionally laden memory in the mind vault and don't feel anything at the time, when we recall a previous event that made us angry, everything in the past with the same emotional label is likely to come flooding back. Thus our anger, rather than being an alarm for the present moment, is likely to become a trigger for memories of everything that made us angry, intensifying and prolonging the emotion and turning it into a mood. This can then lead us to explode at anything that then makes us angry.

Although having a pool of negative memories sounds painful and has the potential to intensify negative moods, the idea of having a pool of happy memories, in contrast, appears positive. It would then seem possible to bolster these and this could then become a place we could escape to as a place of comfort when paramount reality was getting too much to bear. If perhaps we did not label negative emotional events, we could perhaps consider structuring memory around positive ones instead. It could include our favourite holidays, our friends, the things we enjoy doing, our triumphs and how special we feel ourselves to be. Rather than constructing the resetting point around stripping all emotion away, which sounds like hard work, this offers the prospect of emotional escapism. Yet, rather than readying us and preparing us for the unavoidable paramount reality, this would seemingly divert us from it. It could then render paramount reality a place to avoid, instead of a place of hope. Thus, we could try to remain in our resetting point. Positive emotions, if then strung together into a story, will rapidly become an elongated linear narrative. If we construct a story of our life around positive emotional memories that expanded who we are or who we felt ourselves to really be, it will become regression. Yet, the happy memories will habituate and fade and will leave us running after our past, which will always remain out of reach. When this inevitably fails we could find it difficult to manage and we retreat even further. Thus, although superficially this appears attractive, we need an alternative thematic memory system.

Humanity has been successful because it is able to communicate successful algorithms it has discovered to its members. This creates a large repository of potential memories that each successive generation can keep adding to. Far more is available to us if we use the multiple resources of wider humanity than ever will be if we were to rely on our memories of the journey of the self. Such a memory bank will be termed the collective memory. It isn't a story of a particular group. Nor is a collective memory some mystical force, where all we have to do is practise for years to attain a particular state of mind in order to be able to plug into a universal consciousness via telepathy or some equivalent force. We have to accumulate information through the front door of the self–other boundary and then work hard at retaining that information. If we cannot compact the occurrences of a lifetime into a single mind, how less likely are we to be able to do that for the information that has been accumulated by the many lifetimes of humanity? We therefore have to be selective about what we can retain. Besides, our memory is probably hardwired to be linear and emotional and to retain collective learning takes effort. We thus need to be sparing and concentrate on what is important to recall. It is what we turn to when nothing else is indicated. The most important memory the self has is its model of paramount reality and that this is best formed, at least initially, through taking in information from the widest possible sources and as time goes on this can then be refined. Information is taken from the collective memory of humanity and then needs to be incorporated into the self and translated into an individual memory, even if its accessibility has been made very easy through new technologies such as the Internet. In order, though, to place as much useful information within the vault as possible we need alternate structures than that of an elongated linear narrative or emotional classification. The best way to arrange this information is on the basis of how it is related to each other through categorisation and the construction of trajectories within the wider model we are using within paramount reality. It means that when we are crossing the road we recall the relevant information filed under crossing the road, not because it has a particular emotional label or was done at a particular point in our life. We need a label by which we can then stop this falling into the vault and beyond our recall. The only alternatives to using emotion or story are by repetition or by hooking onto something we already remember. We then associate the new piece of information or skill with the hook. For example, if we want to remember a mathematical equation we could hang it on the hook of the person who taught us.

By repeating things, we can create lines to memories. Initially, learning to ride a bicycle takes conscious effort, but eventually with practice our muscles can learn how to balance and pedal at the same time and over time the process becomes automatic. We no longer have to think about what we are doing. This principle can apply to anything. We may repeat our times table or the names of the bones or muscles of the human body, we may know certain laws backwards or the elements in the periodic table. By repeating things, eventually pathways can be constructed into the vault of the mind that do not rely on a position in our elongated linear life story or having an emotional label attached to them.

Repetition is the core of how we learn a skill. Skill has previously been discussed and is formed with a kernel of talent which is then built upon and developed through the hard work of repetition. Skills are necessary to get us through paramount reality. Many skills, though, have as a goal the achievement of social recognition through having a role or demonstration at an event where we receive the applause of others. This is something we have been wary of as it will fix to an identity, yet we do need to be able to judge our performance. The alternative is through improvement from our previous performances, but we need to be wary we don't turn this into a progression. Yet, if we compare with our last performance or our last best, we do not require the elongated narrative that is necessary for a progression.

We could, though, repeat almost anything. There are, though, lots of things that don't bear repeating but we continue to do so; addictions are like this. Many repetitions are sited within paramount reality and amount to trying to grasp hold of something that seems good but turns bad or habituates and doesn't last. We then repeat doing it in the hope of getting back the feeling of happiness. This sets up a memory as something associated with emotion. Such repeated actions are done primarily not to train our memory but because we associate the actions with past happiness. They are then performed to try to get back to that feeling of happiness. We associate them with bringing good into the self and thus are an attempt at an elongation of emotion and to delay habituation. Memory results as a by-product of repeatedly doing something in the search for happiness. If we cannot perform these repeated actions this causes distress and results in inflexibility. We could eat the same sort of meal every day, or watch the same television programme or visit the same pub, a comforting ritual in a scary and unpredictable world. Such repetitions could provide the reassurance that at least in some corner of our lives some things are staying the same and are largely harmless. Yet, we need to remain adaptable and in some cases may be directly self-destructive as when we find comfort in drinking too much alcohol each day, or gamble our savings away. It also constructs that emotional shelter that draws us away from paramount reality. Thus, we should be wary of repetition that is associated with directly getting something. In creating memory from repetitions, we are not primarily concerned with repeating the cycle of the hedonic treadmill.

The repetitions we should perform are primarily about trying to build a skill which then aids us when we reach paramount reality. Repetitions that look after the self, such as exercise of mind and body, rest, meditation, sleep and eating well, are also important to sustain. In many cases we will be performing these repetitions on our own, prior to getting to paramount reality, and will amount to a private rehearsal of repeated actions or thoughts. In paramount reality we should be concentrating upon the present moment and be predominantly concerned with other. Yet we undoubtedly get information in paramount reality that can aid rehearsal, such as in a lecture or tutorial. Such situations, though, are often about registering new information, which we then need to take away and process and work out how this fits in through exercises such as writing an essay or through argument. Yet, there are also many skills that we only get to perfect when we actually do them with others. It is the interaction of repetition in paramount reality and the distillation and reflection when away from that reality by which we learn the skill. For example, there are some skills, such as if we are to rehearse a dance sequence, which we cannot do entirely on our own and require the presence of a teacher and dance partners. Thus, we need to combine the rehearsal space with paramount reality, although often this sort of paramount reality will be given a particular designation. What we are trying to do in all these cases is take something in so we can then give something back that is better of ourselves. The repetition is what enables us to do this, whether this is with another person or on our own. Emotionally, if what we are doing requires effort but in the end is rewarding this is probably an indication we are in the right area. If, however, we are anticipating something but find it ultimately a bit of an emotional let-down maybe we should question this repetition.

Anything that is repeated is by definition the formation of a trajectory loop. Repetition will thus occur when cycling between the resetting point and paramount reality, for example. If we are going into the resetting point repeatedly, then we are practising repetition as we dismantle emotions and strip emotion away from objects, events or ideas. So this would be something we will be doing over and over but also forming memory at the same time. This is clearly a helpful strategy but if our memories need to enable us to manage in paramount reality we need to do more than just this. We can add an extra point between the resetting point and paramount reality, the set point. This enables the building of a specific space where we can build memory away from the resetting point where we are dismantling memory and paramount reality where our focus is not on memory building. It also means we can focus on things that will be helpful to remember. The repetition we practise must be a site for making connections away from emotional tags and the linear narrative. This could amount to trying to cram as much in from the collective memory as possible. Yet, such rote learning is limited and can lead to our memory becoming a repository for lots of bits of disconnected information or actions. We may be able to recite certain things backwards but with little understanding of the meaning and makes little sense to our paramount reality. It is not enough just to take a wide breadth of information into memory. We need to be able to organise it in a way that makes sense. Therefore, we have to keep going back over our memories and form trajectories and algorithms that make sense of the experience, to construct models and theories of our reality. We take in information or skills from other but we then need to put them together in imaginative ways through the act of creating. Then, we need to test them out in paramount reality. This is not the same as seeking applause but instead finding out whether they have predictive or explanatory power. Memory then cannot be a static filing system but needs to be a place where we are always putting together new connections. Often those connections will not work. Failure is as important as success, but creativity is the essence of why we memorise. We need to be able to move from the resetting point to the set point with confidence in the model we have of the reality we face. The caveat is that we remember if we repeat things but we are likely to forget again if we then stop repeating it. At a point in time we probably had mastered all sorts of mathematical formulae or geographical terms but if we do not use or practise them, then most will have likely fallen to the wayside. We can only have a set number of things we keep repeating and thus we need to use our time well.

What we repeatedly do could be seen as a candidate for what our self primarily is. This suggests, though, that the set point, which exists in between the resetting point and paramount reality as a sort of limbo, could be the site for the essential self, a core. It is what we do when we are on our own and the cameras are switched off. We could turn this space into a forum for all our gripes and whinges as to how the world has let us down, as a space where our fears and anxieties run riot; it could be a space for doing all the things we think we can get away with when others aren't watching and think will bring us happiness. It could be a place so dark and scary we avoid it and try and keep some form of paramount reality going continually. Alternatively, we can see the set point as a rehearsal space for when we enter paramount reality. We could endlessly recite lines from a book, walk for hours, sing a particular song or go over words from a foreign language. This could be for a specific task such as for our job, or learning or to practise a hobby. What we are probably most concerned with, though, is the overarching skill that helps us with life in general and developing that skill. To be able to enter paramount reality with confidence that endures no matter what and is well placed, to be able to manage the setbacks and knock-backs. We must be flexible and adaptable and to be hopeful for the future despite our inevitable demise. It is the very skill we have been describing in this book, of dissolving the self and rebuilding it again. They are the repetitions that look after our mind and body, the exercises and the learning and the place of studied calm. This is a viable alternative strategy for memory.

HOPE AND THE FUTURE DERIVED FROM THE ELONGATED LINEAR TRAJECTORY

Thus, there are alternatives to the elongated linear trajectory of the self, in constructing memory. It is after all just one story we tend to keep repeating over to ourselves and we have options to repeat other things. Yet, the elongated linear narrative doesn't just provide a hook for memory. It also provides a framework around which we can construct our goals and skill development. The narrative can become a line by which we can link the self to its future. In the chapter on truth two basic questions were introduced: 'Who am I?' and 'What am I here for?' and it was said that the question 'What am I here for?' leads to a conception of the self as a trajectory. More than this, though, it leads to questions about the purpose the self has for the future. If we construct an elongated narrative that covers our past, we are seeking to explain who we are and make sense of the self for others, to have an identity. An elongated narrative to the future says to others what we want to be and what matters to us. It also constructs an identity but one which is about what we want ourselves or our world to become, a reason for being. If this is about ourselves, this will often be about developing a skill. When acquiring a skill, we can either focus on repeated behaviour as when we are forming a memory or we can focus on the end product, what we will become. In making acquiring a skill the aim of an elongated trajectory, we are taking a line from where the self is now and imagining somebody who has become proficient and by definition has a role. The idea of throwing the imagined self forward into the future can have emotional advantages. We can be imaginatively liberated about who we could become. If the present existence is an imperfect mess of contradictory impulses, the future can be where it is possible to imagine something different. The idea of the future being a better place makes possible the emotion of hope which many would find difficult to live without. If we do construct an elongated linear narrative, the self is colonising the future instead of leaving it as other and unknown. Once we have a line going forward, we have turned part of the future into the self. We can thus construct the self as primarily existing in the future, where we can become who we were essentially meant to be, whether it is a famous writer, a great politician or a creator of world peace. In the future we can also transcend our limitations and become more than what we are today. Hope is a positive mood state but it is not an elongation of emotion. Rather, it is a disposition we are inclined to have so long as we can feel positive about the future. It motivates us to look towards the onward horizons. The elongated linear narrative is one means by which we can achieve hope.

Some versions of the elongated linear narrative concentrate on the future and seem particularly good at inspiring hope and inspire us to develop skills and to have a role. These have previously been introduced as the elongated progression and the truncated progression. Which one we use depends a bit upon our starting point. If we feel things are going well but still have scope to improve, we will tend to use the former; however, if things are badly and we are more desperate for an improved future we will tend to use the acute narrative. We have previously discussed value dualisms where we add values to the self–other boundary. If we create a 'dynamism' we move those values and place the negative in one place in time and the positive somewhere else. By constructing a progression, we put the positive value, which attaches either a core or firmament idea, as somewhere in the future. In doing so, however, we risk undermining the present and making that less good compared to the future. What we construct those values around can also be varied. Thus, if we value skill but see ourselves as unskilled now, we can see ourselves as moving from unskilled now to skilled in the future. If we value truth but see we don't possess this now but would see this as something we want to achieve in the future, the aim of life would then be to get from untruth to truth. Therefore, dualisms when applied to a progression make possible the idea of emotional transformation. Yet constructing good in the future means that what is now or in the past is devalued. Similarly, if we construct good in the past and in some way wish to recreate this it devalues the present. It is also possible to value the present and fear the future as something negative. In all these examples values are not defined by conceptual boundaries but placed within time. Dynamism makes possible goals and value within time. That we can move from a less valued state to a better one or vice versa.

Time could be seen as the passing of a series of events until the arrival of death as in the simple elongated trajectory. Dynamism therefore is not inevitable but the idea allows us to value points in time differently.

Different sorts of progression have already been introduced such as the acute progression and the elongated progression. The hopes these progressions can inspire allow us to make further distinctions depending on where the value emphasis is being placed. One version will be termed salvationism. It is a value dualism with an emphasis on overcoming the negative rather than moving towards the positive in its own right. This can be explained more easily by way of example. If we look at happiness, we can achieve happiness through what makes us happy – pursuing a hobby, going on holiday, talking with friends – or we can reduce unhappiness by eliminating what makes us unhappy, leaving an abusive relationship, distracting ourselves from worrying thoughts or challenging unhelpful repetitive behaviours. Salvationism is grounded in eliminating painful emotion such as fear and anxiety. It is concerned with identifying and naming the negative state we are currently in rather than overly concerning itself with the state we are moving to. The elimination may be a necessary precursor to happiness but of itself does not create happiness. Salvationism is also related to the idea of conversion. People are seen as living in a negative state from which they need saving, hence the word salvationism. At some point, the person comes to a realisation of the negative state and finds the means by which to move into a positive state. This is the point of conversion, at which point the person is saved. Conversion is a real event in time and not something that exists in an ill-defined future. It therefore suggests a real passing from a negative state into a positive one. This potentially leaves salvationism vulnerable if the supposed positive state proves to be less than positive. The archetypal model of salvationism stems from evangelical Christianity. This posits that we cannot be certain of our salvation until our final judgement at death and therefore makes conversion into something continuous. It also posits that once individually converted then there should be an effort to communalise your personal experience through evangelism. Therefore the danger of living life without further goals or dynamism is averted. Salvationism, however, could as easily be used to describe ideas other than evangelical Christianity, such as communism or many advertising strategies. There is always a description or explanation of a current negative state; there is then a description of a means of solving that negative state, which is possibly not as nearly elaborated upon and a means of getting there whether it is the buying of a product, a set of rituals, the belief in particular ideas or the taking of a cure. Yet the issue remains: salvationism is good at providing an emotional description of problems and yet that solution can often be vague or untested.

By contrast, utopianism accents the positive within the progressive narrative structure to arrive at hope. Rather than overcoming negatives it is about detailing the structure that enables the achievement of a better life. Yet, in doing so the present will always be seen as imperfect, otherwise why bother to improve the current situation? This means utopianism can be seen not as the opposite of salvationism but its elaboration. Salvationism is often conceived of as personal and individual. We look to solve our individual issues by means of getting a future. In utopia we need to have a feasible positive target that will resolve our current negative feelings. A popular positive target is to achieve a socially applauded role based on a skill. This shouldn't be too easily realisable, otherwise it is unlikely to seem an achievement, but if it is too distant it can seem unreachable. If a role appears unreachable despite our best efforts we can become discouraged. Other people's applause and recognition are often attached to the target of a role. If we are concerned with our own individual progression the target will often be something for ourselves but we either get there or we don't. If we do, we then need another target and then another, or if not we then have to give up with damage done to the self. It also needs to be a target that is big enough to be meaningful and hang our life's meaning on. Role can seem too small a target to be a utopia; it seems too personal and narrow to be able to cope with our expectations. Skill and role become something we habituate to as well as being dependent upon the applause of other.

If we expand a personal goal beyond the achievement of a role, though it can appear even more morally troubling, it will often involve dreams of infinite wealth, social riches and status, eternal life. Such fantasies can wreak personal and social havoc. The only dreams of personal utopia that appear morally acceptable are movements towards being a better person, but these inevitably involve adopting beneficent attitudes towards the other. As such, the dreams of utopia are often portrayed as collective. We may imagine a world at peace for example where there is no bloodshed. We may imagine a world of untold riches where want and poverty have no existence. We may imagine a world where there is perfect justice and morality. We may imagine a world where suffering and ageing are no longer present and a world where constant friendship and fraternity are the norm. Such imaginings can be likened to the idea of heaven. A realm posited to exist within Christian ideas after death and only entered if we have lived a righteous enough life on Earth. Yet utopianism can also position the idealised realm before death. In part this may be because there is a sneaking suspicion that life after death may be a fantasy. Besides, a postponement of utopianism can mean we try to make nothing better in this life and simply provides succour for our pain. Utopianism, though, suffers from the same issue as salvationism in that hope is a relatively easy emotion to inspire but difficult to reach. What we believe will give us the perfect life may only satisfy for a limited time. It can therefore be an advantage to have utopia always slightly out of reach.

Thus, an alternative to an individual progression is to attach the self to a bigger story. An easy way to get to a big object, particularly one that is communal and involves others, is to attach ourselves to a group. When discussing self as category, there were two boundaries, the core and the firmament. By going into the firmament, the self merges to become something bigger. One way we can do this is by merging the self into a group. Yet in doing so, the self cedes control to the group. However, if it is part of a group, this enables the objects imagined to be bigger and further away. An individual hope is often quite limited. Such hopes with their emphasis on personal futures do nothing to link us to the specialness of others; we either get them or we don't and they must be placed before our demise to be meaningful. Bigger hopes with grander themes, can connect us with others. If the goal is unobtainable individually it doesn't matter as much because there are others around us who can take our place. We can hope our team does well, that we find a cure for cancer, that poverty is removed. As they will hopefully exist as goals beyond our demise it is sufficient that we should feel part of the journey to their fulfilment. Yet, even as part of a group we can end up feeling the goal is beyond us. The bigger the goal, often the harder it is to realise and, although we may accept we may never achieve something in our lifetime, to be meaningful we want to feel we are making progress towards it. Thus, although there may be some attractions to having a group-derived goal this doesn't overcome the issues inherent in a progression as well as with being in a group. Yet, we can be so attached to the progression we can be reluctant to leave the idea. Rather than the idea, we can conclude the problem is us and what we are doing wrong. We can fall into the failure of belief camp or the failure of planning camp or it could be a combination of the two. In the former, to be successful in bringing about a progression we must firmly believe in what we want to bring about. If this fails it is because we didn't have sufficient belief. In the latter, we fail because we didn't sufficiently plan for the future and didn't work hard enough at developing the plans, getting the knowledge to formulate them. What we are attempting to do by extending the self or a group into the future is to enable us to have a foothold of control so we can make it less scary and more predictable. Yet, it has been said previously that extending control where it shouldn't be can end up being problematic.

Thus, hope is a fragile entity that if we ever reach will vanish into thin air and yet if it is too hard or unobtainable we can give up in despair. This fragility, it can be argued, is an inevitable consequence of adopting the elongated narrative as a means of getting to hope. It may seem that this could be overcome by selecting the right object. Yet, an object will always be either easily obtainable or too difficult. The issue is that, by constructing a line of the self to any object whether near or far, we are extending the self into the future. The bigger the goal, the more associated with firmament concepts it will be, the narrower and more specific the more with core concepts. We are thus placing claim upon this future; to own and control it as part of who we are; if we do not control the future this will be perceived as a direct assault upon the competency of the self. Our firmament or core is being constructed on this future space. It will then matter intently what happens to this and makes the self and its confidence extremely vulnerable. If the goal is deemed too easy then it will not merit being a target but if it is too hard this will be experienced by the self as frustration and potentially lead to the self becoming inverted. The self is being blocked from attaining its future and its salvation. Even if the goal is achieved and is deemed sufficiently difficult we will still habituate to this and will need to defend the extension of the self. Using the elongated linear narrative, particularly the progression, means we have set up our goals as the pinnacle point of our life, not as a staging post, which we can pass and then move on from. It matters whether we achieve a particular skill or role or move a story forward. We have formed it as part of who we are, what we turn to when things get tough, what justifies our continued existence on the planet. It will matter if other people share our goals and dreams and if they don't this will potentially cut us off from them. This is potentially a vulnerable thing to hang our hopes and dreams on. Elongated linear trajectories, particularly those that inspire hope, are too vulnerable and whatever object we choose, even one that is very big, will potentially undermine the self and we can become inverted or barricaded or both. Thus our hope is undermined. This is ostensibly because we are over-extending the self and consequently the control we have.

Yet, by having hope at all, arguably we are storing up disappointment, whether this is structured through having an elongated linear trajectory or not. As has been said, hope can be bought at the expense of undermining the present and lead us to a sense of dissatisfaction with how things are now. It can also be a disappointment when we reach it, much like chasing the end of the rainbow. The complexities of the world can be simplified into an emotional feeling of discomfort and the future offering the solution. We imagine that when we reach our target things of the present will be put right, only to discover that all the dissatisfactions are still the same. If our hopes are achievable and we reach our destination, we will still become habituated. Hope is the happiness of obtaining something placed into the future after all. Nonetheless, it is still that happiness and will behave like it if we ever reach it. The hope we will have built our life around will have evaporated and needs to be replaced with something else. Alternatively, we can pin our hopes on something that is too far out of reach that is impossible, such as the utopian ideal, where everything is good and bad is abolished. Whatever we place in front of us as a hope, whether it is to acquire a skill, personal success, that our country does well or the achievement of world peace, we must care about it otherwise why hope for it? Thus to some extent hope must become part of who we are. Otherwise hopes become meaningless platitudes where we say we want this future or that future but do nothing to strive for it. We might as well be without hope. Yet we can have aims but recognise we do not control the future; that our aims are not part of the self but are part of other. We can only hope to influence what happens and that we must adapt to what comes our way in order to achieve our goals. In getting our goals, we must also recognise we will need to replace them. Disposability of aims doesn't necessarily represent the uselessness of hope. What we can do is to have overarching aims such as world peace but then recognise we need to do little things to get there.

Thus, we need hope. If we have nothing to look forward to we can end up in despair. This leads the self to either becoming barricaded against a hostile other or the self becoming inverted. We can become overrun by fear and anxiety not of hope, a place not of utopia but of dystopia where our dreams have turned into nightmares. Dystopias are a common theme of films and stories that throw us out of taken for granted comforts and show us how easily our world could be undermined. This could be the result of collective disasters such as war, autocracy or invasion. This includes the possibility of encounters with something, another species perhaps, a pandemic, an extreme calamity. Dystopias can be something that affects a whole community but they can also be personal as well. It could be about the death of a loved one, the breakdown of a relationship, the loss of a job, bankruptcy or poverty. We do not have to go too far to find examples of these dystopias; there are plenty throughout human history. To invent a dystopia for our future all we have to do is raid our collective past. Dystopia represents taking what is bad in human history and throwing it forward as a possibility for our future.

This inversion leads to the dynamisms where the future is feared, and the positive is placed in the past. We end up in a regression where we hope in the future to return to the past. Yet, we can imagine we can recreate the past. Human history can also be raided to create what will be termed a 'golden age'. This involves creating utopia but not as a place in the future but as a place in our past. The Garden of Eden would be one such place. Many peoples have founding myths that celebrate their origins or successes, whether this was in having a great empire or a pre-eminence in science, trade or culture. Golden ages, though, can be more personal as well. They could involve a time of great personal success, a better period of our own life where we had the opportunity to make different choices or avoid certain fates, when responsibilities were less and opportunities more. A golden age provides a desire to recreate things as they were in the past in order to solve perceived issues in the present. The dream of restoring a golden age acknowledges dissatisfaction in the present and the dream of something better. Yet, it also is dominated by the fear of dystopia that those dissatisfactions are likely to get worse. The only escape then becomes backwards. The irony is that backwards is no escape at all and the fantasy of the golden age is probably even more elusive than that of utopia. For there is one place we cannot travel to and that is the past. We can only learn from it and go forward relentlessly into the future. Change happens not least because we grow, mature, age and wither along with everybody around us. In modern society, change is an inevitable part of time and renders stopping change as a project doomed to failure and its outlook if adopted one that condemns its holder to fear and anxiety. To get to this point, though, will almost always not only require a lack of hope but also a lack of confidence as well. It comes from founding our confidence on things that are vulnerable and then are undermined.

THE FINAL END – DEATH

The elongated linear narrative is over-extending the self to achieve hope. Yet, we need hope. If we do not have hope, when we look into future horizons we may not only see dystopia and chaos. By having an elongated linear narrative which extends into the future it will by definition bring death within our purview. The term 'end' describes the overall goal of a trajectory. When applied to a trajectory of the self the end is detected through emotional motivation. It is the pinnacle of motivating forces when any action is traced to its justification. Thus, if I apply for a job, I do so because ultimately I think this will bring me happiness down the line in my life trajectory. Yet, end also means the finish of a trajectory. Any talk of a conclusion of the trajectory of the self must include some mention of that ultimate human end, death. Death is a certainty of human existence. If though it comes into our purview as our ultimate end, it hangs over all endeavours as a shadow threatening to take away all plans and hopes in an instant. All our cares and concerns become nothing compared to the finality of death. What does it matter if I have spent my life in abject misery or a state of joyous euphoria, if our ultimate end is the same, as rotting corpses in the ground? What justifications do I have to act and to achieve if everything I do will turn to dust in time? These questions are fundamental to constructing a future and hard to ignore when we conceive of life as an elongated linear trajectory.

Death has the potential to destroy all our hopes and motivation. It also threatens to render the self as puny and into inversion. If we draw a line going forward from now into the future to hang our hopes on, it is difficult to disguise what lies behind the place of dreams. We may well dream of being world famous yet the achievement of our dream will undoubtedly be positioned before our infirmity and death. The importance of our dreams is made more significant because death lurks behind them. Indeed, the presence of hopes along the elongated linear trajectory can be used to obscure death and means we can face the future with enthusiasm. Death, though, is liable to come into view at any moment, puncturing our horizons. This could be because we sense our own progression is reaching its end and perhaps we are faced with our own weakness and failing body. Humans, though, with all their capacity of imagination, have been trying to come up with answers to facing our own demise for millennia. Yet, as we shall see, often in attempting to solve the problem of death new problems seem to arise. One way of coping with the idea of death has been to try to solve it. We have a problem; therefore we need to find a solution. We have made giant strides in medicine; improved hygiene achieved through modern sewerage systems and the availability of clean drinking water; fuels that can effectively heat or cool homes; laws to control the selling of food fit for human consumption. All of this has succeeded in massively extending human life expectancy but none of it has brought the likelihood of immortality any closer. There are those who freeze their bodies in the hope science will progress to a point where we can healthily be revived. Even if this were to be successful we will only be revived to die again, just later. Our bodies are finite. Yet, we talk sometimes as if immortality is still the ultimate agenda, not a postponement of the inevitable. It is as if we live by forgetting our final end and hope that sometimes, by staving it off, we may ultimately defeat it. Another science-fiction possibility uses computer metaphors. We can view the self as a software program that runs on the computer hardware of the brain. It is then conceivable the software of the self is transferable to other hardware devices. The self then could be replicated multiple times in different bodies. Whether this is mere science-fiction fantasy or scientific possibility, only time will tell. It is probably more likely that the mind is impossible to disentangle from our body and consciousness is not so easy to transfer. The dream, though, represents yet another attempt for immortality. This is a notion that has been around for millennia and persists amongst us now in different forms.

Alternatively, rather than leave immortality to the forlorn whims of science, we can try to create for ourselves an enduring legacy, so that something of us survives after our death. This is our reputation, the evaluation others attribute to us whether it is through our fame, our fortune, our families and friends, the ideas we believe, the monuments and legacies we leave behind. Reputation has been much discussed previously. It has been previously argued that reputation is something we should not attempt to control. The opinions of others are whimsical and ultimately up to them. Yet death gives a special reason to appease the judgement others have over us, for in our reputations we can live on in the minds of others and have meaning for them. This gives the prospect that a bit of the self could carry on even after death. There are many sorts of reputations we could seek. So, we could be compassionate and caring, we could be tough and courageous, we could be fun-loving and joyous, we could be dedicated and full of conviction; we could be imaginative and creative. Wealth and fame seem to hold attraction for some in the creation of reputation; a means to purchase a legacy, whereas fame is the description of extending reputation as widely as possible, but this could be spread thinly. Others prefer to have a self given only to a few who know us very well. Many attach great importance to those special relationships of family and friendship. Some seek to continue themselves through their children who they try to bring up to have their values and interests.

There is a question, though, of what it is worth being remembered for. What is it exactly we want to be passed on after our death? If we have fame we may have more likelihood of our social presence continuing after our death, although there are no guarantees, but even if we have a social presence or not, it is unlikely to be anything we could control. After all, we are passing on legacies to others who are also mortal and who must pass on our memory again and again. Wealth would be dispersed to whom we thought were those most likely to use it well at the time, but again with no guarantees. The ravages of time will distort memories. Others will only remember what they want to for their own struggles in life. This is very far from the immortality we crave. Some may be genuinely upset by our departure but this could be mainly for themselves, their reminders of their own mortality, their own disruption for their plans and projects. Yet would we want to mean so much in the lives of others that they all committed mass suicide or to send millions into depression and mourning for years? To have achieved such a cult of personality means other people projecting their own fears and fantasies onto us and giving God-like properties which cannot be possessed. Relying on the continuing social self is like having a memory we can no longer control. All in all, we will eventually be consigned to history and what would any of it really matter if we ourselves had gone to oblivion?

So, if our social selves cannot defend us against death, maybe we can build ourselves to immortality. A giant monument that will last for a thousand years should do it, or perhaps a great invention or discovery to which our name can be attached forever. Perhaps we could make a huge charitable gift which eradicates a disease or ends hunger. Maybe we could command a great historical event, a battle perhaps, so that our courage could be proved for all eternity. These are more than the reputation we fight for in the everyday world of our interactions; this is the world of the grand gesture. The gesture makes light of the rest of our lives, so much so that the rest of our story doesn't matter. Our memory can be etched in a moment on the minds of the public and can linger for generations, never mind that we were a tyrant to those who knew us best. Yet is this really a memory worth having? With so many clues left around such reputations are apt to be pricked by some upstart whom we have never met finding out who we supposedly really were. To be sure, if we had no grand gesture in our life, nobody would even be giving the story of our life a second glance. Yet everything is destroyed eventually and even the monuments will decay, even our inventions will be superseded, battles will look pointless to subsequent generations, the causes and the peoples we fought for will become antiquated and cease to exist. In the end, if we are lucky, we will be reduced to a name and perhaps a few bones. Such is the fate of all humanity and one day humanity itself will die out. Then, what will my life mean to anybody?

None of the dreams we have so far come up with seems able to cope with the awful majesty of death. Maybe, though, it is possible for us to subscribe to one of the many supernatural stories that seem to give hope that death is not merely an ending, but a transformation, a beginning of a new and better existence. Such stories told to comfort mere mortal human beings awaiting their inevitable fate are abundant, although basically are of two types. I may either be on an eternal conveyor belt, doomed to return in repeated lives, rewarded with better status if I have performed well. Alternatively, I may be on my way to somewhere else never to return, perhaps to an ultimate judgement, where I could be cast into the pit of damnation or ascend to paradise, again if I have performed well. These stories will only work to console if they offer the incentive of something better. If they offer a picture of something worse, then people may prefer simple, natural annihilation to the story on offer, which may be the case if people think they are on the way to hell. There is also the need to account for how life after death supposedly happens. The body perceptively decays and disintegrates at death. Many cultures posit some essence to the self that is eternal, that can survive death. It is but a short leap to then claim this essence or soul is immortal and can enjoy the benefits of any lives after death on offer.

We have previously discussed utopia as a place of happiness postponed. Paradise is a description of what that utopia could look like. There are many ways to conceive of paradise, often dependent on how the present life is perceived. Paradise though generally involves entering a permanent state of bliss. Such a conception relies on our environment being altered in such a way that we have all our needs and wants gifted to us without effort and we are not overcome with the effects of habituation and rivalry. Paradise often envisages a life freed from the worries of risk. If our experience has been of a life full of bloodshed, then paradise may be peaceful. If life has been dull and bland, paradise may become an exciting place. If life has been sexually repressed, paradise may become a garden of free love, full of beautiful people. If life has been full of poverty and squalor, paradise may become full of riches and unending wealth. If life has been full of loss, paradise may be the place where you are reunited with those whom you have loved; if life has been full of failure and disappointment, paradise would become the place where you are raised up and lauded. Paradise then is the place of our dreams, one which is a state of unending happiness yet still tied to getting what we want. Our escape from painful reality, turned into the prize but one usually placed after death.

In many versions, however, paradise is not a place enjoyed by all. How could it be paradise if it were populated not by those who I loved but all my mortal enemies? Then paradise would end up looking much like ordinary life, unless of course my enemies were somehow magically transformed into my adulators. No, far better and safer to condemn my enemies to fit and deserving punishment in eternal damnation. Hell, the place where this sentence of damnation is to take place, is the antithesis of paradise. It is full of everything in life that is painful, only more so: dystopia plus. The function of such stories is not merely to console, but to correct the perceived injustices that result from the ebb and flow of mortal life. This can offer further consolation to those who feel they have acted justly in their life but have not been adequately compensated for their efforts. There are further questions as to where this heaven and hell are situated. Some would have them exist physically in actual places. The trouble with this idea is that it makes heaven and hell open to refutation. For if I say heaven is above the clouds and then go above the clouds and there is no heaven, it does leave some awkward questions. We then have to begin to locate our afterlife in untouchable realms where the material world cannot intrude upon our dreams.

The idea of judgement, heaven and hell came late in the day. The archaeological evidence would appear to suggest that for much of human history death marked a transformation into a new form of life. Life after all is full of transformations from birth, through to adolescence and changing into adulthood, and the experiences of ageing. From this to suggest that death is but one more transformative stage is not too far to leap. There are many examples of burials in the ancient world where the dead are equipped with all sorts of goods needed in the afterlife. The correct goods and accompanying rituals are necessary in order for the person to get there and thrive. Death then marks the beginning of a new voyage or journey. Apart from a lack of evidence, the major problem in positing death as a transformation is that it can lose its seriousness. If death is the end and means that life comes to a full stop and life is seen to be of value, then death is something awful that we should try in every way to prevent. It is the supreme bad. If death ceases to be the end and becomes a route to paradise it potentially destabilises this evaluation. Let us take one potential view of death where earthly life is of little value. What matters is what happens after you die, when you are judged. This makes life of little value ensuring the inversion of the self and death of supreme value. According to some versions of Christianity if you have sworn allegiance to Jesus Christ, asked for forgiveness, then you will be admitted to heaven if not, you are damned. This potentially makes light of death. This may be an advantage in a society and culture where life is short and cheap, offering some consolation, but it could also make it easier to end lives of others as they may be dispatched to judgement either to paradise or hell quicker. It could therefore make killing appear an act of mercy. Now there are plenty of prohibitions in Christianity as well that mean life is seen as sacred. Yet, these counterbalances need to be introduced if we come to overvalue an afterlife. For we risk by inventing an afterlife making death less serious. The trouble is if death becomes a portal for something better, which if true for everyone, not only can I cheapen my own life but I can also cheapen the lives of others. Let us take the example of discovering if a person is a witch or not. I could fling you into a pool of water and if you floated you must be a witch but if you drowned then you must have been innocent. Yet, if you believe in an afterlife, such callousness doesn't really matter, for you will now be with the angels. Belief in reincarnation can also be used to devalue life, for if somebody dies they are merely moving on to the next part of their journey. If your moral actions cause you to be reborn into high status then clearly you deserve that from your previous life. The corollary is that if you are reborn into a lowly life you must be being punished for your actions in a previous life. Thus you deserve your fate.

The original intention in devising stories of an afterlife may have been to offer consolations regarding death having conceived of life as an elongated linear narrative. Yet, the inadvertent effect is to cheapen life. Supernatural stories upset the delicate balance between life and death. We may want to conclude from all that we have examined that by removing the sting from death we also subtract value from life as well. In the common sense view life has positive value and death has negative value. Any attempt to alter the negative value of death appears to alter the value of life as well. It is as if life and death are on opposite ends of a see-saw. As we raise death up, the value of life comes down. In order to overcome the problems of the see-saw effect it is possible to introduce a notion of a counterweight. If you have a doctrine that lightens the seriousness of death, then you must also have a counterweight that adds value to life. Such a counterweight could include a doctrine on the sacredness of all life for example. We are valuable because God created every one of us. Life then is valuable until the point of death, when one of the other options so far considered could take over. Those who do not readily believe in God may also have reasons to add value to life. So we can consider that all are imbued with specialness, by virtue of having personality that we are capable of empathising with. We may try to buttress this by devising legal defences such as human rights intrinsic to all of us. These, though, tend to stem not from an afterlife but from interactions with other where people have been turned into property or placed in a group which has been evaluated negatively, which consequently has led to their disposability. Both a person's life and death have become trivial due to their commodification. In these circumstances, the see-saw effect does not apply because we are being judged by other and not placing value along the elongated linear narrative.

Another situation where there appear to be issues for the see-saw effect is in a thought experiment where death loses value because we are immortal. In such circumstances, life also then seems to lose its value. We would possess the properties of the ancient gods. Removing death seems to lead to a situation of constant play, of games and trickery, of petty rivalries and squabbles. It is almost as if all gravity and meaning are sucked right out of life. In short, it is a life many young, affluent people can afford to live for a time where we have almost been too successful in hiding death from view with our hopes and dreams. Perhaps we have become too preoccupied by where we are in relation to our fantasies and how others are looking after our reputation. Life can become trivialised into a series of petty squabbles and arguments. It is only when life becomes punctured by the inevitable spectre of death that the ground of such flippancy is shaken, where others are seen as mattering. This can give reason for us to try visualising our own death, even if it is for a short time and at a distance. We normally find death too difficult to visualise and place a shroud over it. Yet, if we are so caught up in our dreams and preoccupations, death can be so remote we can barely consider it. Visualising death in a controlled way can puncture this hubris. Otherwise we can be in a position of taking life for granted, taking what is superfluous and superficial as important. It can also mean that others' lives are devalued and seen as cheap and disposable. If this is done, though, we must be aware, if taken too far, death can also paralyse us, fill us with dread and fear and mean we fail to live our lives. Death needs to be acknowledged, given due respect but ultimately put out of mind as we cannot let it overhang us in every moment. Life and death then can end up seemingly dependent upon each other for meaning. If one becomes valueless, then so does the other. Yet, this doesn't invalidate the see-saw effect. It is by removing death as a possibility, we have changed the nature of life. This, though, suggests we are in a position in the elongated linear narrative where if we gaze upon death it is too much but if we are too successful in hiding it life can become trivialised.

There is also an argument, though, where life is seen to have lost all value and death therefore comes as something of a release. This is what can happen when the self becomes completely inverted and exemplifies an experience of depression. This thinking posits no need of paradises or reincarnation to gain value in death. Death gains in value as a result of directly devaluing life: when life fails to reach expectations. Such a position, though, is usually hard to maintain in the face of having to deal with the true horrors of death. It may well be maintained by means of fantasy. These may include death as a means of finally being taken seriously by people, so that others may finally appreciate our existence or to get back at others who will finally miss us when we have gone. This is a dangerous position which so lowers the value of the self but sees that it could be raised up by hurting those who are seen as having done us harm. This position is also amenable to generalisation. It is possible to lower the value of life for all and see death as a general release for everybody. This is even more pernicious. Not only do you see death as an escape for yourself but as an escape for everybody else from continued pointless existence. This is a slippery slope of inversion.

What is being sought is a way by which life can be valued but death is accepted as an inevitable part of that valued life. This is the good death, which results from living the good life. If this is attempted whilst keeping hold of the elongated linear narrative it will be because we have managed to tell a good story and achieved what we wanted to. This in part depends on the story we have been writing. It could be because the death follows from a life of achievement where the plans have all been fulfilled. Alternatively, it could have been because life has culminated in a death of sacrifice which has ensured the betterment of the rest of the group we have committed ourselves to. The person has sought to give their life over to others. In either case the good death represents the attribution of value to death at the same time as giving value in life. Most people, however, fail to achieve all their plans and we often fail to have control over when death chooses to come for us. A good death therefore appears a rare thing. The eulogy is often the severe editing of a life so that it can appear a good death was achieved. Besides, although theoretically, the good death allows the overcoming of the see-saw effect; as previously indicated, the means of doing so, namely achievements in temporal life, will usually not live on much beyond our death or, if they do, do so without any form of control. The good death will be something ascribed to us by others who may well have their own needs for doing so. This doesn't fundamentally alter the value of death or life.

The issues of death have arisen because we are constructing a future for the self. However, we can imagine the self and other in different ways. One alternative is the claim there is no self, which has already been discussed. Therefore, so the argument goes, when it comes to death, there is no self to die. Death then cannot harm us in any way. Yet, we cannot remain permanently in a state of 'no self', as previously discussed. People need and want to construct a self, even if temporarily. The minimum we need in order to manage in our world is to construct paramount reality. In such short-term time horizons, our gaze will rarely be far enough to be able to see death unless poor health or infirmity brings it into view. Yet, this arguably is little different to the situation with the elongated linear trajectory. We may hide death by having dreams or because our gaze falls short but arguably it all amounts to the same thing: we can't face looking at our own demise directly. Paramount reality is about now and the immediate future, not speculating too far ahead. Yet, it is possible to see paramount reality as not only a description of a trajectory in time that connects us to the future but as a line that connects the self to other. We are always moving towards other but when it reaches us it becomes part of who we are. The self relates to other by taking from it, transforming what it has taken and then giving back. We must do this in order to survive. Other will become part of the self for a time only to be let go again. It is possible then to see an endless cycle of self forming and dispersing, of other coming into and out of. Death in this understanding is merely one point in this cycle where self permanently returns to other whence it was formed; the point where the self finally loses control to other and lets go.

It was the Epicureans, an ancient Greek philosophical grouping, that linked most of the problems of humanity to a fear of death. Their main argument was that non-existence is not a matter for our concern. Most people do not go around fretting about the fact I was not around before my birth. Death could be seen as merely returning to a state that pre-existed our birth. A second strand of the argument looks at the qualities of non-existence and asks what it is about non-existence that we fear so much. If we no longer exist, we can no longer feel pain and nothing can harm us. Therefore it is not death that should induce fear but the process of dying. If somehow the knowledge of dying and the accompanying pain can be overcome then death can be managed. It can become a process much like anything else. This was a consolation designed to bring mental equanimity in the face of dealing with our own demise. It does not deny the gravity of death. We need to keep the full majesty of death, in order to keep the importance of life. The enjoyment we have of life should not lessen. Emotionally we should acknowledge the true horrors and death for what they are and then still be able to come away from that experience smiling. For if we are primarily constituted from boundaries that are made up from other, the skills and objects we have acquired from other on loan simply means the dissolution of the boundaries and the returning of the good we have taken back to other.

ALTERNATIVES TO THE ELONGATED LINEAR TRAJECTORY IN THE CONSTRUCTION OF HOPE

A life without hope though becomes suffocating. Even if we do not construct an elongated linear trajectory to the future and concentrate on being in paramount reality, we will find this draining without any hope. Hope must sit at the end of any trajectory of the self, heading towards the future. Thus, much like memory, having hope is too important to discard. Yet this hope will be quite limited if it is just applied to getting through today and achieving what we need to do. We will need something more than this. What do we want to get through the day for or achieve? The question then becomes how we go about getting hope if not through the elongated linear trajectory. We need to construct a trajectory that relates to the future but is not the self or a group of which the self is part. Rather than seeing the self as an elongated trajectory, we can instead see the self as either receiving trajectories from the future or we can see the self sending out trajectories. This means we do not need an elongated trajectory. Paramount reality can become the site where these communications from the future are received or the launch pad to send things to the future. If the relationship the self has to the future is seen as primarily passive, the future will be regarded as something that comes to us and which we can do little about. The self receives algorithms from the future, and must respond accordingly. The self can either accept these or somehow expel them, to drift into the backwaters of mind. In this example, the self does nothing to shape the future and merely responds. If there is hope it is that we are blessed with good fortune or if we get bad luck we are not tested too severely. The alternative is an active relationship to the future where the self sends its own algorithms into the future. This is different to the elongated linear trajectory, where the self is projected into the future. If we send out a trajectory, it no longer remains part of the self. It will have impacts in the future or maybe it will fizzle out into nothing, yet it will have been fully placed into other. It is no longer for the self to control. We can learn from the trajectories we have sent out and try and repeat or alter them depending on the result. An analogy can be made with archery. We are constantly sending out arrows trying to hit a target in the future. Some arrows will fly past and others may hit. We must then learn how to try to hit the target more frequently. It is the target that will inspire hope.

To accept this idea, we must view the future as yet unmade and that choices made in the present can change outcomes. If we do not accept this we will become passive and fateful. The future will offer us little and will be something to be defended against rather than something we can help make and contribute to. Alternatively, we can see the future as something that sends us things that we need to deal with and defend ourselves against. This is because we are too weak or puny to do anything about the future. Our emotions will be shaped by what we expect. Expectation is not an emotion like anger or love, yet much like the experience of preoccupation described in the previous chapter, it heavily influences what we feel. That which is expected does not lead to emotion, but that which is unexpected does. It therefore matters what is expected. If we expect something, it mitigates feelings. Expectations are shaped by how we see the self and how we see other and will often be built from what has happened to us before. If a lot has happened before and we have developed for ourselves a comfortable protected bubble it may seem as if everything is constantly repeating. Thus very little happens that is unexpected and we don't look for anything that might challenge this either. If we see other as potentially threatening and alien we will want to develop defences against this. If we see the self as bad and useless and that nothing we do makes a difference this will lead to expectations of failure and not trying. Alternatively, if we do not have much of a past or are trying something very different from our norm, everything can seem unexpected. In facing the unexpected, we can either emotionally accept this with anticipation, as an opportunity to change who we are, or we can fear it.

If we predominantly fear the future, one way of severely managing expectations is to claim that the future is preordained and therefore there is nothing the self can do to alter the future. This is more extreme than just being fateful. Rather than not being able to shape the future because we are too weak or insignificant, it is because the future is fixed. This may have emotional advantages for the self. As such the future might be either inevitably good or inevitably bad. We could inevitably be heading to utopia or dystopia irrespective of what we do. This has a powerful impact upon our emotions. If we believe we are inevitably headed to utopia this could help allay our fears but leave us resigned and passive. Yet, if we are inevitably heading for dystopia, we are also resigned and passive and ironically this also may allay anxiety. Anxiety is heightened because of uncertainty about the future. If we feel the future is certain this is allayed. Yet, if we feel we are certainly heading for dystopia the self will almost certainly be inverted. It becomes a means by which we can cope with that inversion. The self is inevitably heading for badness and there is nothing we can do to stop it. We have allayed anxiety, though, at great cost and removed hope. In order to have hope we must believe the future can be changed. Even if we believe we are inevitably heading for utopia this may make us optimistic but means the self needs do nothing to achieve it. We have no hope things could be better. The future is already mapped out. If the future is unmade and we can alter the outcome, what we do matters, which both heightens fear and means we have responsibility. There appears to be a pay-off between a sense of freedom and action and heightened anxiety. The future is not singularly good or bad but depending on choices made could be either. If we fail to do anything, though, we won't have any say in how it turns out.

We can though lessen our anxiety if we are not using the elongated linear narrative to frame our hopes. Much anxiety stems from the wish to control the future self, our future reputation and to manage our fear of the process of death and dying. If we leave go of attempting to manage this as beyond the self to control and concentrate on what is within our purview we can more easily manage our anxiety without eliminating hope. Once those arrows are fired they become other and we cannot do anything except see what happens. Those arrows may be about making the world a better place, they may concern our reputation, or they may be about developing a skill we can use. We can, though, only fire arrows if we think they will make a difference to the future and we have a suitable target. What that suitable target might look like will be discussed below. Once we have loosed our arrows we can then see what has worked and then perhaps fire some more arrows in response. The assertion that we can either be passive and see arrows as coming from the future or we can be active and shoot off arrows is an oversimplification. Everybody will be doing a degree of both. Yet this means of envisioning the future and hope means we can set up hope within the trajectory of paramount reality, without needing to elongate it. It also means we can maintain a broader sense of hope than just getting through the day in one piece.

Seven

THE REAPPEARANCE OF HAPPINESS

MODELS OF EMOTION

The end sits at the finish of a trajectory. Although we have considered other possibilities, the preferred trajectory of the self is paramount reality. It is enough to handle our past and our hopes, without over-extending the self. Paramount reality is a short-term gaze that faces towards the future with limited time horizons, sufficient to get our day-to-day activities completed. The end of the self is the ultimate motivating point of paramount reality. If it just concerns paramount reality, it will be what primarily concerns us day to day. We could just get caught up in minutiae, though, without seeing the bigger picture. Behind these day-to-day aims, though, will be other motivations. This will be the target at which we are firing our trajectory arrows. Initially, we considered happiness as the potential end but there were issues of truth, of the good and of the future self that were problematic. We have looked at each of these areas in turn. Truth is primarily conceived of as the construction of trajectories and categories. When put together these can form a predictive model that enables us to function in paramount reality.

It will, though, need constant improvement and refinement. This can be part of what gives us confidence but in itself it will not form the end of paramount reality. The good was also introduced and a distinction made between value and ethical good. Value good was about defining what is good for the self and makes us happy. The ethical good concerns the identification of specialness and is concerned with empathising with other. This is about the giving and receiving of happiness but in and of itself is not the end. We went on to examine the self, which can be conceived of as either a category or as a trajectory. The conclusion reached was that the self needs to spend time in both paramount reality and the resetting point. In the resetting point, the self–other boundary collapses; good and bad drop away and drift into the space of mind. This leads us to be able to loosen emotional labels. Once we have emerged from the resetting point, this can lead us to confidence that we can manage any bad that befalls us. We also need to structure our memory through repetition of useful algorithms that aid us back in paramount reality. Thus, the importance of having a set point. The self, though, must ultimately be able to manufacture its own good if it is to not be dependent on other for its supply. Whilst in paramount reality in addition to confidence we need hope. It is the ability of the self to establish a disposition where the self is good but other is also good. We need no more than to be sandwiched between the boundaries of confidence and hope. As long as these are secure, the good of the self will be secure. We then need to use paramount reality as a launch pad to set off trajectories directed at the target of hope. Hope is happiness placed into the future, even if it is not our own, and thus we return to where we started, back with happiness.

Happiness is an emotion. Understanding emotion is a good starting point to explore happiness more fully. We have already previously discussed mood. Mood has been understood as primarily an elongated emotion or as a disposition. The two primary positive dispositions we have been concerned with have been confidence and hope. Other moods should be avoided. Yet what we haven't fully addressed is the nature of that emotion. Emotions focus us on paramount reality and help us distinguish being in it from other states and give any situation an emotional immediacy. Emotions are primarily alarms that indicate when good or bad are about to cross, are crossing or have crossed the self–other boundary. Thus, in order to have emotions we must have a self and we must distinguish that self from other through having a boundary. We must also recognise that there is good and bad and that we want to bring some of that good into the self but keep out bad. What will also alter our experience of emotion is how well we believe the self can handle any situation. Emotions then help us bring our attention to what is important in the self and in other and deal with it. One reason for experiencing happiness is because we feel something good is either crossing the self–other boundary from self into other or could potentially make that crossing. There are other forms of happiness that will be discussed below. This form of happiness, though, has been previously introduced as pleasure.

Yet, we do not just experience happiness; we have a whole variety of emotional alarms that help detect good and bad. There are different ways of understanding these emotional alarms. One hypothesis is that an emotion is a feeling. We can call this the 'feeling equals emotion' hypothesis. By a feeling, what is meant is the physical reaction we have when experiencing emotion. So, for example, when we get angry, we may experience a surge of energy through our body. Our heart may beat faster pushing blood quickly through our bodies. We may feel hot and tense. It can be argued that each emotion has a unique feeling signature that defines it. Therefore, each separate emotion is determined by a unique bodily response, a feeling. We know we are feeling angry because there is a particular bodily feeling we get. That feeling is like a reflex, much as we would experience if somebody tapped us just below the knee and our leg jerks upwards. If we accept the feeling equals emotion hypotheses there becomes little we can do about these reflexes. Something happens and we get the feeling. The only thing we can then do is respond. Once we have responded in a particular way expressing what we feel, say running away or hitting out at somebody, the emotion dissipates. If we do not respond then the emotion will build up within us. There is a model of an emotion which is called the hydraulic hypothesis where the experience of emotions is regarded as much like the pressure building up in a boiler. In some cases, we will be unable to respond in such a way that the emotion is driving us to. We might be angry at our boss but know if we respond we will be fired. We might experience the grief of losing somebody close to us. The emotion will be telling us we need to find them and bring them back safe but we know that we can't. Emotion becomes an automatic programme that we have to follow and if we can't this will cause us distress. According to what is termed the 'hydraulic hypothesis' we can feel lots of emotional reflexes but if we stifle them in some way then they will find a way out somehow, often in more destructive impulses. So, for example, if we have emotions such as fear, anger and lust but then don't give them expression, they will wreak havoc with us later on. Having emotion leads to a loss of control. In these circumstances it becomes common to see thought and emotion as opposites. Emotion can be characterised as representing our more animal natures and thought our higher, more rational natures. Emotion cannot be controlled and is dangerous. Thought is amenable to control and therefore emotion should be subordinated to thought. Reason becomes valued and lauded over emotion.

There has been a long tradition of seeing rationalism as superior. The ancient Greek philosophers recognised two philosophical approaches to the management of emotion, of which the achievement of apatheia, where the aim is the extinguishing of emotion, was one. In apatheia, from which the term apathy is derived, the extirpation of all feeling appears both difficult and potentially joyless. If we extirpate all emotion, this will include happiness. This will mean sucking out one of the main reasons for living. A possible result of imagining what an emotionally extirpated individual would be like leads to pure rationalism. We are left with Mr Spock from *Star Trek*. Mr Spock's existence was then contrasted negatively with the rest of the human crew as it was emotion that made human life worth living. The issue is that what most people want is not the expunging of all feeling but to remove troublesome and upsetting ones and those that lead to social actions that then cause hurt and regret. Further, it can be argued that it is essential we feel a whole gamut of emotion in order to make better decisions about our interactions with the world.

Thus, perhaps in a reaction to rationalism, the more romantic reverse the dualism and side with feeling as closer to our true natures compared to our over-controlling reason. Emotion is what gives life meaning and flavour and it is thought and reason that dampen and destroy feeling. It could further be argued that cultural rules that dictate an act of self-presentation for the benefit of others, the construction of identity, ultimately lead to self-destructive emotions down the line. Potentially destructive feelings, such as anger, lust or fear, have to be masked and confidence and assurance projected instead. This interference can be argued stifles what is human in us. It is possible to see our problems as being the cultural suppression of natural emotional responses. Yet, the dangers of emotional feelings uncontrolled remain. There is another emotional theory in contrast to the 'hydraulic hypothesis' which is the 'learnt response hypothesis'. In the second model the opposite position is taken. If we respond with anger in one situation, we are more likely to respond again in the next until there is a build-up of angry responses. It will almost be as if we can no longer control our anger unless we can learn to moderate our response. The more we act on a feeling the more we follow the same pattern until it becomes a learnt response. Excessive anger for instance can wreak emotional havoc if there are not some boundaries to these feelings.

Thus, there can be characterised two views, one lauding emotion over reason and the other seeking to suppress emotion with reason. Neither seems particularly satisfactory. One possible response is to seek a middle way. Apart from apatheia, other ancient Greek philosophical thinking suggested moderating our emotions and pursuing the middle path. This was favoured by Aristotle. This appears another possible response and is something closer to appropriateness. Here emotional responses are seen as pairs of extremes and the preferential path is to choose the moderate one. We need to feel but not excessively. Yet, in order to achieve this, we need to have a mechanism to do so. Emotion needs to be characterised as a continuum with extreme feeling at either end and the preferred solution steering a middle course. It is not clear that this best represents all emotional situations. One school of ancient philosophy, the stoics, made an adjustment to the ideas of apatheia. They did not give up on the extirpation of all passions but did not give initial emotional reactions the status of emotions. These were more like reflexes for which we could do nothing. What we could do was recognise them as reflexes and not prolong them unnecessarily. Ekman (2003) states something very similar when he says that emotion is a good thing but he can see no useful purpose in mood. He seems to be using the term mood here in the sense of an aftershock as discussed earlier.

Rather than seeing emotion and thought as opposites it is possible to view emotion as involving thought as well as feeling. Thought becomes integral to any emotion along with any actions they lead us to. Thoughts and actions that can then provide leverage over the emotions we experience. It is also possible that the feelings we have are not so defined as we think. We know the emotion we are having not by a particular bodily signature. Instead, we interpret our bodily arousal because of the thoughts we are having and the circumstances we are in. Thus, our body tenses up but our interpretations will decide whether this is anger, fear, anxiety or something we can safely ignore. This way of viewing emotion potentially gives us much more control over it but does not minimise the importance of emotion either. Yet not all thought is emotional; only some is. The particular thought that carries emotion is made possible through connecting to a few important concepts. They are, what has been referred to earlier as self and other, good and bad and where this is situated spatially and in time. As stated, emotion is what detects good and bad in relation to what we consider to be our self and situates it as a category or a trajectory such that we can either steer the good towards the self or push the bad away. These though are thoughts and suggest that emotion is formed out of an appraisal or an idea about a situation. So that accompanying an experience of anger will be thoughts that I have been slighted or wronged or interrupted in some way from what I was doing. My actions will be to fight for what I consider my rights and position. This may mean verbally raising my voice, taking a hostile position or even preparing to fight. If emotions do not have unique bodily signifiers but general bodily responses that are then interpreted in the light of ongoing situations, I may by changing my thought process change the emotion. Rather than being slighted or wronged, I may feel threatened and fearful. If this is the case, seeing feeling and thought as opposites, fighting for the terrain of our souls, is unhelpful. This is important because of what we can then do about the emotions that we experience. Rather than having no control over emotion or expunging all desire, we may have more leverage in bringing our emotions under conscious control.

The exact configuration of thought, action and feeling that goes to make up an emotion is possible to debate. For example, it can be argued that a perception or thought comes before any feeling. I can hear a loud noise; I interpret this as a threat and I feel fear. As a result of feeling fear I decide to take action such as running away. In this example it is the perception or interpretation of a loud noise as a personal threat that leads to the experience of fear. It is also possible that, rather than a single thing called thought or perception, there are multiple perceptions, some acting quickly like reflexes and others more slowly. This can lead to rapid reappraisals of what is occurring, leading to different emotional responses. Thus, I may hear a loud noise, which I experience as an immediate threat to the self and feel fear but then look around my environment for more information to support or disprove my initial perception. I could find that the loud noise was a car exhaust backfiring and then as a result of my reappraisal find my fear rapidly dissipating. It is possible, though, to change the dynamic of the elements involved in an emotion. I experience a bodily feeling and interpret this as fear and I then look around the environment for a reason I may be frightened. In this example it is the feeling that precedes the interpretation. It is also tempting to conclude that the action is the last thing that follows. We feel the emotion and therefore we act but there is also some evidence that by performing an action, say in a ritual dance to express anger, then anger may be felt to arise in us. Rather than getting bogged down in endless speculations as to the exact relationship, it is probably better to see all the elements as somehow integral to emotion and that each tends to lead on to another and that by interrupting one of the elements all the other elements will also be interrupted.

The relationship between thought, feeling and action, even if we are not so concerned with the exact order they come in, is suggestive that emotion is not something that happens in a moment but is a process evolving over time in response to ongoing events. It means that each emotional episode is different, even if the alarms themselves are recognisable as particular. The time we flushed with redness will be different in some respect to the previous one. Yet, for all that each episode is unique, there will always be an underlying process of feeling, action and thought which we have a choice of sustaining or escaping. Emotion is a label that attaches itself to an arrow of trajectory or category coming towards us when we have identified it as good or bad. Yet for emotions to act as alarms they need to be quick and automatic. If I see a truck coming towards me, which is bad for the self and immediate, I do not stand and think what to do; I jump out of the way. That is not to say there is no thought but the thinking is not conscious and deliberative; it is automatic. What we can do, however, is realise we are in that process from an early stage and use whatever skills we have to reflect and halt the situation if it is inappropriate. This is easier said than done because the thoughts and actions that follow are likely to be commensurate with any emotion we are already having. So, for example, when we are nearly hit by the truck our thought may be what kind of idiot was driving so recklessly as to nearly kill me. I may go further and imagine it was a deliberate action of another towards me. Such thoughts are likely to intensify feelings of having been wronged in some way and therefore to intensify the feeling of anger. It is only by interrupting such thoughts by saying something like I was not really paying attention to what I was doing and the truck driver was only where he should be, that those feelings are likely to subside. This control or lack of it was given by the thoughts we had after the event and it is this that can perpetuate, intensify or dissipate any emotion. Human beings are not unique in the animal world in having emotion, but our capacity to think and to express our thought in language does give us a unique ability to reflect upon what we are both thinking and feeling. Rather than just having a reflex-type emotion we can cut it short or intensify it for long periods. We can think things such as I am very angry with the truck driver, but I also know being angry is not doing me any good. This ability is termed reflexivity.

Such reflexivity is used in cognitive behaviour therapy (CBT), where people learn to interrupt problematic emotions by disputing the appropriateness of any thought to a given situation. To have this skill, the minimum we must be able to do is to know we are experiencing an emotion, to distance ourselves from the emotion we are experiencing, and to be able to reflect whether this is helpful or appropriate. If an emotion is an alarm, it will alert us to something but we don't necessarily need the alarm to carry on sounding. It merely means we should put our attention somewhere and it is no longer needed to be able to switch off the alarm and then reflect upon the best course of action. We can question given what has been said the various methods of switching off an alarm. If we see an emotion as primarily a bodily feeling with a reflex response, the self will often feel bad. We don't want to feel inverted and therefore we want to get rid of that feeling as quickly as possible. We could project our pain onto somebody else, express our anger and get rid of our bad. Yet we are getting rid of our pain by moving this bad onto somebody else like a game of pass the parcel. This may give us a temporary sense of relief and we may even feel good for a while. Yet that good will dissipate; we have simply moved the bad around. This is likely to bring us substantial social difficulties in the long run and will also still leave the bad lurking, potentially to return. If we use the 'hydraulic hypotheses' it will mean we are likely to vent off but this will potentially mean we keep dealing with bad by passing it to others. If we conceive of emotion as having a thought component it makes it more amenable to interrupting the cycle of thought feeling and action. It means we can reframe situations. Thus, anger relies on the perception of threat to the self and that there is an individual that is threatening us and that we have the power to overcome that threat. By looking at the components of perception that give rise to an emotion we can disrupt the emotion. Yet, at a more general level, all emotion depends upon being sustained by identifying self and other, good and bad and a movement in time. By altering any of these components we will at least significantly disrupt the emotion. Thus, if we cause a collapse in the self–other boundary and enter a state where all is mind and strip away the labels of good and bad and a sense of time as has been recommended in the resetting point, we can strip emotion of its power.

Yet, we do not want emotion to lose all power, all of the time; we need to feel those signals when we are in paramount reality in particular, so we can feel when we are facing something bad. What we want is to be able to feel negative signals, act appropriately and then turn the alarm off. There is a whole gamut of emotions that detect what we see as bad for the self. Thus, if we feel anger, it will be because we feel something bad is about to happen or has happened and we feel able to stop it or expel it. We don't always experience anger as negative. It is an energising feeling which prepares us to fight. To do this, requires a certain amount of confidence in the self. We can get this wrong and overestimate our abilities. Although anger can start as an energy it can quickly get out of hand as it tends to trigger the same response in others. It is thus potentially dangerous and if anger becomes a default first response to every perceived sleight it will become a problem. Anger needs careful containing. If we feel fear, it will be because we feel something bad is about to happen and we do not feel able to take it on and the only options are to run, hide or cower. Fear and its relation anxiety are future-focused: they are about things that may happen. Fear, though, will usually have a target, whereas anxiety is usually more general and is often related to more ephemeral things such as how our reputation is being kept by others. Fear and anger are very close to each other and the only difference is how capable we are in dealing with a situation which can vary very quickly. We can thus find ourselves feeling anger and fear in quick succession. What is changing is our perception.

Some emotions face forward to the future and anticipate what may or may not cross the self-other boundary. There are other emotions such as guilt, embarrassment, sorrow and depression, which result from when something bad has already happened and the self has been in some way damaged by this. They indicate pain and badness inside the self. That something has been incorporated within who we are and we have the need to expel this. Emotions then don't just indicate that good and bad are about to or have crossed the self–other boundary but also indicate when that good and bad have arrived. Emotions ensure that good is experienced as an emotional reward and bad is an internal punishment. We may try to hold onto good for as long as possible but it will habituate and the feeling will dissipate. If, however, we feel something bad has been incorporated within the self, unless we do something about it, then we will continue to feel the emotion. We risk the self becoming bad and inverted and that these emotions will elongate and turn into moods. The same is the case if we feel something bad is outside of us permanently and continuously threatening to invade the self. The bad then needs to be driven out of or away from the self. If good or bad is driven out of the self, emotional alarms will also be felt. In relation to bad this may be tied to feelings of relief but may also be tied to feelings of vengeance, getting back at others, who are seen to have done the self wrong, a sense of justice or restoration.

What we don't want is to allow negative emotions to stay within the self and elongate. Emotion can become a preoccupation such that it becomes an elongation and turns into a mood. If this happens, we cannot live in the present moment of paramount reality. We become distracted by the emotion. If we have incorporated something bad within the self and see this as integrally damaging to who we are, we won't readily be able to get rid of it. In order to suffer inversion, there must first be a self. One way we could ensure inversion doesn't happen therefore would be to cease to be a self. If we did this permanently, this would mean we would never be able to enter paramount reality or construct a self–other boundary. We could, though, barricade the self–other boundary, such that we don't need anything from other and thus no bad could enter. Yet, we know we need things from other in order to survive; we have drives and we have hopes. Thus, we need to enter paramount reality in the first place. Having drives, though, will create deficiencies within the self. What we can do though is keep the self–other boundary as small as possible, and we can mark self and other out to be as good as possible. The more we expand the self beyond what we need in order to function in paramount reality, the greater the chances we can get happiness as pleasure but, unless counterbalanced by increased confidence, this will also create greater deficiency and will also increase the chances we will incorporate bad. We can grow the self–other boundary because we tie self to a space, with objects we accrue, with reputations to keep, which then will need defending. As the objects break or lose their lustre, we will constantly have to replenish them. As the applause of our audience turns to derision we can find ourselves having to run off stage, leading to inversion. We can tie self to an identity and have a story we tell others and to ourselves as to who we are. This can make us feel good and give confidence, particularly as a progression, but if this becomes damaged it can lead us to be vulnerable. We can knit our self in with a group either spatially or as part of a wider story. This can lead us to feel stronger and have a wider purpose but we can lose our individuality and will end up alienating anybody who does not feel they belong. It will thus multiply the emotions we can feel and make negative emotion more likely.

Yet, so long as we are able to cope with negative emotion, respond when we hear its alarm and then turn it off this won't be such an issue. Negative emotion, though, is pointing to things in the self space that are bad and need to be got rid of. As we grow the self space, there is a greater chance that there will be more in the self space that will need to be expelled. We can either expel the bad as described in the 'hydraulic hypothesis' or we need a mechanism by which we can strip emotion from that which has been incorporated into the self. We can do this through the resetting point. The problem, though, is it can take time to process emotion through the resetting point. If we have too much or too intense bad that won't go away, this can become difficult. We could then find the negative emotion residing in the self and becoming a preoccupation. At this point an emotion elongates and we are unable to stop the alarm. Thus, we need to feel negative emotions whilst in paramount reality. Our attention needs to be drawn to what is bad in our environment so we can then deal with it. Yet once our attention has been drawn, we need to be able to switch off the alarm. It is like pain. We need to feel pain, but once we know about it, we don't need to continually feel it. That is why we take analgesia. Having a resetting point is our analgesia for emotional pain. Having a well-working resetting point that could process all our bad into good could be seen as meaning it doesn't matter whether we have to face bad or good; it is all the same and doesn't matter. Yet it takes emotional effort to remove bad and isn't easy, particularly for highly personally traumatic events or frequent bad occurrences. We can eventually be overwhelmed.

MOVEMENTS IN RELATION TO THE SELF–OTHER BOUNDARY THAT CREATE HAPPINESS

In paramount reality, unless there is good reason, it is better to seek happiness, to feel positive and to avoid what is bad. Thus, we have less chance to be preoccupied by negative thoughts. One way of being positive is to have confidence when we enter paramount reality that we can manage well within it. This is best achieved by constructing a sound model of reality, by having the maximum amount of good in both self and other, through using the resetting point and having a good rehearsal of our memory. The point of being in paramount reality is to engage with other. We are enabled to deal with the categories and the arrows of trajectory that befall us and to send some trajectories off into the future. Managing these all well can cause us to feel happy. Being in paramount reality is our source of happiness. It is the site after all where emotions are brought about, so it will be where all our happiness is generated. To have happiness there must be a self–other boundary. All other positive feeling will be self-derived dispositional mood. We can either feel happy by moving something good in relation to the self–other boundary or expanding the self–other boundary into other. In this section the movements of good in relation to the boundary will be considered. In this situation, emotion is primarily created through movements across or in relation to this boundary and happiness is the emotional alarm that detects what is good. Movements of the boundary itself will be considered in the next section. In the English language, happiness is often used as an overarching term for all positive emotion. By contrast negative emotions have specific meanings, such that anger, fear, guilt and sadness are highly differentiated to particular circumstances. This does not mean, however, that because positive emotions are not as differentiated, that they cannot be. It could be that happiness as a whole is not best as the end but that a form of happiness is.

One form of happiness is related to the feeling that bad has either crossed into the self from other or may do. This will give rise to the plethora of negative emotions such as anger, fear and anxiety. If we think something bad is about to happen and it then doesn't this will lead to a form of happiness. Thus, if we see a lion and think it may attack us but instead it walks away calmly then, as the anxiety dissipates, we are likely to feel a form of positive emotion. Similarly, if something bad has happened and we manage to expel it we will feel happy. We could process this through the resetting point but if we can it might be quicker to expel this from the self directly if we can. Thus, if somebody has slighted us and we are subsequently vindicated then this will lead to positive emotion. We can call this experience of happiness 'relief'. In one case we see the bad outside the self and fear it may damage us but we manage to avoid it. In the second case, bad enters the self but we manage to expel it back across the self-other boundary. Both of these movements will lead to a sense of relief. Relief, though, is reliant for its effects on experiencing either the threat of bad or bad having been incorporated in the self first. It means unpleasantness is experienced first and then subsequently we experience happiness. It is an emotional trajectory marked with pain at the beginning and happiness at the end. This is an unpleasant way to get happiness. It also doesn't last and is likely to make us more fearful and watchful of bad in the future. We may have been able to expel bad in the past but may not be able to do it another time.

We can also feel happiness through pleasure, the bringing in of good to the self across our self–other boundary. This movement has been much discussed previously. By originating from the other side of the self–other boundary means we can never fully control this emotion. Once a pleasure has crossed the boundary, we will stop getting the feeling of happiness due to habituation. In order to get the feeling again we will have to repeatedly get goods to come across our boundary. This is what is termed the 'hedonic treadmill'. It means that pleasure does not last. Yet, we are fortunate to live at a time when there is a plentiful supply of goods. So long as we have the means there are often ample opportunities to bring in goods; we may for a time not be too concerned by this effect. This may mean we can have one pleasure after another. Each pleasure, though, will create a deficiency, a gnawing emptiness that will need to be filled. This is a consequence of having drives and goals which have previously been discussed. We will also increasingly habituate to pleasure as a whole so that the experience over time of happiness will lessen.

Pleasures can be singular emotional experiences. This is the case if something good arrives unexpectedly. We will then have a singular experience of feeling good about something which will then dissipate with time. Most pleasures though will be experiences which occur over time and will be marked with different emotions along their trajectory. Once we have identified something as good in other, we will often feel we need that good within the self. This need will cause us discomfort from feeling the self is deficient without having that good. Drives and goals mean we are drawn to particular things in our environment as good. These things that will assuage our discomfort we will then label with good. Assuming we can then bring this good into the self, this discomfort will ameliorate and we will often get an intense feeling of pleasure. If this is a relatively short act of bringing a good into the self, this will be when the trajectory stops and then the pleasure will dissipate as we habituate to the object. In the case of drives though the trajectory we will have another feeling to indicate when we are feeling satiated and need to stop. In drives, emotions will come as pairs as they act both as indicators that we need something and then act to shut off that need when we have had enough. This, though, also ties in with the idea that within many objects there are elements of good and bad. Therefore, some objects are likely to stimulate more than one alarm. We need to have food but it is also possible to have too much of it. The issue is in being paired we can begin to see all objects as emotionally complex and therefore the alarms we receive when experiencing them can reflect this. Thus, pleasure is an unreliable way of achieving happiness because we habituate to it over time, we cannot ultimately control it and the happiness is frequently sandwiched between discomforts. Besides, when we do habituate to any pleasure and assuming we don't destroy any object in the process of consumption, it will then potentially become a source of pain as we fear we may lose the object. Yet, we should not fear pleasure either; we should welcome it when it comes and move on. Pleasure and relief are probably the most obvious movements from which to derive happiness, but there are alternatives.

Perhaps surprisingly, we do not, though, have to bring something into the self in order to feel happy about it. It is enough that we can identify something as having potential to be brought into the self as a good. We could also bring something within the ambit of the self and return it to whence it came. It becomes a loan as in the case of mysteries which was previously discussed. Mysteries, though, was a residual category, which applied to anything we cannot possess or control, a subset of which could be positive. Yet, the attitude mysteries can imbue can be had towards anything as long as we are content to experience other as good without the need to assert control over it. Control has been discussed previously. When we align control with determining what is good and bad this leads to a desire for the self to dominate other. It can cause us to expand our boundary and in doing so it can multiply what we find bad in other. If controlled–uncontrolled is kept to describe the self–other boundary, but is separated from describing what is good and bad, this means it demarcates just what the self is to be responsible for. We no longer need to move the self–other boundary and are happy to keep other as other. It means that good is no longer defined by what we control in other. Previously, we have discussed how to minimise the bad in the self. All things being equal, the larger amount of good in the self, the smaller we want from other. If we view good from other as being just what we desire for the self, either to satisfy our drives or hopes, then minimising what is good in other is good for the self. Thus, by minimising our drives and having appropriate goals, this minimises the deficiency that is created in the self, minimising the bad in the self. This is patently a good thing. Yet, it means that much of other will be regarded as bad.

Yet, so long as we are content to leave the good in other, we can create as much good as we like. It is not enough, though, not to find large amounts of bad in other; we must be able to positively value what is there. The ability to find as much good in other as possible will be termed appreciation. We just don't want appreciation of other to be at the expense of good in the self. Thus, to be happiest we want the largest amount of good in both self and other that is safe. If we labelled everything as good, we would in theory feel happy all the time. Theories such as pantheism which see God in everything will usually end up taking this position. For if God is in everything and God is good, everything must be good. Yet this is an unrealistic and potentially dangerous position. There is bad in our environment and we must be able to identify it in order to survive. The point we can turn everything good is after it has passed into memory and we can learn from it. It is good because we can learn from it and we can then improve our model of paramount reality. We remove labels of good and bad in the resetting point, and thus they cease to be part of a personal story. Yet, we can revisit these situations to learn how to approach paramount reality better the next time. Both good and bad exist in paramount reality. Yet, whilst acknowledging this, as long as other is relatively benign and not a direct threat to the self, it is important we can appreciate it. If we come to take what is in other for granted or become so distracted that we fail to see the good, we will be liable to miss out on happiness.

The starting point for appreciation is to observe closely. In observing, the purpose is to know it or become familiar with it, not to own or control it. Knowing something well can be a prelude to control, so if we are appreciating something we must be careful that this should not happen. We have previously discussed a boundary that can be used to demarcate the self, knowing–unknowing. It, though, is neither a good descriptor of self–other or of good–bad. What it does do well, though, is when applying it to the space of other that we want to appreciate. It describes other neither as good nor bad. It is good that we know some things well but it is also good that there are things we need to know. It is bad if we are in a situation where we think we know everything. It is also bad when we are in a situation where we think we know very little. We need to steer a middle course keeping the extremes of this continuum in balance. We will discuss this further below under synchronicity. Knowing something, though, is only a prelude to appreciation. Unless we carefully observe something, we cannot appreciate it, but observing or knowing about something does not necessarily lead to appreciation. We must be able to cultivate a further emotional attitude to turn what we are observing into something that is good and we can appreciate apart from its utility to the self.

The main way we create good is to compare it to bad. Thus, by creating good we automatically create something that is bad; we create a dualism. This will split other down the middle into good and bad. Even if we want to leave it there, it will mean large swathes of other will be left as bad. We have previously discussed the creation of continuums where both ends are good. This could be another option. It means we can always try to find good in anything. Yet, in creating good in one place, we are always displacing bad to somewhere else. The continuum is always underpinned by other dualisms, which will include bad. So, although we may be emphasising the good, the risk will be that bad is always somewhere. If we are creating good, bad will always also be created; we just need to create good in a way that it is constrained. If we create good now, one place that is relatively safe is to put bad in the past. We can do this by creating a progression for the good that has arrived before us. A progression was seen as problematic for the self but the object in front of us doesn't need a future, just an explanation of how it arrived to us, and how if something had been slightly different, how any component that had gone missing, this moment wouldn't have happened. Another option is to amalgamate other into something very big. We have been suspicious of placing the self within groups, but as long as an amalgamation doesn't result in the de-individualisation of the self or the exclusion of anybody then it can be done. Let us start with things that are easy to appreciate, mysteries. Most of the mysteries are good because they are awesome; because of their size or splendour they are amazing. Yet, to have a mystery such as this it potentially renders everything else as mundane and ordinary. We then see what is awesome as good, but having returned back to the ordinary it has the potential to appear mundane again. The only way we could make everything awesome would be to cast it as part of something much bigger. This is possible. Everything is part of a system that is the Earth, the Sun, Moon and stars. What is good is that everything is part of the system and works together as part of a whole. We must, though, make room for bad, otherwise we end up with the pantheism of earlier, but that bad must be constrained. If what is good is the system working, then what becomes bad is the system not working. At some level, though, the system will work, which reduces the possibility of bad. Yet, within this the self becomes the observer of the system, so if something happens to the self then there will be no longer an observer of the whole, thus bad can happen to the self, but that bad is constrained.

Another movement relies not on the expulsion of something bad but the giving of something good. Losing something good usually will occasion sadness as discussed under relief. If we have a favourite object and it breaks, we can become upset. In our discussion on deriving happiness from pleasure once we have habituated to the object, we feel nothing towards it until something happens. Then we can feel pain. Thus, we actually become liable to more negative emotion than positive. This emotion is grief. Yet the movement of good from the self to other can also occasion the self to feel positive. This will usually be a deliberate action of the self as opposed to an accident or the deliberate action of others. This giving of good away will be termed generosity. We have come across some of these movements before. In some cases, we give the good of the self in order to be able to enhance our reputation. In these circumstances the positive emotion results from somebody whose opinion matters to us judging us positively. This comes back to the idea of having a reputation and believing that having evidence that others are keeping it well will give rise to happiness. Yet, we cannot control how others regard us and the pickings can be fleeting and fickle. Alternatively, we can give the good to others to show compassion. We can feel good at giving a present to somebody else we care about, or having made something good that somebody wants, or giving time to a charity. This relies on somebody who is usually in a weaker position than us showing us gratitude. It can also reinforce our feelings of superiority and how good we are. In both cases if we feel we give good in anticipation that we will get something back in return. This may just be another's appreciation and it may be in the future but the expectation is there. We have allowed our good to be in the hands of others to judge. This will be termed conditional generosity as our feeling of happiness is contingent upon the response we get from other, which we cannot by definition control and may be illusory. By being conditional, it means the happiness we feel does not result directly from the good we give out but from the reaction we get back from others and the feeling we have enhanced who we are. Thus, such actions usually stem from our own feeling of inadequacy and the need to affirm our own good in ourselves. Yet such actions may fail and such conditional generosity makes our feelings about the self vulnerable. The previous recommendation was not to allow the bits of the self that reside in others to matter. They are no longer ours to control and so we shouldn't try. What we can do is be our own judge but to do this with fairness and accuracy. This is difficult and requires a fair degree of self-honesty.

Yet, if generosity can become a movement of good from the self that is not contingent on the response of others, this has many advantages. As opposed to receiving good from other or escaping from bad, if we are giving out the good, we have control. This gives the prospect of the self being able to control happiness. If we conceive of happiness though as our measure of good in the self, we will only be able to give what we have already got. In these circumstances, if we have a finite supply and if we give this away this will drain us of the good we have. We will end up depleted and inverted. Yet, if our good habituates over time it could still be argued that this is not a bad thing to do with it. We might as well give it away as let it rot and become our pain if we lose it or it gets broken. If the self, though, can manufacture its own good then it will have an endless supply which it can attempt to give away. Good in the self is measured in confidence, so, as long as we place our confidence in something which is endless and doesn't interfere in our ability to give out good, we can create endless good for the self. By placing confidence in our ability to manage what is thrown at us and not what we do, we can have an endless supply of good. In entering paramount reality with a target of hope which doesn't undermine the self now, we can have an endless supply of good. By giving something good away we challenge the notion of happiness as something we keep an accountant's ledger for: of getting as much positive for the self and avoiding the negatives. Using such unconditional generosity means we will potentially derive most happiness in paramount reality from giving away good. This should not be contingent upon the response we get but it should genuinely be good. Using our skills of empathy which we relate to specialness and the golden rule we can attempt to give as much good to other. We may have an unlimited supply of good in the self but we probably don't have an unlimited supply of goods. This means that giving out good from the self isn't a matter of giving things although it doesn't preclude this. The least we can do, though, is to keep other's specialness well, have genuine concern for them and we can let them know this.

Yet, there may be some circumstances where giving out good to other may have dangerous repercussions for the self. These are circumstances where the other is not indifferent to our efforts but may actively be hostile. This may be because the other does not acknowledge our specialness and sees us as property. They may well be deficient in skills of empathy. The world they see may have been chunked up into groups which they are either with or against. Thus, the person they see in front of them is not an individual underscored with specialness but a member of a potentially hostile group. They may see us as a fellow performer on stage and consequently a rival to the applause of others that they crave. Their own self may have become inverted because they haven't for whatever reason been able to process the pain they feel. They may displace this pain onto us in an attempt to rid themselves of that inversion. The inversion may have interfered with their ability to tell good from bad. It may mean they have barricaded their self–other boundary in an attempt to stop any more bad coming in. Paramount reality may have become so unpredictable and hostile for them so all they can do is shut off from it. This means they cannot hear or relate to anything we are doing and cannot tell if what we are doing is good or bad. There might be multiple reasons why if we give what is good to other, we get back bad. Yet, this should not undermine our ability to give out good but may make it more difficult to determine what would be good for other. It must always be underscored by the golden rule and our empathy but should be directed to helping the individual see themselves as a person of value, who can be good and sees themselves apart from a group, who can lower their barricades and not depend on the applause of any given audience. If, though, there is a genuine threat to the self from other, we have every right to defend ourselves.

A further movement or more properly movements across the self–other boundary will be termed synchronicity. This is where our actions in sending out trajectory arrows are met with positive returns immediately. The giving of good from the self gets immediate rewards from other for what we do. It can feel in this situation that we don't have to do the hard work of creating our own good. All we have to do is give it away and then we get it back again. Good is endlessly recycled across the self–other boundary. This experience most often occurs when we are performing a skill which is sufficiently challenging but we feel is within our capabilities to master. We do something, we perform it well and there is a reward of executing a wonderful piece of art or playing well at a sport. This form of happiness is called a flow state and was described by Csikszentmihalyi (1992). The flow state, though, in general is rare. Unless we manage to perfect a skill to a high level it will be something we experience occasionally. It can also occur in particularly environments of benign communities, where people give spontaneously and look after each other. When we experience it, though, it gives a sense of profound pleasure, that self and other are in harmony and that the sharp division between self and other has collapsed. It represents the synchronicity of giving and receiving in the moment and is worth savouring when it does arrive. Due to its desirability, we are apt to develop ways where we can get greater access to these flow states. For example, many video games are often designed to induce flow and give a sense of mastery over a simulated environment. These simulations, though, can take us away from paramount reality rather than engaging with it and the flow state although worth appreciating should not be chased for its own sake. Although the flow state is worth savouring, when it does arrive, there is an aspect of it that is worth noting. Rather than existing at the boundary of self and other, or at the boundary of good and bad, it exists at the centre of what is known and unknown. It involves steering the middle course between the familiar, where we know what we are doing and bringing this up against the unfamiliar in an attempt at mastery. This zone won't necessarily bring about the flow state but unless we inhabit it, when in paramount reality, it definitely won't arrive. Yet, it is also to fall out of the zone and lose the state, which leaves as quickly as it arrives.

MOVEMENTS OF THE WHOLE SELF–OTHER BOUNDARY THAT CREATE HAPPINESS

Pleasure, relief, appreciation, conditional and unconditional generosity and synchronicity are the main ways we can achieve the emotion of happiness, whilst in the trajectory of paramount reality, with a simple self–other boundary that faces other to the future. Of these, the most sustainable are unconditional generosity and appreciation as they are within the gift of the self to generate independently. We can also feel happiness, though, by moving the self–other boundary entirely in the direction of expansion. If we are successful in expanding the boundary, this in itself will lead to happiness, but, much like pleasure, it will also habituate. In order to keep getting any effect we must keep moving the boundary. It is a one-way process, so having moved the boundary once, in order to keep feeling happy, we must keep moving it outward, further and further into other and away from any core of the self. By making the self–other boundary outward we will be making it longer, making opportunities for pleasure more likely. There will be more opportunities to locate good in other but we are also expanding the opportunities for bad. The boundary will also be harder to police. The narrowest the self–other boundary can be is as a line that separates the self from its future. It is difficult to move this sort of imagined boundary and it is fairly fixed. Yet, as has been discussed, there are many different ways to imagine the self and its boundary to other which make its movement far easier. If the good–bad boundary is overlaid on top of the self–other boundary or otherwise becomes enmeshed with the definer terms controlled and uncontrolled this will encourage us to push into other to control it as much as possible. This will meet resistance from other and leads to a situation where either the self seeks to dominate other or retreats from it. Often, the main reason for moving the self–other boundary is the search for greater control. Yet, as control can never really exist in other and only in the self it will always become a search that is illusory. Once expanded, though, the self feels impelled to continually expand itself in search of a locus it never seems to get to. This was where the self–other boundary and the good–bad boundary had exactly aligned.

In situations where this is not the case, we can still end up in scenarios where we can expand the self–other boundary. It has also been argued that any conception of the self as a spatial category expands the self–other boundary from being a narrow boundary that faces forward in time to one that encompasses a place. The self–other boundary is moved to entirely surround the self. Other is conceptualised as something that encompasses us and the self is staked out from it. Paramount reality becomes more of a lookout tower from which we have to survey any space we inhabit. It faces no longer just towards the future but in several directions at once. The danger of such a conception is the fear that we could be overwhelmed by other. It thus becomes imperative we form a defence: a core of who we are. Core becomes our essentialness, which then translates as our foundation. The core and the foundation become the same thing and will be from where we get confidence. We need a firm marker which will keep otherness at bay. Otherness will be on every side and could be felt liable to overwhelm the self at any point. If we have a spatial concept of self, it matters as to what space we then occupy and control. For the moment let us concern ourselves with siting the self in physical space, where we are, the home we have, the places we go, and leave the more ephemeral spaces we can inhabit, the relationships we form, the connections we have, the ideas we share, to later. In this conception of self, we may add in a trajectory but we will primarily be a category moving through time. Time is something that if it exists will just trundle along in the background with minimal awareness.

The definer terms mine and not mine, though, make possible the idea the self can accumulate possessions and that we can site the self in more than one place at a time. They make it possible to define the self as a category with an ever-expanding boundary over what is covered. This enables the self to expand in terms of the objects it possesses and means the self could almost have a limitless possibility of expansion as long as it has a supply of objects deemed good, can afford them and adequately store and protect them. Expanding the self in a physically defined place is limiting, in that we require those in other to recognise our rights over any physical objects. Although it doesn't require ownership as such, we will need to abide by certain rules and conventions. To define the self by a home we must be able to afford one or have a relationship with somebody who can provide one for us. To define the self by a workplace, we must first have work. None of this, though, obviates the rules of habituation. We may attach the self to more and more objects but they will only make us feel good when they cross the self boundary and will then recede from mind. We then have to bring in more and more objects to get the same feeling. Having more and more objects also places the self at more risk as, rather than feeling pleasure, we are more likely to feel the pain of loss as all the objects inevitably degrade or are lost. Expansion, though, is not mainly in the number of objects the self attaches itself to but in the places where we site the self, associated with a home, which either can be expanded or multiplied. We can have holiday homes, or a second home, for instance. Yet having more space means that not only will a home be usually identified as necessary to the self but so will other locations. We can also site the self at a work place, at a leisure space, the places it visits frequently. All this can mean the self becomes highly dispersed physically over large territory, which can all be difficult to manage and will all be degrading.

Defining the self through physical space and objects is limiting. Yet, other ways of defining the self could offer more flexibility and be easier to expand our boundary. For example, we can expand the self through having and keeping a reputation where the self is placed with others to keep. Thus, if we give our reputation away, and allow our happiness to depend on how others regard us, whether this is through liking us, them doing what we say or being grateful to us for our help, not only can we be happy when this happens but we can feel happy when our influence is expanded. We move our self boundary outward into other, into more and more people. This is fame. If we feel happy when we think others regard us well, the more people we do this to, the greater the potential to feel happy. Yet, the corollary of this is that the more people who can think badly of us, the more people who can judge us harshly, the greater the potential for us to feel bad. Thus, although we have expanded the opportunities for happiness, we have also expanded the opportunities for negative emotions as well. In addition, we can never really be certain how another really regards us. We can end up second guessing and giving import to all sorts of things. If we want more than fame, though, and instead we want power, it won't matter so much what others think of us but whether they do what we say. Yet, if people do what we say and then curse us then this may be uncomfortable. Our happiness will then rest on the power we can exert and the accumulation of power will create enemies and rivalries. Life will only have meaning to the extent we can have and maintain power and history teaches that, even if we get power, it will dissipate eventually and often at moral cost.

Yet, we do not have to regard the self as spatial to be able to expand the self–other boundary. If we primarily see the self as existing temporally, we can lengthen the self–other boundary in time through having an elongated linear trajectory. This means shifting the self–other boundary from its narrow position facing into the future into longer lines which connect the future and the past. We create a story for the self that links together important events in our life. The boundary is what ties those events together and usually develops that story in a positive direction and separates the self from other. The storyline will then encompass what is self. Everything else that is other will then fall outside the line of the story. Once we have formed the story, shifting the self–other boundary means changing and developing the story in some way. It will also often mean having a future self, that which we want to become. The past is already written, although it is possible to change how we see the past as we move through time and our perspective alters. We can also cross the firmament to merge the self into a bigger group story. Thus, the boundaries of the self become that of a wider imagined group. As the story of this group changes and alters, so do these boundaries. We do, though, cede control of the writing of the story of the self to others.

Shifting boundaries outward as a means of achieving happiness, though, is ultimately unsustainable. However rich we become, however popular, however powerful, however much we achieve our personal goals and become the person we want to be, we will not forever be able to move our boundaries infinitely into other. The self will become constrained and will eventually disappear. Besides, all movements of expansion will lead the self away from the self–other boundary that is easiest to control and is most present in paramount reality, the narrow focus of the immediate future. It is, though, possible that we shift boundaries in the opposite direction towards contraction; this will often result in the opposite of happiness. The loss of somebody who we thought was keeping our reputation well, having to sell a property or having to rewrite our story because something happens that challenges who we thought we were. Possibly we could experience feelings of grief, loss or anger, for example. Having expanded boundaries, though, will result in a more complex self. Contraction will result in the boundary moving closer to the core of the self towards greater simplicity. Thus, in losing complexity of the self, as long as this is something we control and choose, could lead to happiness. Yet, this would be a single movement, much like an expansion. Having contracted the boundary once, we will habituate to this and in order to feel happiness again we will have to contract it again. We will have a finite position to which we can contract the boundary to, namely facing narrowly forward into the future. The only possibility, having done this, to feel happiness would be to then expand the boundary again. This gives the possibility that the self could go through cycles of expansion and contraction which in turn would lead to happiness. This would make such happiness sustainable, but would mean, for instance, we would get fame only to then try to give it up again, then try to get it again. A reputation may not be that easy to expunge or control. Alternatively, we get lots of things only to then give them away and then get more things. We could join the self to a group and then leave again to join another one, bearing in mind that some groups are easier to join and leave than others. We could imagine the self story and then give up imagining the self story and perhaps imagine an entirely different story. It perhaps would be simpler not to embark on the expansion and contraction of the self–other boundary in the first place. In which case, we are left with having a narrow self–other boundary when in paramount reality that demarcates the future and divides self from other and three main ways of achieving happiness when we are there: to focus on unconditional generosity, to maintain a balance between what is known and unknown in other and as far as possible to contain the bad in self and the bad in other to an absolute minimum and see the bulk of both as good.

Eight

THE FINAL END – HOPE

SETTING UP A TARGET FOR HOPE – THE AGGLOMERATION

We are now in a position to review the question we began with at the start of the book. Having voyaged around what truth is, journeyed around good and circumnavigated the self, on the premise that these could be alternative ends, we have arrived back at happiness. Yet through these journeys, hopefully a more developed and nuanced understanding of both the end and happiness has been gained. The end we are concerned with sits at the horizon of paramount reality and is hope. Hope is happiness postponed, so it is happiness but in a different form. It is a dispositional happiness based on looking forward to the future. Yet, it is easy for the self to become invested in that future and undermine its present. The future should not be bought at the expense of the present. The ideal way the self should enter paramount reality has been much discussed already. At the beginning of this trajectory, the self must have confidence. The construction of paramount reality will, by definition, create a boundary between self and other, which should be kept narrowly facing the future. Paramount reality will also cleave good from bad, but we should look to keep as much of the self as good and as much of other as good as possible. Happiness is our detector of good, so we can know we are doing this when we are happy when in paramount reality. Yet, in order to persist through paramount reality, none of this is enough; we need to have hope. Hope sustains us and provides the target of what we are aiming for overall. If we are sending out arrows of trajectory into the future, it will be what we are aiming to hit.

Hope is a profoundly difficult mood state to get right and can easily go awry. It is a mood that needs something powerful to attach to. If we have nothing to aim for, we risk entering a state of listlessness and passivity, having no sense of direction and failing to act. Yet, in setting up an object of hope, although it motivates us, it does give rise to potential problems. It is easy to become emotionally invested in achieving any object we set up, such that it devalues where we are now. To begin to live in the illusion that the target we have is part of the self rather than of other and believe we may be able to control the future for the self. We can then become diverted from living in paramount reality and risk intensifying any emotions we feel. It has already been said that emotions should be kept at the boundary of the self. If we become emotionally invested in hope then we will end up seeing good as anything that furthers our hopes and what is bad as what detracts from them. We become preoccupied not with now but what may happen in the future, extending our emotions whilst we wait and watch what happens. Whilst we plan and turn our lives into a game of strategy that may or may not achieve our desired outcomes.

Hope has been discussed earlier on in the book in the context of constructing the elongated linear narrative. There are several ways in which this could be constructed but in relation to manufacturing hope we throw the self into the future. This means we imagine the self as different to what we are now, a better self. We then draw a line to the new self and see what we might need to reach that point. It is the self colonising the future. We turn part of the future into the self, a road which we need to tread upon to get to our hopes. This, though, will devalue the self we are currently. The goal in this instance is personal, meaning it only applies to the self and is not about creating anything better in other. With such a personal goal, we either achieve it or we don't. If we achieve it, we can feel good for a time. We may even change our life trajectory, which enables us to tell a different story to the one we could have told. Yet over time the happiness it creates will dissipate and we will adjust to whatever trajectory we have taken, often barely giving the alternative story a second glance. We will habituate to any goal achieved. In doing so we will have created an identity, which then will need defending from other. We will also cease to have a target to hope for, so, unless we can then create a new self we want to become, we will lose hope.

It could perhaps be argued it is better to have something to hope for which is bigger. By having a bigger target what is meant is something that is more difficult to achieve. Thus, there is less risk of getting to our target, bringing it into the self and therefore experiencing the effect of the goal dissipating. One way we could have a bigger target for the self is, instead of maybe getting a new job or a completing a course, we could make it much more difficult. We could imagine being a perfect self that never makes mistakes and lives a hermit-like existence away from the pollutions of other. Yet, if we put our goal too far out of reach that we never achieve it we can become easily discouraged and give up even striving. Alternatively, we could view a new self as an inappropriate target to pin our hopes on. It will either be too small or too impossible. One way we have previously discussed of having such a target would be one we share with others. A way of doing this has been previously discussed, by attaching the self to a group, whether this is a single other or a multitude. We enmesh the self with the story of a particular group we can identify with. It then is not the self that colonises the future but the self becomes part of other. We then imagine what it would be like to live in a better way together. This makes the dream we are having about other and so it is less about the self colonising the space of other and more about how we can organise other in a better way that would also be of benefit to the self. This may still be a difficult or impossible target but it matters less that the self cannot reach it on its own, as long as the self can be part of the story of reaching it. Yet, such an imagining will still devalue the current situation any group finds itself in. We are still constructing a progression with all the problems this will create.

Constructing hope through attaching it to an individual future self or group is thus problematic. In paramount reality, we are facing towards other. The end we are facing should remain as other and not be transformed into the self or an extended self as in the case of a group. Thus, the self remains the self and other remains other and the responsibility for control stops at the self and its actions. Rather than seeing the self in the future through the metaphor of a road, instead we can use an alternative metaphor of a target to which we send out arrows of trajectory. This gives a better relationship as to what the self can be responsible for and means we are not over-extending the boundaries of the self. Once we have sent something out into other, we can no longer control it. We can instead keep sending out more trajectory arrows in response to the results of what we have sent out previously, having learnt from what has gone before. Hope becomes what we are sending our trajectory arrows to. What the self can do is hold other well and maximise the good seen in it. Within other are those with specialness. In order to maximise good, the specialness of other must always be underpinned by good even though individuals with specialness can originate bad, particularly if they have become inverted. The self must hold this specialness well. If we deny specialness to some, we create bad in other. Dividing those with specialness into groups of good and bad divides other as evenly as any dualism. This is so even if the self remains apart and doesn't identify with any group. There will still be those in good groups which the self is happy to engage with and those in bad groups which the self seeks to avoid. Instead of creating groups of those with specialness it is suggested an agglomeration is used. An agglomeration does not seek to put people into categories of good and bad which the self can then choose to relate to or not. It is an addition of those together within the space of other, without seeing good or bad, other than the possession of specialness. An example of an agglomeration becomes the utilitarian approach to morals and happiness. Thus, one target we could use for our arrows is to maximise the happiness of those in front of us so long as they have specialness. What we are trying to do is send out as much good as possible and prevent others with specialness from becoming inverted.

THE SUM OF ALL OUR HAPPINESS

Hedonism can be seen as what happens when an individual seeks to maximise their own happiness through getting as much pleasure as possible from other at any given time. Yet, opportunities for pleasure can only be made widely available if the self can interact with a well-functioning other, where goods are manufactured in bulk, made available and accessed easily. If this doesn't happen, then the pool of potential pleasure will be narrow and hedonism becomes only possible for the rich and powerful. This suggests that in order to have sustainable pleasures we must develop the idea of an agglomeration, that those with specialness must work together in order to produce what is good in order for us to be able to enjoy it as pleasure. If we just take from other without somehow also contributing to the wider effort, then there will be no good to have for anybody. It is possible to imagine a finite pool of the world's goods from which we can derive pleasure. Pleasure represents the drawing down on the pool and, unless there is a means of also adding to the pool of goods, eventually that pool will run dry. Hedonism doesn't concern itself with any of this. There is no communal holding of potential future goods, because it is about maximising pleasure taken by an individual in the now. This position cares little about how the wider supply of pleasure is formed in the future and is merely concerned with obtaining this for the self by the easiest means possible.

To have a notion of an agglomeration, we must be able to recognise at some level that our own happiness is dependent upon the well-being of other. We must also have in mind that happiness that is sharable is probably more sustainable than that which is exclusive to the self. From this recognition we can then ask how it is best to sustain a communal holding of happiness. One way we could conceive of an agglomeration is as a store of future goods. We, along with others, can put aside things for the future, through delayed gratification, as we recognise that this will ensure a more plentiful supply of good in the future. This introduces into the system one of the other main ways we can create happiness other than pleasure: generosity. That generosity, though, is conditional. We are hoping to be able to give pleasure to our future self, at the expense of pleasure being taken now and are doing so by putting into a pool with others. This will be then kept safe and then drawn down on in the future. This form of agglomeration will be called the 'sum of all our happiness' and it functions a bit like a communal bank account. We put in our good now, mix it with others' good in the hope that it will be safe and we can draw down on it in the future. Such an agglomeration requires an idea that sometimes it is best to delay pleasures being taken now and of a conditional generosity; that by giving now we can get something back in the future.

The 'sum of all our happiness' is a simple agglomeration of goods that everybody who contributes has put in. It is different, though, to the utilitarian idea where we measure the greatest happiness at any given time. This makes no distinction over how we come to be happy just that we feel happy. Thus, all the happiness when we have become inverted is included, which fails to measure value reliably. This includes people deriving happiness from sadism, masochism and doing each other down. Such happiness is usually derived from relief: the form of happiness that relies on the avoidance of bad or its expulsion. This includes displacing our pain onto others and spreading bad around. If we have become inverted, we can also invert bad as good and then become consequently happy. The utilitarian idea simply adds up all the happiness at any given time however it comes about. The 'sum of all our happiness' does not include this relief as a means of happiness. It focuses on pleasure and conditional generosity and is concerned solely with good and not displacing bad. It is about happiness being a store for the future not about taking happiness in the now. The 'sum of all our happiness' has at its centre the idea of the self being concerned with its own happiness and could be seen as primarily selfish. It relies on pleasure and conditional generosity, balancing out. As a result, morality becomes being somebody who plays by the rules, and takes out no more than they put in. A more moral person is somebody who puts in to the pot but then takes very little out. In contrast, immorality will be somebody who breaks the rules and wants to take out of the pot of communal good without first contributing. So long as we are concerned with being a moral person, the guide to our actions would be to maximise the total amount of good available to the wider community, however the wider community define it. As well as those who give to the pot, another moral action could be those who defend it from those who fail to contribute. Thus, conditional generosity will add to the 'sum of all our happiness', whilst pleasure will drain it. Assuming we do choose to be a moral person, our generosity will add to the 'sum'. An issue, though, is that we could find a mismatch, where few people add to the sum and most people drain it, leaving very little communal happiness to go around. Pleasure will still be seen as the preferred way of being happy and generosity, a necessity to get more pleasure down the line. We know that many people prefer to derive their happiness from pleasure rather than generosity and the schema provides no means for balancing this out.

Conditional generosity as opposed to unconditional generosity is the giving of good from the self, in the anticipation that this will result in future good accruing to the self in the future. Unconditional generosity focuses on the act and although it is hoped it will do good it is not concerned ultimately with the results. Yet, what we can hope to achieve with our generosity can vary. So far, conditional generosity, in the idea of the sum of all our happiness, has focused primarily on giving to a future self. This could mean we invest in the future, say, so training the self up with a qualification, or saving money up to put a deposit on the house. This doesn't seem to involve other that much, except for providing the framework which we use to be able to do this, so the recognition of training and qualifications or a savings account to put money into which we can then access when we need to. Yet, generosity, the giving of good from the self, is generally held to mean more than giving to a future self. It is normally conceived of as being good to another person. We can feel good because the person in front of us is judging our actions positively, by, for example, accepting our gift. This has been discussed above and means an act of generosity is experienced by the other directly as pleasure. The reaction of the other is experienced as a judgement and the act of generosity would be an example of a performance. We feel happy because of the approval we perceive of our performance. We could also feel that the other person is happy from our actions and we feel happy back. This relies on the mechanism of sympathy. Sympathy means we reflect whatever emotion is felt by other, in this case happiness. This route focuses on the feelings we perceive of other. In each of these cases, generosity becomes more like an exchange where something is expected back in return in order to feel good whether this is another's smile or their favourable judgement. Here, we only feel positive about generosity if it is appreciated there and then.

In these cases, the pay-off from generosity and the reason we feel happy str fairly immediate. There is no storage of our generosity within the wider community creating the need for a 'sum of all our happiness'. Generosity, in each case, is defined by other and happiness is only felt because we feel that the transaction has been successful. This turns generosity from being a good we give out to a good we receive back and it resembles more of a transaction. Yet, it is limited in scope and doesn't represent the placing of value into a store. A further reason why we might feel happy, though, is because we have put others in our debt, which they are expected to repay with generosity in kind at a future date: a means by which we can store up future debts that we can be owed to ensure a ready supply of goods in the future. We can then become affronted if this exchange goes badly or is seen as unfair. If our generosity is seen as being abused this can become a source of anger and upset or if we are seen as too generous then this can appear weak and open us up to exploitation.

In order to make generosity more sustainable, it is better to reconceptualise it not as an individual exchange but as part of a broader system of exchanges. So, rather than seeing generosity as the placing of an individual whom we have done good to in our debt, with the expectation they will do good to us in return at a future date, we are creating a store in a wider system held by a given community that can then be taken by anybody in that community so long as they have the correct rights. If we do this communally, this magnifies the potential future pleasure and makes it more available. When generosity is seen as benefitting wider society, we are primarily concerned with how our reputation is being kept by a given community. It is reputation that will give us rights to access the communal store of happiness. This moves the 'sum of all our happiness' to being a tally of our trustworthiness. In these circumstances, it is now not so important what the person in front of us thinks of us as long as there is a broader community that can judge us and hold our reputation well. It is how trustworthy the self is viewed that will get us access to the 'sum of all our happiness' in the future. This conception of generosity is to view social life as maintained by a web of reciprocation. If this web of reciprocal action begins to loosen and we become concerned solely about the self, the whole basis of cooperation and the wider social order begins to break down. If people are no longer generous towards each other society can easily disintegrate into mistrust and hostility. This conception still, though, maintains that generosity is part of an exchange for which happiness comes back either now or in the future through pleasure. It only works, though, if there is a community that guards the rights on the broader store. Such a conception relies on the view that such a future store is under constant threat and future pleasure needs to be defended. The 'sum of all our happiness' becomes a pool of debt of gratitude that needs to be repaid, sustained as a result of the exchanges that are necessary to receive future happiness. It means that in order to feel good from generosity we need to get something good back and this looks a lot like pleasure.

This conception of 'the sum of all our happiness' makes construction of a group much more than likely. It relies on maintaining direct knowledge of a group of people around us. Such direct knowledge will mean we are only able to keep a limited number of reputations and we will need to differentiate those we know from those we don't. We will form in our mind a group of people who are trustworthy and are entitled to draw down on the pool of happiness and those that aren't. Those that do will need some means of defining who they are, and we begin to have the foundations of group formation: those who are seen as good and those who are bad. If the group becomes very large, we must rely on broader proxies, such as economic tokens or broad assumptions about other. The perspective we have on the community will often depend on our perception of our own access to the store of pleasure. If we regard ourselves as a participant in the creation of the store our perspective will be that of protecting our future rights upon it. However, if we regard ourselves as somebody who is being denied access to the store, our perspective is then likely to change. We will often see those who guard the pool and grant access to it as our problem. In either case, the manufacture of a group with personality traits becomes much more likely rather than having a system which encompasses everybody.

Although 'the sum of all our happiness' sets up an agglomeration, it is one that is built out of two forms of happiness that we have already stated the self cannot fully control, namely conditional generosity and pleasure. We can never fully control what is given to the self from other in the form of pleasure. We can never fully control the results of our generosity, whatever we are seeking to accomplish by this. Thus, if the self were to adopt the narrow version of this agglomeration as its hope, our emotions will become tied to the achievement of the agglomeration. If this agglomeration fails, and our generosity isn't recognised and the good we put into storage for our future is not repaid, we risk disappointment and inversion. Indeed, if we do not inhabit a benign social environment, such a conception of an agglomeration could be more precarious than relying on immediate pleasure. Having something we can take in the here and now is often more certain than something we may or may not be able to draw down on in the future. The latter is only feasible if society is set up in a particular way that makes this more likely than not and ensures that when we need something we have the rights to draw on the communal pool. Generalised reciprocity, though, is of such an advantage in order to allow society to function that often every attempt will be made to encourage it, even if the eventual promise is not forthcoming. It is the act of generosity that is encouraged in the belief we can draw down in the future that is important for society. If we then come to need to draw down and find we do not have access or the store is closed there is little we can often do at that point but it will leave us feeling dreadful. It means our happiness will be dependent upon the ability of society to get most people to believe they can guard and store the pool of future happiness, so it will be available to them in the future. The belief in the efficacy of conditional generosity can lead to us looking foolish. Yet, for all that the 'sum of all our happiness' fails as an agglomeration, it is useful to consider that it does deliver many of the things we are seeking from an end. It gives a target we can aim our actions to and a reward and a framework for ethical and moral behaviour.

THE ARCISTRY

If, however, we take 'the sum of all our happiness' and examine the elements the self can directly control, we are left with the generosity of the self putting into the pool of happiness but without any expectation of return. This is unconditional generosity. Unconditional generosity makes no commitments to receive payback now or in the future. We have already said that if we deliberately send good from the self this potentially feels good. Yet, the removal of good by sending out an arc, though, represents a diminishment of the good in the self potentially letting bad in. It therefore is a risk and the default position is usually that a loss of good to the self is bad. This is, though, dependent upon how the self supplies its good. Often, we are dependent upon other for our supply of good. Happiness is our alarm to let the self know that good is arriving into the self. We also have a variety of emotional alarms that will let us know when good leaves the self and if that represents a diminishment of good within the self these emotions will be painful. It is only when the self has a plentiful supply of good, such that when given out deliberately it doesn't represent a diminishment, that we can then experience the positive emotion of unconditional generosity. We can do this by the self manufacturing its own good, through ensuring as little bad is in the self as possible. If there is minimal bad in the self, then the self will be good and through this confident. Otherwise, if generosity ends up diminishing the good within the self, even though it will feel good initially, we will feel exhausted over time. This is why if we keep giving without much being received in return, we can end up feeling burnt out and we feel less and less happiness as a result.

Even if our happiness is derived from sending out arrows of good, we still need a target to aim for. We could send out anything and call this good. To be good, arcs must be directed towards something, intended to benefit other and show the good of the self. It is no harm to 'the sum of all our happiness' if somebody chooses to contribute far more than they put in. Indeed, this will benefit everybody. Thus, we may hope that we would be able to draw down on the sum but we do not expect this as a right and our happiness will not depend upon it. To differentiate this agglomeration from the 'sum of all our happiness', this will be termed 'the arcistry'. It will be the place where our arrows of trajectory are fired in the hope that our generosity will have an effect but without expectation. We can imagine it as the place as where all our arcs and the arcs fired by others will meet in agglomeration. There is no difference to how 'the arcistry' is conceptualised compared to 'the sum of all our happiness' other than what the self cannot control has been removed. We are still doing so because this is the only way we can manufacture the largest amount of happiness for everybody, including for the self. Whether it succeeds or not, though, is not up to the self but will be worked out in the agglomeration. Yet it remains the only mechanism available. Thus, the 'arcistry' is what ideally will sit at the end of paramount reality and become the target of our hopes. As with 'the sum of all our happiness' it still represents the pool of communal future happiness, but we approach this with the wish to take from it as minimally as possible. We will need to take some good from other in order for the self to carry on and get its sustenance and the like. Yet, this will not be the way we get the bulk of our happiness; although pleasure should not be seen as bad, it needs to be contained.

The majority of our happiness should derive from unconditional generosity. Previously, love has been seen as a potentially problematic emotion. It either causes the self to over extend its boundary into other in an attempt to take over and control it. Alternatively, it leads to the surrender of control of the self–other boundary to other. Unconditional generosity can be every bit as powerful as love. We can give unconditionally from the self, but no longer with expectation that we either need to control other or that other needs to control the self. We don't know in giving, though, whether this will feed the arcistry or not. What we do know, though, is if we don't send out any good, then the arcistry will not be fed and if everybody does this then there will be no sustainable happiness in the future. The arcistry is something positioned just out of reach, the end of the rainbow, so to speak. It represents the best goal we can have when in paramount reality and is the best means to obscure our eventual end, namely death. Unconditional generosity, though, could be dangerous to the self. It could suggest to be happy we should be generous to as many people as much of the time. To do this, though, we need to make sure we are able to manufacture sufficient good to be able to give out. If we are very generous to everybody, we will give to those who deserve it and those who don't. We may give to those who may exploit us and see our generosity as weakness; those others who have become inverted or who misplace their confidence. To offer generosity is relatively easy when we are cosseted in a privileged and benign situation but becomes difficult and endangering if other is hostile. Thus, we could be generous and receive hatred, indifference or be taken for granted in return. When faced with somebody who has become inverted, we must always attempt to give them good and teach them to be able to manufacture their own good. We must not dismiss them as intrinsically bad and then either avoid or attack them. As stated, somebody who has become inverted has lost their bearings in how to value and there is a likelihood the good we give out could be seen as hostile. There are times when perhaps we cannot manufacture enough good for ourselves that we could find ourselves taking on board the bad others give us. We have a right to protect the self in these circumstances. People can set themselves up so they are so barricaded that it is difficult to find any way to reach them, yet we should never give up. As previously discussed, though, we are not stating the self should ignore what is bad and dangerous. It should be able to defend itself. It should do so, though, from the standpoint of maximising the good in other as far as possible.

In being generous, we usually use the reaction of the intended receiver as a guide. This is to see whether our generosity has meaning to the other or is an arrogance of the self, determining what is good for other. We have already said though the reaction of others can easily mislead, be a form of politeness or a fickle reaction made up in the moment. The other could have become inverted or founded their paramount reality in a misplaced confidence. The information we get back from other is important but we should not attach our happiness to any reaction or find our confidence there. The reaction of other is not a good to the self but information. Rather than allowing other to be our source of happiness we are free to see how effective our generosity has been and adjust the next arrow of trajectory we send accordingly. We must target with a mixture of empathy we have for other, the golden rule and an idea of the greater good. If the immediate happiness of other is not going to be the goal of our generosity we then will need an agglomeration to make sense of our actions. Our generosity must initially be based on benefitting the person in front of us but always with an eye on the bigger picture, to make sure it doesn't harm others or the person's longer-term interests. It no longer matters, though, if the agglomeration holds a memory that we can draw down on in the future. Memory and rights are significant when we are operating to a system where we are concerned our generosity may be abused. Instead, the aim by giving away our good is to encourage others to do the same, but our happiness will not depend upon this. It is enough that we are generous but our actions should encourage others to do as we do.

By being generous, what we are attempting to do through modelling and education is encourage more of those others as possible to derive their happiness from generosity as possible. What we are aiming to create with our arcs of trajectory is a situation where the vast majority of those with specialness are deriving happiness from generosity in the same way the self is. We are contributing a small amount of generosity into the system in the hope that this will reverberate but without any expectations. Generosity is founded in the recognition of the good we either have received or expect to receive. If we privilege the latter, we will only give generosity when we expect something in return but in the former, we already recognise the good we have been given and the vital part this has in sustaining us and wish to acknowledge this. This slight change in perspective means our generosity is no longer tied to the whims of the person in front of us. Instead, we have a view that recognises that our very existence hangs by the ability of other to provide and sustain us. Generosity becomes a response to this, a giving of the self that is not measured by the whims of happiness of the person in front of us. We are generous to the person in front because we are impelled to, because of the good we have received already and, although they may not recognise it, we are still giving this back to the greater whole. If we are to do this it means we need to found generosity upon appreciation. Appreciation is either the recognition of good we find in other without the need to grab or control it or the recognition that what we have received is a loan from other and we need to return this in the form of good. This form of happiness arguably feels different to pleasure when we receive something to control and dispose of. It is calmer, less euphoric but ultimately more satisfying.

In doing this, we are also additionally filling the space of other with as much good as we can. Other needs to encompass everything. In addition to providing a target for our hopes, an agglomeration acts as an idea of bigness that is different to merging the self into a group. If paramount reality just becomes a narrow bubble that we immediately engage with, good will only exist in that bubble and everything outside the bubble will become bad. We need some way of making sure not only that we have a target to aim our trajectory arrows at but also that we will stop bad becoming anything that is unfamiliar to us. As previously discussed, to keep our engagement with paramount reality, we need to have a balance between familiarity and unfamiliarity. It is by ensuring the biggest concept of other we can that stops paramount reality collapsing into a bubble of familiarity. So, for instance, we can imagine the biggest category we can make sense of in our day to day, the planet we are on. The planet is not a static, unchanging entity but a dynamic system made up from teeming components, all having their own trajectories and all interacting with each other. It is from all these dynamic interactions that the trajectories that come towards the self derive. Although what comes at us from the planet will be both good or bad from the perspective of the self, we are still grateful for the planet to exist, for without it there would be no possibility of good and we could have no existence. That would be the supreme bad. It is not enough to imagine an 'all' and not care how that 'all' functions. 'All' if thrown forward into the future suggests a dynamic location where all is unformed, uncategorised and yet to be developed. It is a horizon point where all trajectories come from and also where those trajectories we create go. This makes more sense as something that should exist in the future, a totality in which everything is merged together, waiting to be born, a potential. If this is placed as the end it could also be a description of death. As well as a place where everything is formed, it is also the place where the self disintegrates as an imagined boundaried entity and merges back into the greater whole to continue a journey transformed.

Thus, the arcistry, our preferred end, is made up of a gigantic system of which the self is but a speck. We do not just imagine a flattened category that encompasses everything but a system of constantly moving trajectories which are forever interacting with each other to produce reactions. A system is defined by being made up not of a merger of categories but a merger of trajectories that come together. It is possible to see all life as sustained through systems and feedback loops that interact with each other in this way. The arcistry is a gigantic all-encompassing system of flows of trajectories that have multiple impacts on each other. We are not trying and can never have control of such a system. Our relationship to this system of flows is defined by its all-encompassing complexity. We can only have an influence, often a very small influence over this system. The vastness and complexity of what we are witnessing is impossible to control and in the face of such a system we could suffer paralysis. We could take a view that it is impossible to determine what the best course of action is likely to be. There are so many variables, it is difficult to say whether any given action is preferred or not. Yet, by not doing any actions we make some outcomes in the future certain. If I plant a tree now, it is possible there will be a tree in a hundred years. If I build a house now it is possible in a hundred years there will still be a house standing. If I have an idea that world peace will be brought about by spreading kindness to as many people as possible, down the line there might be a better world. In all cases, though, there may not be. There are no guarantees but if I do not act in such a way, we are guaranteed not to have a tree or, a house or I will not be part of bringing about a better place to live. Therefore, we have to take some action in the face of such uncertainty and some action is more likely to have certain outcomes than others. The only way we know this is through the accumulated knowledge and memory transmitted to us from the wider community and through the skills we have been taught to manage in such an unpredictable environment. What we can do is recognise that all our actions and thoughts have consequences in the system; some may be very small and some may be large and we often have no way of knowing which. We can also see the whole of the system as good, even though it will throw both good and bad at us and we have to deal with both. The ultimate bad, though, would not have a system at all. Those with specialness within the system should be underscored by good as well, even though they may do bad to us. This way we can face other as predominantly good and have hope that we can keep it that way.

Nine

THE ELEPHANT IN THE ROOM

ADDING GOD INTO THE PICTURE

We now have suggestions as to how we could configure the self and its boundaries to make happiness more likely. Yet, so far, we have been ignoring an important issue. As such, it is the elephant in the room: an idea that has dominated thinking about the profundities of life for centuries; the belief in the existence of God or gods. Belief in deities has been around for all of recorded human history and not to pay some heed to their ability to shape ends and all the other boundaries of the self would be a great omission. According to believers it is only through such a belief that we can experience true and meaningful happiness away from a fleeting and temporary world. Through God we can experience truth and deities can also be seen as what underpins morality and guides ethical behaviour. For many who believe there can be no reason to behave ethically apart from a religious sanctioned system of justice. It is through a belief in God that we are drawn away from the immediate needs of the self and into consideration of the needs of others, where we can also discover who we really are, finding our real self and who we are meant to be. It is this belief that gives us hope for the future and a sense that our lives matter, that we are destined for something better than the life we have now. Belief in God places at the core of the self something eternal and unchanging in a world of flux, giving potentially both the enlivenment and resilience that makes up confidence. God is other and yet the other is always within us. Our future maybe death but we can be made for eternity. Happiness may be fleeting but within us is the joy that doesn't change. A refuge we can continually return to. Thus, a belief in God or gods can infuse everything that has been covered in the book so far.

A traditional way of depicting gods or God is as a part of a supernatural realm that capriciously intervenes in the lives of humans, demanding they follow a path of sufficient prayer and devotion. Such gods may love us one minute and then turn against us the next. We constantly have to appease them to keep in their good books. Otherwise, these gods have such power over us they could snuff us out in an instant. In addition, the existence of many religions means potentially there are many gods all with different personality attributes, vying for our attention. This raises the question as to what basis, other than accidents of birth or emotional affinity, are we supposed to decide which gods merit our attention, respect or worship. Gods can be morbidly jealous and want to wipe all others from the planet. This logically means that followers of this god cannot tolerate followers of any other. In this situation followers are forced to choose. It could lead to gods being seen as egotistical megalomaniacs dependent for their emotional well-being on getting as many followers as possible and worshippers forced to endure this. These gods are powerful but not in the thrall of death. They are immortal. Having such a god on your shoulder could be useful if they are sufficiently powerful. Somebody who could give you confidence. Yet, it will not be a confidence derived from the self but from a childlike dependency on another being, whose favour could change in an instant if we fail to appease them. God is a fixer, the righter of moral injustices done against us, the disposer of luck, the bringer of fortune, and the controller of destiny. The fixing in question is all about a better future and therefore a changing in the trajectory of life. This may be about the righting of perceived wrongs; it may be about wanting a better future for the self or my family and friends. In return for fixing our trajectory of life and changing it for the better, God will want something in return. Part of that bargain may be a demonstration of our affection in terms of a sacrifice. Such a sacrifice may range from small tokens to blood sacrifices of yore. The minimum spend usually required is absolute faith or belief in the power of God and total obedience. It turns the relationship between God and worshipper into a transaction. God gets the attention and worship and the worshipper gets their life advancement. God is seen as having the capability of intervening in our life and making it better and if this doesn't happen it indicates we may have backed the wrong god. For many thinking people, such a way of depicting God or gods is problematic. Even if such gods were to exist, they are unloving. Such gods could just as easily undermine confidence as give it.

Alternatively, rather than God being viewed as being capricious and in need of appeasement, we can see God instead as the embodiment of perfection. This is how the idea of God tended to evolve over time, from capricious, flawed superhero to an idea of the perfect. Such a god, although still given a personality, tends to end up as rather remote within the realm of other, heaven. The self can just about communicate with such a god but it is unclear why such a being of perfection would be concerned with such a puny and weak self. God, as the embodiment of perfection, means it would be difficult for such a being to change. Any change would indicate either that the being was less than perfect in the first place and needs improving or instead is becoming less than perfect. Thus, such a perfect god is usually imagined to be timeless and eternal. It is also difficult to imagine the existence of more than one perfect god. If there is already one perfect god, why would we need any more? So having more than one god becomes unnecessary. If we can have a relationship with such a god of perfection, the god is portrayed as a rather remote father. This, though, is a problematic relationship, for how can such a weak self respond when being loved by perfection? However much love the childish self gives back it will never be enough for the perfect parent. The self can often experience such love as suffocating and controlling. The child after all is deemed a product of the perfect god. God is confined to the realm of other, as a guardian on your shoulder. We love God to compensate for our own perceived weakness. The self becomes dependent upon God because it is weak and bad and doesn't know what it is doing really. Thus, the self is maintained in a state of permanent childishness.

Not only is God the potentially all-loving father, but God is perfect in every other way as well. For a start, God is all-knowing. From the vantage point of heaven (originally conceived of being above the clouds, but, since it could not be located there, subsequently banished to some invisible realm), God can see everything that goes on, not only in the visible world but within our hearts and intentions as well. This makes God rather like the best surveillance system that has ever been invented. God could track where we are, what we are up to and what we believe. We had better do whatever God wants us to do, because, immediately we don't, God will know about it. This also makes God the perfect judge who will be able to punish us. Not right now, though. God is going to watch us make all our mistakes, may or may not intervene to help us or not, but come the end of life we will face God, and either be sent into heaven or condemned to eternal torment. Having such personality traits, though, creates its own logical inconsistencies. As much as we project certain ideals onto God, we have also turned them into personality characteristics, such as being all-powerful, omnipotent, and all good. This is a problem if God is seen as supreme controller of the universe and supremely good. God cannot be all these things without setting up a string of contradictions. For if God is all-powerful and all-good then in theory we should live in a utopian world, yet we patently do not. This is the moral problem of evil. One possible answer is that this good and loving god is not particularly powerful and is unable to prevent the evil and suffering in the world. The problem with this notion is then who would want to worship a weak god. It challenges the very notions of what a god ought to be. Another possible answer is to say that the evil is really humanity's fault. It was humanity that brought in evil and God values human freedom and choice more than eliminating human suffering. This is all right up to a point but it cannot account for evil that is not authored by humanity such as natural disasters, plague and pestilence. Another answer is that we are all part of some larger plan which will all work out well in the end. This may lead us to the conclusion that we cannot possibly know the mind of God and therefore when we see suffering we should shrug our shoulders and exclaim that God knows best and that we cannot possibly know God's purpose. Suffering here could be seen as a test for our own self-improvement or righteous judgement on our immorality. This, however, allows God to do practically anything moral or immoral, our role is to trust him whatever. Alternatively, the evil in the world is the result of an eternal battle with the Devil, in which case God cannot be all powerful. There is no real satisfactory resolution to the problem of evil. Yet, this is only a problem that arises as long as we wish to attribute personality to God and specific traits of being all-powerful, all-good and all-loving. We could then reject this but we are then potentially left with the capricious gods described previously.

God has also historically been seen as the creator and sustainer of the universe. This means that the existence of God is also a theory as to how the universe works and is sustained. It gives an explanation for causality and the creation of algorithms that we face in paramount reality day to day. Thus, if it rained on a particular day, it was because God willed it; if we had an abundant harvest it was because God willed it; if we triumphed in battle it was because God willed it. Yet, as alternative scientific theories have come into being to explain how the universe works or how life evolves this has challenged these personality facets. It was once supposed that God inhabited heaven and yet we can find no physical evidence of heaven. God is banished to an invisible realm whose existence we can only imagine. It was once supposed that human beings had a soul which linked them to God. Yet there is no physical evidence for a soul. Most evidence that was seen for God's intervention in our day-to-day lives is now attributed to other causal explanations. It rains because of particular weather patterns, the crops flourish because those patterns along with a particular environment allow them to do so and we have an abundance of reliable food as a result. We win or lose battles because of preparation, human psychology and the weaponry we can deploy. We no longer look to God for any of this. God has been such a predominant idea, however, that, as scientific explanations have come to the fore, one response has been to strategically retreat to what is still feasible. For example, God is regarded as Creator but then has disappeared and left us to get on with it and is no longer seen as intervening in the world. This is a god of the gaps. As more and more explanations, though, become available, these personality aspects attributable to God become less and less; the very existence of God can become questionable. God becomes an emotional crutch we turn to when our conventional explanations and means of dealing with things have failed. God has become like complementary medicine. So, this way of envisioning God as primarily a separate being with specialness will be put aside.

Instead, we will examine God in five different ways. The first is as an idea or concept, which is placed as our end, where words fail and concepts melt away. This is a god of philosophers. The second way is as an experience imbued with emotion, so profound and life-altering that we can no longer keep living life as we previously did; we are changed forever. The third way is to experience God as a person, but rather than the capricious gods of yore or as a remote being of perfection we will cast God as a means by which we can keep, store and intensify emotions. The fourth way also means conceiving of God as a personality but as the expression of an ideal person who we would wish to become. The fifth way is to regard God as so alien to the self that God becomes supremely other. Although each of these sections will have different ways in which God is being described, they are all interlinked. Yet, for the purposes of explanation, each perspective will be introduced separately but it is with the view that they will tend to run into each other.

GOD AS IDEA OF THE END

One of the most important ideas posited in this book so far is of the end. It is possible, rather than conceiving of the arcistry as the end, to see God instead. The arcistry was the target used for our trajectory arrows whilst in paramount reality without extending the self into other. We could call this arcistry god but this would be substituting one name for an end for another. Yet, what the idea of God potentially allows us to do is reintroduce elongated linear narrative as a progression. There have been several reasons given as to why creating a progression is problematic. It elongates the self-other boundary colonising other, it extends control beyond the self, what is valued becomes that which helps the self along the progression and anything that doesn't is bad. Adding in an idea of God, though, will tend to alter the way we can view the elongated linear narrative. For a start we often posit with an idea of God, the idea of an afterlife, of a heaven. So rather than obscuring death, which we want from our hope, we place the object of hope beyond death. There was much previous discussion about the relative values of death and life and, if we value death too much, we devalue life. Let us put this aside, though, for the moment. The advantage of positing the object of hope as being beyond death means that life doesn't immediately end with illness, decrepitude and demise, but can be seen as a progression into something better. It makes possible the continued use of the progression even as there seems to be little left to look forward to. That progression, though, is towards God. Often that will mean, rather than getting a job or being regarded well by our community, our primary concern will be to become as close to God as possible. Life becomes a journey towards God and it is this journey that marks our progression.

Apart from the risk we could end up devaluing the present, and life in general, having God as the end then begins to beg the question as to what sort of end we now have. This end could be any of the sorts of ways to God we have outlined above. It could be as a profound life-altering emotionally based experience; it could be as a person onto whom we can hang our hopes; it could be as a journey into the void of other. Let us for the moment, though, concentrate on the ideas of end we have previously introduced. One possibility is that ends and God mean the same thing and therefore, for example, God simply becomes truth. This proposal means God could exist as an end in the same way as truth or good and, so long as we accept the end exists, it negates the issue of the existence of God. To say God does not have existence in these circumstances would mean much the same thing as saying I do not believe in truth. So long as you accept the existence of truth so God must exist as well. The issue then becomes about being able to define the concept and establish its usefulness in a wider context. Yet, although God being an end may make it easier to accept, it is difficult to see what other advantages this would bring. If God means truth, it is hard to justify using one term over the other. It would also mean that God acquired all the difficulties so far expressed about the nature of truth. All ends so far discussed have issues about their suitability and renaming them 'God' would not solve this.

Another possibility is that ends could be amalgamated together under a conceptual title, which could be termed God. Although individually ends may be problematic, it is a possibility that if they were amalgamated these issues may be resolved. In order for amalgamation to become a possibility there would need to be a means by which ends could be put together successfully. As with the suggestion around multiple cores, the danger with having two or more of anything that forms a concept is that they can contradict each other, which can then lead to splitting and internal conflict. Most of the initial issues with happiness were thrown up by examples whereby truth and happiness or morality and happiness were in conflict. The possibility must be that, by putting together the various candidates for ends such as truth, morality and happiness, rather than resolving issues they will simply conflict. There is an additional issue, though, with ends. What is being searched for is the ultimate motivational pinnacle. By requiring two ends to balance out each other, the very idea of a motivational pinnacle is undermined. The problem in each case is that it is unclear what the end is. It suggests that when we aim for happiness, we need instead to aim for something other such as truth and vice versa.

However, God could be placed above all other ends, so, rather than happiness, truth or morality, all end in God. God could therefore be seen as the ultimate end and all other ends merely derive from God; other ends become changed through this encounter. For example, truth becomes the pathway by which we can understand God. Happiness becomes the way we experience God. Goodness becomes the way we can measure God. Yet, if we regard God as this supreme idea, which encompasses truth, good and happiness, what we are discussing is the creation of an all-encompassing category in which the best of everything is placed. This all-encompassing category then becomes what we regard as God. It doesn't just include truth, happiness and good but the best of everything we can imagine. This is then placed as our end, either at the horizon point of paramount reality or, if we have created an elongated linear narrative, a bit further out of sight. We have previously imagined a place where all boundaries to categories collapse entirely. This is the resetting point, where we experience mind, without the constructs of self and other, but also remove good and bad as this strips away emotional labels from objects as we consign them into mind. Yet, once we have turned such an all-encompassing category into God, it becomes the supreme good. In this case we have collapsed everything except the boundary between good and bad. If we have a good there must always be a place to have the bad, whether this is an opposite category or a place in time along a trajectory. When we discussed the agglomeration, we could view this as a good because not having an agglomeration or totality was bad. When we create a supreme good through categorical collapse, this means not being in categorical collapse is bad. So, when we are in paramount reality, living in a world of conventional categories and distinctions, we are experiencing what is bad. In doing so we have created a progression. Where we are now is the supreme bad, mundane existence; at the other end of the trajectory lies what is good. We are not concerned with launching trajectory arrows but dissolving the self and the categories and trajectories it perceives, so that it becomes mind. Thus, we are largely unconcerned with interacting with other or understanding it.

Thus, if we ever achieved our end, we would be forced away from paramount reality into an almost permanent resetting point. God becomes analogous with the resetting point. Before, though, there was a purpose to being in the resetting point: we destroy the bad within the self and this enables us to return to paramount reality. Yet, such an idea of God necessitates the destruction of boundaries permanently. The resetting point becomes what is good and paramount reality is what becomes bad. To get to the good of God we need to be dispense with paramount reality. Such an end, though, is difficult to conceive of as heaven or life after death; it suggests the achievement of a permanent disintegration of the self. As such, although we may have a progression up to the point of disintegration, if we were ever able to achieve this, we would then have to destroy the progression as well. There is no requirement for a life after death. If we ever achieved the goal of the disintegration of the self, we arrive at the valuing schema where other becomes bad and the disintegrated self is good. Other is bad because it represents those who are in paramount reality and haven't merged categories together. As such they are of the world and the world as categories and trajectories is bad. It is only when we can experience everything apart from this as mind that we can become good, apart from the world. Although, it is possible, having reached the point of permanent total categorical collapse, good and bad would collapse as well. If, though, we were to find the self reforming, which it will always have a tendency to do, that self would be inverted and bad. We would have to become forever watchful and guarded against this inevitable tendency. Such a rarefied existence would only be possible in highly protected environments away from the hurly burly of everyday life, perhaps associated with monastic cloisters or the life of a hermit. For we know already that we need to be in paramount reality for at least some of the time. Otherwise, this is unsafe for the self. We also know that it is good to enter for a time a place where we can experience categorical collapse, but we do so in order to be able to experience paramount reality more clearly, not as an aim that we should experience this state permanently. Let us then discard this as a practical option and look instead at other ways in which God could be added to our understanding.

GOD AS EPICENTRE OF MEANING

Rather than viewing God as a means of placing the resetting point as our end, and experiencing categorical collapse, we can view God as heightened emotional experience and place God as an alternative to the core of the self. This is God as the epicentre of meaning. Here, emotional preoccupation is the main pathway into God. As previously stated, emotional preoccupation gets to the heart of self; it is but a small step to argue that what preoccupies us becomes like a god for us. Preoccupation, though, is often with what is negative and concerning. We can drive out such negative preoccupations with confidence. Confidence relies on mood as a disposition and is based on the trust in something that we will be able to manage in paramount reality. Thus, confidence enables us to face paramount reality as it is. Alternatively, we can drive out negative preoccupations using positive preoccupations. These are positive emotions that fail to habituate. Emotion is something that we experience in paramount reality and is an indicator of an interaction between self and other. It is possible, though, to elongate that emotion so that it becomes a mood. Thus, positive preoccupations are moods that result from elongated emotions rather than dispositions. Positive preoccupations will tend to take us away from facing paramount reality as it is. We know paramount reality can be harsh and one way to deal with this is to not face it directly. Rather than having a resetting point where we allow the experiences we have to drift into mind through categorical collapse, it is possible to build an emotional haven away from paramount reality. Such a haven is built from elongated positive emotional experiences; pleasures which are extended. We hold onto them and constantly bring them back to mind.

Negative emotion can take longer to habituate than positive emotion. In order to remember positive emotion, we have to work hard. We could just try to remember the emotion, by recalling times when we were happy, for instance a holiday, a wedding or favourite film, and engage in practised recall of these times. Even then it is likely to recede into mind. To create an epicentre of meaning, we place an object within the self that we are able to hang particular emotions on, to stop or delay habituation. These will invariably be objects on which to hang positive emotions such as happiness, joy or love. That object can be anything, yet, as we have discovered, objects or ideas will eventually lose their lustre. One of the main ways that positive emotion doesn't habituate is if we are frightened that we may lose the good it is attached to. The good will have come into the self in the form of pleasure. One way we can be frightened to lose what we have is if we believe the good is not really ours to have. If this is the case, we can either accept it and give it back when the time comes or cling on to it ever more tightly. We could attempt to build a haven for the self without an idea of God, but doing so would leave us in a state of fear of loss of what good the self already has, so that it doesn't habituate. Using the idea of God will give advantages. Let us regard God and good as synonymous. God is the ultimate good. God is also other and cannot be self. This means by default other is good and it is the self that is bad. This will lead to an inverted self that values unpredictably. Yet, the good of other can be incorporated within the self if God is allowed to reside in the self. So long as we let the good of God into the self, the self will then become good and also will have a continuous supply of good. That will be the good manufactured by God for the self. If the good of God, though, were to leave the self, then the self would revert to becoming bad. This means the good in the self, is not the self and could leave at any point and return to other. Such an emotional set-up, so long as we accept it, will mean that self is predominantly good, but only by virtue of having God within it. Without this the self will be bad. All pleasure such that the self receives and the ability to value will be dependent upon God. This will inspire a fear and a thankfulness that is most likely to delay habituation.

This gives a better chance to delay habituation and keep hold of positive emotion. If we have a haven of positive emotion we can bring to mind at will, we know when we face paramount reality we will always have a place of escape we can use no matter what. The concern posited previously is that having such an escape facility will mean we can end up attempting to avoid paramount reality. If we did not have an idea of God, this would be inevitable but with an idea of God it makes possible a variety of positions. God is other. God is also good. Logically, therefore, other will be good. Thus, we ought to be able to face paramount reality where other is. It is the self, without God, where bad will be located. Yet, our experience can say otherwise. The reason we often want to hold onto positive experiences and create an emotional haven is because paramount reality is difficult. If we posit the existence of both God and the Devil then it becomes possible that other contains both good and bad elements. This risks a turn away from paramount reality as potentially bad. Yet, the good inside the self can be seen as giving protection against the bad in other. As well as giving an elongation in positive mood it can also be seen as a source of confidence, that the good inside the self can overcome the bad in other.

For those that can, this can be a highly emotionally intense way of experiencing God. For if we can delay habituation, the positive emotions we experience can accumulate over time. Although initially pleasures will have come in the front door whilst in paramount reality, so long as we can keep hold of them and store them in a positive emotional memory bank to recall at any time, we will no longer become reliant on front-door pleasures. If also the god inside of us can manufacture good, then again, we no longer need pleasure. We can be confident in having a store of good from within the self. We have a situation where potentially there is an ever intensification of positive emotion which is generated by the interaction between the self and the god inside. This is God as ecstasy: a centre of meaning so strong that we can forget all else. A god that gives within the self an experience described by so many mystics over the centuries. That takes us away from the mundane and everyday concerns of life to somewhere significant. It is possible, therefore, to regard such overwhelming positive emotion directly either as God or an indicator of the presence of God. This is unlikely to be just mundane happiness. The happiness that comes from the normal everyday preoccupations and pleasures. Such happiness as has been previously stated is too fickle, too self-centred, too short term and can take delight in unseemly behaviour. Nor is it the laid-back joy of giving good from the self or appreciating what is around us that we have been championing so far. This happiness associated with God is far more pressing and urgent. An overwhelming power of joy. In such a situation, we can face paramount reality and it may be predominantly good but potentially we don't need much from it either. Essential drives will still need to be satiated, but these should be able to be contained. Thus, by having such a concept of God we have reached the same point that much of the book has been arguing for but by a different route. We have a self that is predominantly good, albeit in this case through having God inside of the self rather than anything the self has on its own. Other also is regarded as good and thus the chances of happiness in paramount reality are maximised.

Yet, the whole of this edifice is built upon accepting that God as good can reside in the self and transform us so we reach a point of manufacturing a divine ecstasy at will. If we then fail to achieve this, we will be left bereft with an inverted self and an inaccessible god within other. For the edifice rests on a fear that this good may leave us at any point. It thus suggests a lack of control by the self and a ceding of control over to God. So apart from entreating this entity to enter the self and stay there, there is little the self can do. If the self attempts to construct a haven without the idea of God, having a haven will alter how we approach paramount reality and what is good and bad within it. Good will be anything that then adds to the haven and bad will be that which challenges its safety. If the haven though is God, the haven becomes something the self is not responsible for constructing but is constructed by other inside the self. Thus, we cede control and potentially have little concern or care what happens in paramount reality or its end, other than we make sure we protect the refuge that has been created. As long as this is secure, it doesn't much matter what paramount reality is like and we will have little concern to model it or understand it. There is also little point in giving away the good we have to get happiness, except to persuade others to accept God within themselves as well. This would be the most generous thing we could do. Thus, although we reach a similar position to that outlined previously in the book, it is not identical and has flaws that could act to undermine it.

GIVING GOD A PERSONALITY IN CONSTRUCTING AN EPICENTRE OF MEANING

So far, the sorts of god we have considered are pretty abstract; without the attribution of personality, it would be difficult to have a relationship with such a god. It helps to have a personality to focus upon. In considering the addition of personality, this will be different to God as a separate person with specialness that was outlined at the introduction of this chapter. We are either adding personality to the end we wish to achieve for the self or to the epicentre of meaning. Taking this latter possibility first, God existing as an epicentre of meaning is difficult without some form of personality to relate to and engage with. It is therefore common for God to be seen as a person to whom we attribute specialness. It was said previously that we could attribute personality to anything. It is the imbuing of others with specialness that brings them alive in our imaginations so they can live within us. Therefore, it can make sense that if God is to conquer our hearts we would want to attribute a personality to God. Yet, in enabling God to take up residence in our hearts, there are perhaps some aspects of specialness that are more important than others. We could start with the voice emanating from the self that we talk with. The ongoing chatter in our mind. Telling us what to do and what to avoid. It is our voice, but left unspoken. It doesn't take much to change the tone of this voice, maybe to something a little more authoritative; maybe it could be someone we have known. Perhaps it could become an authority figure from our past or the voice of a friend or relative. What we often want if we construct an epicentre of meaning is a god that is going to look after the self and keep it safe from harm, that perhaps will allow the self to make difficult decisions and to allow the self and any others it relates to prosper.

Yet, having a voice in our head that we can talk to and bounce ideas off doesn't give that voice specialness. To have this, we need to ascribe a story, a separate identity, goals and the like. We know that constructing a story makes things more memorable. Although we have been discouraged from constructing a story for the self through the elongated linear narrative, for others we must keep some story to be able to engage with them. We should, though, limit that ascription and not become preoccupied by another's story to the extent of wanting to merge it into our story to either become them or expand the self. Nor become so preoccupied about writing that story when we are not with them or by what they may or may not be doing or telling us. We should maintain another's story just enough so we can update it and add to it every time we meet with them, to enable us to relate to them better and keep their specialness well. This will mean, though, we are not keeping a story for the self or fully for other. Yet we can imagine and make up characters and create stories and plots as fiction as much as we like. We can identify with these characters and in doing so build skills of empathy and being able to look at the world through the eyes of others. As long as we don't confuse these existences with either the self or other, we can extend them back and forth as much as we choose. We may identify with them for a time and then, when the story is run, we can leap out again without consequence. It is one thing to have voices in our head to be able to give us reassurance. It is another to construct stories for characters we create as a practice for skills of empathy. It then becomes a possibility that we can merge these two skills together. That those voices in our head become characters in a story and have an identity separate from the self. They are neither properly the self nor are they properly other. They exist on the side of the self but are not the self, they are liminal existences. We can then directly engage with the characters we have created as voices.

It then isn't too far to turn that voice in our head with specialness into God. The important personality traits to ascribe to God, if we seek comfort and reassurance, are those of friend and lover. Loving something or someone is the main way to bring about a positive preoccupation and thus create an epicentre of meaning. It is possible only to imagine the full flowering of love when focused on another personality. Love is one of the most powerful experiences a human being can have. Yet, there are issues with love as have previously been mentioned. It requires that we either try to become another, which is destructive to the self, or alternatively, we integrate the other into the self as an extension to who we are. Both positions are ultimately unsatisfactory and unsustainable. Having an imagined personality called God leads to a possible resolution of this issue. By having an imagined lover, we circumvent the need to either become another or expand the self into another. Instead, we construct an imagined personality we try to love. This should be easier as we construct it. The issue is that we have created within the self, specialness which is from other, that we then attempt to love as a means of forming an object around which we can then attach positive emotions.

In the previous example, it was the fear of losing the good from other that was the main reason for delaying habituation. The main delay, in this case, to habituation comes about from the creation of specialness. By having God within the self, when we experience something good this can be ascribed to the actions of God inside of us. We have somebody else to thank for our good fortune. We must remember and relate to them and it doesn't matter if we become preoccupied by their story. The good we get can go to them for them to keep for us. They also will protect us from any bad that might befall us and give us strength to be able to deal with it, to be our confidence in facing paramount reality. Thus, giving God a personality may make it easier to construct an epicentre of meaning that we can build a refuge from. In doing this, it means we become less reliant on the fear that God may leave us but instead we rely on the veracity of constructing a believable and relatable imaginary friend. By constructing a deity to believe in will alter the experience of love, compassion and respect. In part that we are now attributing all of these emotions to a divine figure. They could be seen as a manifestation of God that is then pouring from us. So if we are loving, giving respect or compassion, this is from God ultimately. Yet there is an ulterior motive to this goodness. We are now acting as an acolyte from God with a view to showing others the goodness of God.

In having a pretend lover though, this potentially makes us avoidant of paramount reality, and means everybody else will fall short of the pretend lover and leads us to living in our imaginations away from facing other. This projection, although it presumes to be other, is an imaginary version of the self which it is using for its own comfort and protection. That self-projection is turned into a divine entity which could then end up as a tyrant masquerading as God. God becomes part of the self. The self can then create God in its own way to its own designs to meet its whims and fancies. We have a direct channel to the voice of God, who can then give our pronouncements divine weight and authority beyond questioning or challenge. It also means there are aspects of the self that are transformed into not God that are then seen as negative and not part of me. This sets up some potentially problematic psychological dynamics. It places at the core of the self an idealised version of who I am which is divine but also an alienated aspect that then becomes easy to deny or project outwards onto others. This leads to splitting, which could lead either to guilt or denial or both.

It could be held, however, that, once we have created the personality around which we can build positive emotions, it may be possible to eventually expunge the personality element, such that we could recollect and maintain positive emotional states at will. If we could manage it, we are no longer maintaining positive emotion through fear but neither are we relying on the construction of an imaginary personality, except as emotional scaffolding. That is removed when emotional memories become so powerful we no longer need the original story. What is suggested here is that the experience of God propels us towards a divine rapture and a semi-permanent state of love, happiness or bliss unattached to any object. This is derived from an initial love of a divine personality. Potentially, by continually bringing to mind feelings such as love and bliss when we think of God, they become so dominant we forget the initial personality. The feeling that becomes the focus not the initial object. In introducing an imaginary being to attach our love, there is nothing really there to start with. If we project love onto nothing, if we then remove this logically the love would continue. Yet, in order for the love to be there in the first place we must believe in the veracity of the personality. Indeed, the love and devotion make no sense without this. To love at the outset something you know as a projection to be false and untrue would be impossible. So, we are left either with having a psychological conceit as a means of achieving a state of pure bliss or with the same scaffolding as before. We will have to constantly reimagine the personality in order to delay habituation.

In addition, it is far from clear that a permanent state of bliss is even desirable. Moods and emotions, whether positive or negative, are signals to help us interact in our environment, to negotiate paramount reality. Even if it was possible to be permanently in love or a state of continuous happiness it is questionable as to whether this would be appropriate. We would see everything as good, even if a situation was dangerous or problematic. Emotions and moods would be experienced and would be incongruent to our circumstances. Love allows the other to live in us, it also means we trust another to allow them to keep a bit of ourselves with them without feeling we must try to guard or influence it. Love also means that once acquired the object does not degrade within our preoccupations as would our normal attachments. Objectless love suggests there is no object of focus. Therefore, we just experience love for no apparent reason along with any happiness this brings. We could experience the dullness and routine of work, extreme brutality afflicting our family, or winning an important championship, with the same feeling. This is experiencing emotions derived purely from within the self, which it is far from evident is a good thing. Would it be right to stop feeling pain, fear, empathy or happiness in response to outside circumstances? Do these emotions not provide important feedback as to what is going on? It is what we then choose to do with that feedback that is important. We need to be able to process the emotions in the moment, deal with the situation to get as positive an outcome as possible and whatever happens learn from it, take the positive from it and move on.

Thus, even if we could experience constant bliss all the time we probably shouldn't. Yet, we could replace the existing idea of the resetting point we had previously, where we strip all emotion away, with one where we experience rapture. This would make the experience of God temporary, but one we can return to at will. We have managed to turn all memories to pleasant and therefore like a rose garden we can return again and again. Alternatively, we can go and lie on a beach or experience a beautiful countryside, when we turn away from paramount reality. If we know we can do this, then it potentially means we can go into paramount reality, take whatever this throws at us, knowing we always have this enjoyable place we can escape to. Yet, there is no real reason to return to paramount reality apart from satisfying our basic needs. We thus risk turning the self to a blissful good but other into the site of bad. We would then want to spend our time in our blissful retreat as much as possible and no longer need paramount reality as much. It is no longer the main site in which we become happy. Thus, although this sounds a superficially attractive option, if we could bring it about, it will lead us to escape from paramount reality.

GOD AS A MODEL OF IMITATION: THE IDEAL PERSONALITY

God as personality, though, may not just be seen as an epicentre of meaning where we can keep and intensify positive emotions. We can instead construct the personality of God as our end. So, rather than seeing the end as something other, instead it becomes who the self should attempt to be, a better self, thrown forward in time. An ideal self modelled on the paradigm of God. We have looked at trying to construct a better self in the future previously in the form of elongated linear narrative called the progression. It was found that this over-extends the self and what it can control and means we devalue the present. This is often about achieving some kind of future role or status for the self, some possession or skill. These aims for the self can be seen as selfish. We either reach them or we don't and then need new goals or give up striving. If we place some ideal personality traits as our aim, traits that are often seen as godlike, such as being wise, loving, peaceable and just, for example, we are unlikely to ever be able to reach these.

They will be something we have to keep striving to be. These traits were seen in ancient philosophy as virtues. What we are doing is constructing an ideal personality and then modelling the self upon that personality is an attempt at imitation. In this situation, it is not that God is a separate person, but God represents the person we should strive to become. The idealised personality is God; God represents the embodiment of good and in order to be fully good then we must be as like God as possible. This constructs a moral compass to aim at becoming.

Yet we can imagine what constitutes an ideal personality can be very socially relative depending on our culture and position. As previously mentioned, what has been attributed to God is multifaceted. A predominant version of God casts him as male; as a ruler, a king, or lord with ultimate status and as a supreme judge and arbiter of moral order. In order to perform this function, God is often attributed supernatural qualities such as existing outside time eternally, free from the ravishes of ageing and decay, being present everywhere and at all times to be able to know the content of our hearts as well as defining the laws of universe. This is not a god we could ever hope to imitate, but one we can only fall down and serve in the hope of appeasing. Everybody falls short of such a god and all are tainted with sin; however, some will fall much shorter than others. For example, if God is cast as male, around fifty per cent of the population are excluded from the possibility of achieving perfect godliness. Some traits such as being of higher status would suggest that a lord is closer to God than a peasant. Yet, there is considerable variance in how God is portrayed. God is also portrayed as being meek and lowly and as being on the side of the poor. This suggests the nature of the supreme idealised person is likely to vary over time, from culture to culture and from person to person. This opens up the possibility that a culture will create particular traits to be lauded at a particular time. For example, if a culture is under constant threat then it may value strong warriors and thus value personality traits that lead to this and deify those. If, however, a culture is strewn with infighting and injustice a strong judge may be wanted. If a culture has suffered bloodshed a peacemaker may be yearned for. If a culture suffers from want, poverty and oppression somebody who will break your chains and take on the rich may be desired.

Even if we could agree on the personality traits we should laud, having personality traits to emulate as an idea is still potentially problematic. Any attempt to manufacture the good self with perfect traits, such that any reasonable judge would see us to be good, could be seen as an attempt to forge an identity. Paramount reality becomes the place where we are seeking to perfect the self and its traits. The problem is that this sets up the self as striving for perfection which it can never reach. It will always fall short and thus will always be bad in relation to the ideal. Thus, it may always be on the road, striving to get there, but the self never will. It will always be inverted. A future located self transfers happiness from something primarily situated in the present to something to be hoped for in the future. If these hopes are purely personal this can be problematic as all hopes will ultimately fall short. When young, the trajectory of life is often relatively safely imagined to be a long one but as this imagined trajectory gets shorter this may be intensely problematic. The issues of salvationism and utopianism were mentioned previously. Having cast the self into the future it can increasingly look out of reach. We may dream of a moment when life's sorrows are righted and yet they still come to us. We may yearn for a time when anxieties and complexities are banished to simplicity. We may dream of being perfect but we never can be. Instead, it was recommended we see the self as existing in the present making its future by sending out arrows to a target, not seeing the future self as its own target whether made from God or not.

GOD AS SUPREMELY OTHER

So far, God has mostly been placed on the self side of the self–other boundary. This may be as part of other, within the self, or with an idea of the self extended into the future where other is usually located. God is still within the ambit of the self, whether this is a permanent resetting point, personality traits placed as our end or as the good within the self that comes from other, whether or not conceived as an additional identity. In this section, we will explore a god that is not like us and we should never hope to emulate. God is conceived as fundamentally different, so the only response we can have is awe and worship. This is God conceived as firmly within other and the opposite of self. Such a god must be met where the self–other boundary is firmly present, in the day-to-day experience of paramount reality. When God was conceived of as a capricious being or the embodiment of perfection, God is not part of the self, but part of being other. God is another being apart from the self that we interact with just as we would another person. It is just that God has special super-human qualities and the way we interact is different. We can never hope to become this god, we can never possess God as a form of propert; we can never control God, or treat God as just another reputation to hold. God is supremely beyond control and worthy of respect and awe. Such a god of otherness has though been given specialness and personality, as we would also give others specialness and personality. These gods were dismissed as unloving and yet this was to undermine the response to such a deity or deities. Having a god we conceive of as other invites a particular response from the self. That response is frequently one of diminished ego; that we are nothing in the sight of God. It is suggestive that we should reflect upon our own specialness, in particular to leave go of trying to create a reputation for ourselves and have status in the eyes of others. This conception of God as other invites us to continually give respect. If we see the main issues of humanity as a tendency to egotism and selfishness, then having such a god could be a considerable advantage. We will be forced to take on viewpoints other than our own and consider the needs of others around us. This god is a powerful dictator whom we ultimately will need to appease. Yet, such a powerful figure is as likely to imbue fear as much as benevolence. Besides, acting from fear of being caught out hardly constitutes genuine love and concern for other human beings. Yet, another being with specialness is still possible to relate to and not entirely alien. It is possible that, rather than being conceived of as being a super person, God is beyond personality, beyond specialness and is so unlike us that God is beyond comprehension. The analogy can be drawn that we are like a goldfish in a bowl looking out into a universe we can scarcely comprehend or understand.

We shouldn't even attempt to describe such a god because God is other. This specialness, though, cannot be completely estranged and incomprehensible. A god who was beyond total comprehension would be impossible to relate to. We could imagine a scenario of alien life on another planet that we know nothing about, even its existence. That alien life may be very different from us in a galaxy many light years away from us and without any means of communication to us. Such alien life by being so other as to be unknown is meaningless to us. It only has meaning if we can relate and interact with it. Envisioning a god so apart from the concerns of human life becomes too distant. If, however, the alien species was able to communicate for example that it possessed an intergalactic ray gun that would be fired at Earth unless we humans respected each other more, then the relationship takes on meaning. It is the prospect of more and greater communication that enables a relationship. Therefore, in order to be worthy of our awe and respect, there must be the prospect of relationship and engagement.

Such a god forces upon us the idea of other as mystery. Rather than interacting with paramount reality as a means of getting what we want, we do so as appreciation. The interaction alone becomes the means of being happy. This has been discussed before, but is given additional power by the addition of being an expression of God. The interaction becomes an act of prayer. Mysteries, as previously discussed, represents a residual category of things that are untradable and cannot be possessed. It can include that which potentially can harm the self but is not the responsibility of another causer: an act of God. In this context, though, mysteries we are primarily concerned with that which is benign to the self but inspires in us awe and wonderment. Everything that the self gets comes from this mystery and this will become a blessing. Yet, we must appreciate that as much as everything can be given so it can be taken away again. God, in the meaning here, becomes about adopting a particular attitude to other because we recognise we are formed not by our own efforts but from the mysteries around us. Those mysteries could just as quickly remove everything we have obtained. If we have an appreciation of other as this wild, unpredictable, beautiful ride, this can help us accept the inevitable lack of control we have; to reach a place where knowledge, understanding and appreciation are more important than control. Many can find this in an appreciation of nature or the universe. A crazy amalgamation of lots of stuff, repeating itself in a thoroughly unique way that we may be able to influence occasionally but most of the time not, that we cannot shy away from, that ought to scare us but despite this we smile. This could be an expression of God. Yet, we do not need an idea of God to have mysteries, just an idea of the self as not defined by controlling what is other, content to see other as good without the need to possess it. A self that derives most of its happiness not from pleasure but from generosity and has the confidence to see itself as good. Although the idea of God has been used for centuries, the way the idea can be used adds little to concepts used here and in many cases manufactures other issues. It is thus not a necessary idea.

Ten

END WORDS

HOW TO BE HAPPY

The purpose of this chapter is to bring together the themes of the book and to suggest the best way to live life in order to maximise the chances of being happy. The opening chapter of the book introduced happiness as an obvious way to define the purpose of life, the end. For if we track back the reasons for doing anything we can usually find happiness as the ultimate justification. We do things with the aim of making the self happy. To have an end at all we must view the self as being a trajectory, of having an existence into the future. Yet, building life around happiness can lead to hedonism. Hedonism is the philosophy that happiness is what we should pursue in any situation. There is no differentiation made as to the sorts of happiness we can or should experience. The idea of paramount reality was previously introduced as the direct experience of other. It is constructed as a short-term trajectory stretching out into our near-term future. The horizon point of paramount reality would be an obvious place to site our end. It means that, if we adopted hedonism, every time we enter paramount reality, we should seek to maximise our personal happiness. Happiness in paramount reality has been understood as the alarm we feel when we are detecting good either in the self or in other and in particular when it moves across the self–other boundary. Different movements of good could be used to differentiate forms of happiness. Pleasure is the feeling we get when good moves across the self–other boundary from other to the self. Relief is the feeling when we remove something bad from the self or prevent it from entering the self. The problems of hedonism revolve around these two movements of happiness. Some of the problems identified with hedonism in the first chapter can now be seen in this light. Thus, if people find happiness in running others down or making other people miserable it is because they have something bad within the self and are displacing it onto others. If somebody is trying to grab as much for themselves as possible, the biggest house or the most opulent lifestyle, they are doing so because they have identified the self as deficient and in order to make it better they need to grab as much good as they have found in other as possible. If happiness is defined in this way it will often mean that one person's happiness will result in another's unhappiness, whether directly in causing harm or because a small group of people are grabbing everything for themselves. We also now know that if we could construct a pill that would make us permanently happy that would not be a good thing. It would be a very similar situation to living in a state of bliss as a result of a religious experience that was discussed in the last chapter. Happiness is meant to be an alarm primarily related to paramount reality. If we remove the alarm from this context, it becomes problematic. It actually leads us away from paramount reality and avoidant of the very situation the alarm is pointing us to. It leaves us in a permanent resetting point that we no longer wish to leave.

Having examined the problems of hedonism could lead us to a conclusion that happiness is something that needs reining in because otherwise, we would put in jeopardy three important areas of life. The first area considered was reality. It was argued that, if we considered happiness as our ultimate goal, it would probably be better to live in delusion about the situation the self finds itself in rather than face truth head on. That the self is contained in a fragile body, subject to ageing, illness and decay, whose life often won't amount to a great deal. Not only could it be argued that truth is an objection to having happiness as an end for the self, but it also could be an alternate end for the self. Yet, when we looked more closely, we found we can never reach a non-instrumental truth. Truth must always have a purpose and we will always be approaching from a viewpoint. Instead, truth becomes a process in which we must be open to ideas and explanations, must not take a fixed position and don't jump to conclusions without a careful evaluation of the evidence. We often fail to do this because we have set up goals as an end to achieve happiness, we are concerned with the achievement of some reputation we think will give happiness, or we will have attached the self to a group whose goals and aims we take on as our own. Alternatively, we will have allowed the self to become inverted. In these cases, we have a vested interest in manipulating how we view other and setting it up to meet goals, or alternatively seeing other as predominantly bad and avoiding engagement. If these are not present, we have no motivation to skew our viewpoint and can keep a clear sight of paramount reality. We may still get it wrong. We may attribute the wrong cause to things, or string incorrect algorithms together; we may pay heed to the wrong evidence or draw the wrong conclusions. There are no guarantees but at least we can face paramount reality in that knowledge and not because we have a misguided belief about achieving a happiness that will always elude us. It is these misguided ways of achieving happiness that give rise to issues of honesty.

The moral good could also be seen as having issues for an undifferentiated happiness. As stated, pleasure and relief pose particular problems for the moral good. In which case, our own happiness can be at the expense of others. The moral good could also be set up as an alternative end. When examined, though, what is set up as the end will be others happiness rather than our own. This could be just as much a fallible guide. Alternatively, it will be some form of our own reputation as held within the wider community. This could leave us vulnerable to something we don't really control. Another alternative movement to relief and pleasure has been discussed. Rather than receiving good from other, which we cannot fully control and will habituate, or displacing bad onto other, which again will habituate, we can give out good to other. This was termed generosity. We can fully control this movement so long as we can manufacture our own supply of good. Unconditional generosity is no longer dependent upon the reaction of others or how our reputation is held by a wider community. It is merely dependent upon feeling happy at giving away the good we have. This would no longer be a problem for moral good.

The third objection was related to the self and its future. The idea is that we can take happiness now but this can be at the expense of being able to take more happiness later on. In order to get greater happiness, it is suggested we should develop personal goals for the self of what we would like to become. We then construct pathways to this future self as to how we reach this destination. Thus, within paramount reality, these goals would then become our ends. The achievement of these personal goals would then get us to happiness. This has later been questioned in the book. We have been wary of drawing a line from the self out into the future, creating a progression from an elongated linear narrative. Setting up a future self to achieve over-extends the boundaries of the self and what we can control. It is happiness postponed, but when that happiness does come it will still be in the form of pleasure with all the issues this entails. This could mean that we revert to taking our happiness now, whatever the cost to our future self and thus undermining our potential future. In losing the idea of goals and a future self to achieve, this should not be at the expense of striving, effort and hard work. This danger, though, was related to the taking of pleasure, whether now or in the future. If our prime means of getting happiness is through sending out good into other, this should not be a risk. It is just that we have altered our model and expectation of the future so it doesn't undermine the present. With good sent out hopefully there will be more available down the line, which makes our future better.

Thus, rather than seeing happiness as an undifferentiated personal feeling which leads us to hedonism, it can be viewed as a set of feelings that indicate where good is when we are within paramount reality. Of these differentiated feelings it has been argued unconditional generosity should be the main means of achieving happiness, as it is the one the self has the greatest control over. We have also set up a vision of as many people as possible deriving their happiness from such unconditional generosity, termed the arcistry. It is a target to which we can send our trajectory arrows, constantly adjusting to do as much good as possible. Yet, we cannot invest any of the self into whether this is achieved or not. It is the arcistry that best defines our hope and the end of paramount reality. Paramount reality, though, needs not only to have a dispositional mood to define its end but another one to define its beginning, namely confidence. The best way to get that confidence is if the self can remove as much bad as possible. Thus, ensuring that the self does not become inverted and lead to difficulties in valuing. In order to do this, we need to develop a resetting point, where we collapse the self–other boundary, on which all emotion is dependent. This is easier than it sounds. It is much easier to form places in space or time which give us comfort and provide a haven from the vicissitudes of paramount reality. They provide a mental retreat where we can believe we are off stage and not performing and can sometimes feel a lot like being in a resetting point. Yet, they keep us away from facing the paramount reality as it is. Within the resetting point all concepts and ideas must be allowed to collapse. This will strip emotion away from any objects they are attached to and consign them into the vault of mind. We normally use emotion as a mental filing system. This needs to be replaced through practised repetition which requires us to have a set point as well. We can also find attention being thrust hither and thither. Within the resetting point, the idea is that we print it back under control of mind and let it rest. The mind is usually a reflection of what we have set up the self to be. The ripples of this reflection are then mirrored back to us. By setting up the self well, we will find it much easier for the mind to become calm and to have control of our attention. Doing this, though, means we can be confident we have the means by which to face paramount reality. We have confidence because we know we can handle any bad that comes our way and see other as primarily good. Yet, it takes time to remove emotional labels. We need to also ensure we are not overrun by any bad in the meantime. This means keeping the self–other boundary as narrow as possible. It has been suggested that being in paramount reality needs to be how the self is primarily viewed. The self is truncated and not over extended and we have as smaller barrier as possible between the self and other. Other becomes only in the future. It means that we are much less likely to experience bad. Thus, we have a model of the self that maximises a sustainable happiness that is easier to control.

Marar (2003) sees a concern with happiness along with other emotions as a turn towards interiority. A turn away from more collective and social concerns to being concerned with managing our emotional life. This is exemplified in this quote: *With the rise of emotions as inner drivers of human behaviour, coinciding with the rise of the new discipline of psychology, came a turning point of extraordinary significance. The pursuit of happiness, moving from its early connotation of good fortune and good character addressing the*

Socratic question, how ought I to live?, came to require that we answer a brand new question, namely what do I really want?... Only when it began to be possible to see happiness as dependent on a more subjective, personal ideal did the modern term become intelligible. Many would claim that the rampant individualism that makes happiness intelligible to us makes it as obscure to other cultures as it is to other periods in our history... the shift from a moral to a more psychological view coincided with the rise of happiness as a political concept in the late eighteenth century... At the political level the concept is either anodyne or dangerous. The pursuit of happiness can only make any sense when you scale down from the political sphere to the level of individual psychology (Marar, 2003, pp23–27).

Happiness and the emotions, though, can just as easily push us towards other as away. It depends which movements of happiness we give priority to. Often there is a concern to place ideas around the dualism of individualism and collectivism. Individualism can be seen as selfish, with a concern for the self and what it can get. We can see this if pleasure becomes privileged and self becomes defined by what it possesses. Yet the opposite, collectivism, can be as problematic. Collectivism, to those that wish to denigrate individualism, represents a concern for other and their well-being, for the group as a whole. Yet, we have seen that often what a concern for the group means is the self subsuming itself into the needs of the collective and being defined by it. A concern for the group can also mean a concern for reputations and the consequent policing of this, something we can never hope to control. Instead, individualism should be seen as the ability for the self to determine itself rather than have a group to which you belong make decisions for you. Collectivism, by contrast, is where the self and its boundaries are determined by the social group with which it identifies. This has been the most common way of self-definition for most of human history, whether it is as a member of a tribe, a nation, a class, a religion or a sect. Individualism is a privilege that has not been available to most of the human populace for most of its history. Yet, individualism can easily degenerate into social dislocation and crisis if this is dominated by themes of having as much pleasure as possible, trying to get happiness through illusory control or becoming inverted. If individualism appears to lead to unfairness and no form of the greater good then we can retreat into a tribal membership of groups. Further, individualism can be seen as undermining the bonds of society such that people work solely for their own advancement. Only when we take individualism as the privilege it is and derive our happiness from generosity does it become sustainable.

BIBLIOGRAPHY

Annas, J. (1993) *The Morality of Happiness*, Oxford University Press

Argyle, M. (2001) *The Psychology of Happiness* (2nd Edition), Routledge

Armstrong, K. (2000) *The Battle for God*, Harper Collins

Axelrod, R. (1990) *The Evolution of Cooperation*, Penguin Science

Batchelor, S. (1997) *Buddhism Without Beliefs*, Bloomsbury

Belliotti, R. A. (2004) *Happiness Is Overrated*, Rowman and Littlefield

Ben-Ze'ev, A. (2000) *The Subtlety of Emotions*, MIT Press

Berger, P. and Luckmann, T. (1966) *The Social Construction of Reality*, Penguin

Berkowitz, L. (2000) *The Causes and Consequences of Feelings*, Cambridge

Boden, M. (1990) *The Creative Mind*, Cardinal

Boteach, S. (2000) *Kosher Emotions*, Hodder and Stoughton

Brazier, D. (1997) *The Feeling Buddha*, Robinson

Caplan, M. (2001) *The Way of Failure*, Hohm Press

Casti, J. L. (1989) *Paradigms Lost*, Abacus

Christian Community Bible (Translation) (2nd Edition) (1988), Claretian Publications/St Paul Publications/Divine Word Publications

Cloud, H. and Townsend, J. (1992) *Boundaries*, Zondervan

Cohen, S. and Taylor, L. (1992) *Escape Attempts* (2nd Edition), Routledge

Csikszentmihalyi, M. (1992) *Flow – The Psychology of Happiness*, Rider Books

Dalai Lama (with Howard Cutler) (1998) *The Art of Happiness*, Coronet

Damasio, A. (1994) *Descartes' Error*, Papermac

Dawkins, R. (2007) *The God Delusion*, Black Swan

De Becker, G. (1997) *The Gift of Fear*, Bloomsbury

Dennett, D. (1991) *Consciousness Explained*, Penguin Books

Devettere, R. J. (2002) *Introduction to Virtue Ethics*, Georgetown University Press

Dickson, A. (2000) *Trusting the Tides – Self-Empowerment through Our Emotions*, Rider Books

Doyal, L. and Gough, I. (1991) *A Theory of Human Need*, Macmillan

Ekman, P. (2003) *Emotions Revealed*, Phoenix

Fernandez-Armesto, F. (1997) Truth – *A History and a Guide for the Perplexed*, Thomas Dunne

Fernandez-Armesto, F. (2003) *Ideas that Changed the World*, Dorling Kindersley

Ferudi, F. (2004) *Therapy Culture*, Routledge

Feuerstein, G. (2001) *The Yoga Tradition*, Hohm Press

Fromm, E. (1976) *To Have or to Be*, Abacus

Gardner, H. (1993) *Frames of Mind*, Fontana Press

Gilbert, D. (2006) *Stumbling on Happiness*, Harper Perennial

Gleick, J. (1997) *Chaos*, Vintage

Goffman, E. (1959) *Stigma*, Penguin Books

Goffman, E. (1963) *The Presentation of Self in Everyday Life*, Penguin Books

Goleman, D. (1996) *Emotional Intelligence*, Bloomsbury

Gosling, S. (2008) *Snoop – What Your Stuff Says about You*, Profile Books

Gyatso, G. K. (2000) *Eight Steps to Happiness,* Tharpa Publications

Heron, J. (1992) *Feeling and Personhood,* Sage Publications

Jeffers, S. (1987) *Feel the Fear and Do it Anyway,* Rider

Lane, R. (2000) *The Loss of Happiness in Market Democracies,* Yale

Lazarus, R. S. and Lazarus, B. N. (1994) *Passion and Reason,* Oxford University Press

Malkani, V. (2001) *All You Wanted to Know about Happiness,* Sterling Publishers

Marar, Z. (2003) *The Happiness Paradox,* Reaktion Books

Miller, J. (2000) 'Trust: The Moral Importance of an Emotional Attitude' in *Practical Philosophy,* November 2000, Volume 3.3 pp 45–54 (www.practical-philosophy.org.uk/volume3articles/trust.htm)

Miller, W. I. (1997) *The Anatomy of Disgust,* Harvard University Press

Monks of New Skete (1999) *In the Spirit of Happiness,* Rider Books

Morris, D. (2004) *The Nature of Happiness,* Little Books

Morton, A. (1996) *Philosophy in Practice,* Blackwell

Norem, J. (2001) *The Positive Power of Negative Thinking,* Basic Books

Nussbaum, M. (1994) *The Therapy of Desire,* Princeton University Press

Nussbaum, M. (2001) *Upheavals of Thought,* Cambridge University Press

O'Toole, J. (2005) *Creating the Good Life,* Rodale

Oatley, K. (2004) *Emotions, A Brief History,* Blackwell

Oatley, K. and Jenkins, J. (1996) *Understanding Emotions,* Blackwell

Parkinson, B. (1995) *Ideas and Realities of Emotion,* Routledge

Person, E. (1996) *The Force of Fantasy,* Harper Collins

Planalp, S. (1999) *Communicating Emotion,* Cambridge University Press

Poundstone, W. (1988) *Labyrinths of Reason,* Penguin

Power, M. and Dalgleish, T. (1997) *Cognition and Emotion,*

Psychology Press

Putnam, R. D. (2000) *Bowling Alone*, Touchstone

Ricard, M. (2006) *Happiness, A Guide to Developing Life's Most Important Skill*, Atlantic Books

Rouner, L. S. (1995) 'Ecstasy and Epistemology'''in *Emotions in Asian Thought* ed. J. Marks and R. Ames, pp 91–107, SUNY

Sacks, J. (2008) 'Make Heroes of the Moderates' in *Culture*, 20.11.2008 11:11

Seligman, M. (2002) *Authentic Happiness*, Nicholas Brearley

Sharples, R. W. (1996) *Stoics, Epicureans and Sceptics*, Routledge

Shermer, M. (2004) *The Science of Good and Evil*, Owl Books

Smart, B. (1993) *Postmodernity*, Routledge

Smart, N. (1996) *Dimensions of the Sacred*, Fontana Press

Swami Rama and Swami Ajaya (1976) *Creative Use of Emotion*, Himalayan Publishing

Taylor, S. (1989) *Positive Illusions*, Basic Books

Thayer, R. (1996) *The Origin of Everyday Moods*, Oxford University Press

Thayer, R. (2001) *Calm Energy*, Oxford University Press

Tolle, E. (1999) *The Power of Now*, Hodder and Stoughton

Turner, J. H. (2000) *On the Origins of Human Emotions*, Stanford

Vardy, P. (2003) *What is Truth?* John Hunt Publishing

Whybrow, P. (1997) *A Mood Apart*, Picador

Wierzbicka, A. (1999) *Emotions across Languages and Cultures*, Cambridge

Wilber, K. (2001) *No Boundary* (2nd Edition), Shambhala

Wilkinson, T. (2007) *The Lost Art of Being Happy, Spirituality for Sceptics*, Findhorn Press

Wilks, F. (1998) *Intelligent Emotion*, Arrow

Wright, S. G. and Sayre-Adams, J. (2000) *Sacred Space*, Churchill Livingstone